CHINESE STREET OPERA IN SINGAPORE

TONG SOON LEE

Chinese Street Opera in Singapore

UNIVERSITY OF ILLINOIS PRESS
URBANA AND CHICAGO

Manufactured in the United States of America
1 2 3 4 5 c p 5 4 3 2 1
This book is printed on acid-free paper.

Library of Congress Cataloging-in-Publication Data
Lee, Tong Soon, 1969–
Chinese street opera in Singapore / Tong Soon Lee.
p. cm.
Includes bibliographical references (p.) and index.
ISBN-13 978-0-252-03246-2 (cloth : alk. paper)
1. Operas, Chinese—Singapore—History
and criticism.
I. Title.
ML1751.S51L44 2008
782.1095957—dc22 2007019171

Contents

Acknowledgments

Writing this book has been as much an academic pursuit as it has been a process of understanding myself. Working on Chinese street opera is both familiar and foreign to me. The languages of the two main operatic types I worked on—Chaozhou and Fujian—are what I grew up speaking with both sides of my extended families. Growing up in Singapore, I was aware of Chinese street opera around me, but I did not really know about it. I never imagined needing to use my family tongues as the primary mode of communication for my research. This level of familiarity with and working on something so close to home was disconcerting. Yet with the patient support of and assistance from colleagues, friends, and family, it has been a rewarding experience of intellectual and personal growth.

Members of the Sin Sai Hong Hokkien Wayang and Lau Sai Thor Guan Teochew Wayang have generously shared their knowledge and experience in Chinese opera performance with me. My thanks to Chua Kian Hock, manager of Sin Sai Hong, and Johnnie Ng, manager of Lau Sai Thor Guan, for allowing me to spend time with their troupes. I am especially grateful to Goh Gek Lam, who spent much time teaching me about the joy and tribulation of a professional Chinese opera performer in Singapore. Thanks also to Chua Soo Pong of the Chinese Opera Institute for introducing me to numerous professional and amateur Chinese opera troupes and personnel, and to Sim Siew Tin of the Singapore Bukit Panjang Hokkien Konghuay Recreation Club, Tan Ooh Chye of the Thau Yong Amateur Musical Association, and Tan Yang Ngor of the Nanyang Pho Leng Hui Kuan for their assistance in so many ways.

Bell Yung and René T. A. Lysloff have both been integral in guiding my work at the University of Pittsburgh and beyond. Their own research in ethnomusicology and their mentoring of students are models to which I aspire. My foray into ethnomusicology began in 1991–1992 when Robert Provine entered the classroom at the University of Durham's music department dancing and playing the Korean drum. My heartfelt thanks to all three teachers. I am grateful to my dissertation committee members, Nicole Constable, Evelyn Rawski, and David Brodbeck, for constantly expecting and pushing for higher standards from me, and to Matthew Rosenblum for being so supportive of my work.

Judith McCulloh at the University of Illinois Press has patiently guided the publication of this book and I am grateful for her invaluable comments; Rebecca Crist and Laurie Matheson have also helped me in many ways—thank you. Many thanks to Helen Rees, Margaret Sarkissian, Andrew Weintraub, Deborah Wong, and Yung Sai Shing, who have constantly offered advice and ideas to improve my work and myself. Thanks also to Ann Youmans, who copyedited the manuscript, Noridah Moosa for her assistance in fieldwork, Tay Puay Nam for systematically collecting archival documents, Peter Scott and Roger Norris for their indefatigable support in every way, Wang Lan and my little brother, Tong King, for helping me with translation. To Eng Teong: thank you for allowing me to use your photographs, and most of all, for always being there in the last three decades.

Research for this project has been generously supported by the Tan Kah Kee Foundation Postgraduate Scholarship, Andrew Mellon Postdoctoral Fellowship, Singapore Hokkien Huay Kuan Arts and Cultural Scholarship, British Academy Committee for Southeast Asian Studies, International Dissertation Field Research Fellowship, and the Institute for Comparative and International Studies Research and Program Fund at Emory University. Publication of the book is supported in part by the Deans of Emory College and the Graduate School of Arts and Sciences at Emory University.

Sections of the book were written as part of my MBA thesis at the Durham University Business School. Earlier versions fo several chapters have been published previously, and I am grateful to the editors for enabling me to develop my work: "Professional Chinese Opera Troupes and Street Opera Performance in Singapore," *Asian Music* 31, no. 2 (2000): 35–70; "Chinese Street Opera Performance and the Shaping of Cultural Aesthetics in Contemporary Singapore," *Yearbook for Traditional Music* 34 (2002): 139–61; "Chinese Theatre, Confucianism, and Nationalism:

Amateur Chinese Opera Tradition in Singapore," *Asian Theatre Journal* 24, no. 2 (2007): 397–421.

Working on this book project gave me opportunities to delve into my maternal grandfather's life. I will always treasure the times he spent telling me about early twentieth-century Singapore when he first arrived from China as a young man. My parents went out of their way to enable me to continue studying music: this book would have been unthinkable without their unceasing support. Thanks too to my older brother, Tong Beng, who helped me in his own ways. To Ruby, who has been with me since the beginning of this project—thank you.

In memory of our daughter, Wen Ling,
and in celebration of our son, Wen Jin.

Prüfungsthema MuWi: Chinesische Oper in Singapore
↳ Was?
↳ Geschichte
↳ Merkmale
↳ Singapore
↳ Geschichte
↳ Merkmale

Introduction

Chinese street opera is at once anachronistic and relevant in Singapore today. When one talks about Chinese street opera here, the conversation is often tinged with nostalgia for a dying tradition and sometimes accompanied by the question, "Is it still performed nowadays?" Considering that about a dozen Chinese opera troupes perform street opera all over the island city for an average of fifteen days every month, the question may seem odd. What this scenario suggests, however, is that there have been changes in the understanding of Chinese street opera in Singapore. What are these changes and when did they come about? What motivated such changes in Chinese street opera and what are their implications?

Performed by two different groups of performers, the Chinese street opera tradition in Singapore has come to represent more than mere entertainment or an art form. The emerging meanings and values of this tradition form a continuum along which the complexities of nation-building in Singapore are played out. In this book, I examine the cultural perspectives of nationalism in Singapore since its independence in 1965 through a study of Chinese street opera to understand the impact of changing cultural aesthetics on music and society.

The Singapore Context

Singapore is located near the equator with Peninsular Malaysia (West Malaysia) to the north, Sarawak, Sabah (East Malaysia), and Brunei to the east, and the islands of Indonesia to the south and west. It was first known as Temasek (Sea Town) in the fourteenth century and was later referred to by its Sanskrit name, Singapura (Lion City). Singapore was part of Malaya until 1819, when Sir Stamford Raffles established the island as a trading station on behalf of the British East India Company. It was incorporated with Malacca and Penang (in West Malaysia) in 1826 to form the Straits Settlements, ruled directly by the British government, and in 1959, the People's Action Party (PAP)—Singapore's current ruling political party—was granted self-government in domestic affairs by the British colonial office. In 1963, Singapore joined the newly independent Federation of Malaysia and became a sovereign nation in 1965.

According to the population census in 2000, the total population in Singapore is approximately 4 million, with a majority of Chinese (76.8 percent), followed by Malays (13.9 percent), South Asians (7.9 percent, predominantly Tamil-speaking South Indians), and other minority communities comprised of Eurasians, Arabs, Japanese, Jews, Armenians, and Europeans (1.4 percent).[1] The four main ethnic communities in Singapore are the Chinese, Malay, Indian, and Eurasian, corresponding to the four official languages: Mandarin, Bahasa Malay, Tamil (collectively known as "mother tongues"), and English (the "first" language for education, business, and administration). With such an ethnically diverse population forming a complex milieu of social, political, cultural, and economic differences, the state's guiding political principle has been to produce a national identity based on the ideology of multiculturalism.[2]

CHINESE IN SINGAPORE

The Chinese community has constituted the majority of the Singapore population since 1836 (table 1). In addition, the Chinese are economically the dominant group. Geographically, however, Singapore is situated in the Malay Archipelago where Malays form the indigenous majority and the Chinese, the immigrant minority. With its unique demographic, Singapore has been referred to as "a Chinese enclave in the Malay Sea" (B. Chua 1995, 108), where ethnic relations between the Chinese majority and the minorities, particularly the Malays, are of paramount concern in all aspects of the society.[3]

The Chinese played important roles at various junctures in Singapore's history. They were instrumental in organizing anti-Japanese campaigns during World War II and also in Singapore's struggle for political independence from the British colonial office in the 1950s. Between 1963 and 1965, when Singapore was part of the Federation of Malaysia, the Chinese-dominated leadership in Singapore was constantly at odds with the Malay-dominated leadership of the central Malaysian government.

Table 1. Population Percentage in Singapore by Ethnicity, 1824–2005

Year	Chinese	Malay	Indian	Others	Total
1824	31.0	60.2	7.1	1.7	100
1830	39.4	45.9	11.5	3.2	100
1836	45.9	41.9	9.9	2.6	100
1849	52.9	32.2	11.9	3.0	100
1871	56.8	27.1	11.9	4.0	100
1891	67.1	19.7	8.8	4.3	100
1911	72.4	13.8	9.2	4.7	100
1931	75.1	11.7	9.1	4.2	100
1947	77.8	12.1	7.4	2.8	100
1967	74.4	14.5	8.1	3.0	100
1970	76.2	15.0	7.0	1.8	100
1980	78.3	14.4	6.3	1.0	100
1990	77.8	14.0	7.1	1.1	100
2000	76.8	13.9	7.9	1.4	100
2005	75.6	13.6	8.7	2.1	100

Sources: Cui (1994, 12); A. Lai (1995, 16); Statistics Singapore (2000; 2005).

Chinese in Singapore exerted strong political and social influence against the Malay population in Peninsular Malaysia and fueled the tense relationship between the two political parties. Such tensions led to riots and social unrest between the Chinese and Malay, which finally led to Singapore's dismissal and independence from the Federation of Malaysia in 1965. To the extent that Chinese street opera performance in contemporary Singapore aims to transcend its ethnic Chinese boundaries to accommodate the state's multicultural discourse, its social significance needs to be understood against the backdrop of such delicate interethnic relationships in Singapore.

The majority of the Chinese in Singapore during the nineteenth and early twentieth centuries were immigrants from China. Some were merchants with small businesses while others arrived as indentured laborers known as "coolies."[4] The numerous waves of immigration rapidly increased the Chinese population: in 1824, Chinese constituted 31 percent of the entire population, and in 1931, this figure reached 75.1 percent, a level that has been more or less maintained since.[5]

A large proportion of male immigrants arrived during the nineteenth century, while the majority of female immigrants arrived only after 1853. The first wave of female immigrants came in 1822 and until 1900 constituted only 5.29 percent of the entire Chinese population of 232,929 (Cui 1994, 21–23). It was not until the first two decades of the twentieth century that the number of female immigrants grew rapidly. Consequently, there was a predominance of male Chinese opera troupes in the early nineteenth century in Singapore, while female troupes emerged gradually only since the 1880s.

According to a survey in 1840, the four major Chinese groups in Singapore were the Fujian (Hokkien), Chaozhou (Teochew), Guangdong (Cantonese), and Kejia (Hakka) communities (Makepeace et al. 1921, 350). In 1848, Seah Eu Chin (Siah U Chin, 1805–1883), an eminent Chinese businessman, classified the Chinese community in Singapore into six distinct dialect groups, namely, Fujian, Chaozhou, Cantonese, Hakka, Hainan (Hylam), and the Malacca-born Chinese (Straits-born Chinese or Peranakans) (Seah 1848, 283).[6] A significant proportion of Singapore's Chinese community arrived from the Fujian and Canton provinces in southeast and south China respectively. The Fujian community largely comprised immigrants from the southern region of the Fujian province, otherwise known as Minnan ("south of the Min region"), "Min" being the alternative reference for the Fujian province. These included people from major cities such as Zhangzhou, Quanzhou, and Xiamen (Amoy). In his *One Hundred Years' History of the Chinese in Singapore,* Song Ong Siang notes that the first boat from China to Singapore was from Xiamen in 1822 (Song 1967, 21).

Three groups from the Canton province were linguistically quite different from each other. One came from the Chaozhou area in the eastern part of the province, where the major cities are Shantou and Chaozhou, and the vernacular language is known as Chaozhou. Being geographically close, the Fujian Minnan and Chaozhou dialects are mutually intelligible, and both are distinct from that used in the regions around Canton City (Guangzhou). Immigrants from the Canton area, Hong Kong, and Macau formed the third largest Chinese community in Singapore, after the Fujian and Chaozhou. The Hakka community from northeastern Canton (specifically around Meixian), Fujian, and Guangxi provinces, as well as the Hainan community from Hainan Island in south China also have constituted a sizable section of the Chinese community since the mid-nineteenth century. In Singapore today, the dominant Chinese ethnic groups are the Fujian community at 41.1 percent, followed by the Chaozhou at 21 percent, and Cantonese at 15.4 percent (E. Lee 2001). Collectively, the operatic genres of these three communities form the core of Chinese opera in Singapore.

The prominence of the Chinese community in the history of Singapore has meant that it inevitably constitutes a central representation of the Singaporean culture and tradition.[7] An example is the annual nationwide Speak Mandarin campaign that began in 1979, a political movement to unify the different ethnic Chinese communities.[8] In Singapore, Chinese opera has been iconic of the Chinese community as a whole and of individual ethnic Chinese groups in particular. Thus, representations of Chinese culture in Singapore invariably include Chinese opera, be it in terms of actual performances or as a cultural symbol. An example of this is the establishment of the Chinese Opera Institute in 1995 by the National Arts Council as a means to promote Chinese culture in Singapore through the theatrical tradition (Chinese Opera Institute 1996). Specifically, the image of Chinese street opera is given particular attention in the larger context of nation-building in contemporary Singapore, where, amidst national cultural activities that encourage ethnic awareness and assertiveness, traditional forms of expressive culture such as dance, costumes, music, and ritual are enthusiastically promoted and practiced.

Chinese Opera in Singapore

Chinese opera is a multifaceted theatrical genre that acts out a story through singing, speech, movements, instrumental accompaniment, and stage props. One of the distinguishing features in Chinese opera is the concept and use of *jiaose* (role types). The *jiaose* system differs from one operatic form to another among the many extant Chinese opera genres, though certain established roles are similar from genre to genre. Probably the most recognizable *jiaose* are the *sheng* (male), *dan* (female), *jing* (painted face), and *chou* (clown) in *jingju* (Peking opera).[9]

Equally distinctive is the music in Chinese opera, based primarily on the use of *qupai* (labeled tunes) and other preexisting tunes (such as folk melodies) using two approaches: *lianquti* (string-of-tune "medley" form) and *banqiangti* (tempo-variant form). *Lianquti* uses a number of different tunes to form a suite, while a suite in *banqiangti* is made up of variants of the same tune set to different *ban* (tempo).[10]

Chinese street opera, or *jiexi* (street show), refers to Chinese opera performed along the streets, in the vicinity of a temple, or in open areas such as a field or parking lot, on a temporary stage constructed out of timber poles and canvases. In Singapore, Chinese street opera is sometimes referred to as Chinese *wayang,* the Malay word *wayang* referring to a drama or play. Performances often take place in a broader context of Chinese religious events and customary celebrations, deities' birthdays, and special anniversaries of Chinese temples. Twice a day, usually for two to three consecutive days, a Chinese opera troupe invited for a particular occasion performs from 2 P.M. to 4 P.M. and 7:30 P.M. to 10:30 P.M. At the end of an engagement period, the troupe proceeds to another location for the next series of performances. If no further bookings are made, troupe members then take a few days off while the stage paraphernalia are stored in the troupe's headquarters.

The types of Chinese opera performed in Singapore are inextricably bound to the respective Chinese communities, with *fujianxi, chaoju,* and *yueju* (Hokkien, Teochew, and Cantonese operas, respectively) being the most prominent.[11] In studies on Chinese opera, these operatic forms are commonly referred to as *difangxi* (regional opera). Within the *fujianxi* category, the most popular genre is the *gezaixi* ("folk-tune" opera).[12]

Regionalism in Chinese musical cultures is a result of several interrelated factors, such as the geographical vastness of China, cultural interactions along shared national borders, and the diverse Chinese languages (Liang 1985, 212–29). Therefore numerous kinds of opera flourish in different regions of China. Their differences include the use of distinct local dialects, musical styles, preexisting tunes, repertory, and instruments, although they may share similar plays, acting methods, and costumes. Traditionally, regional operas also share three social functions: they serve as a form of mass entertainment, as part of religious rituals and calendrical ceremonies, and as a source of social commentary (B. Yung 1989, 8). Chinese theatre in traditional Chinese societies serves as an integral medium of cultural dissemination (Ward 1977, 193–96).

The origins of Chinese drama may be traced back to *sanyue* (variety music) of the Zhou (1075–256 BC), Spring and Autumn (770–476 BC), and Warring States (475–221 BC) periods, which broadly referred to folk music and dance, drama, and other folk arts (Yang 1981, 36 and 229). In addition, the Han dynasty (206 BC-220 AD) saw the development of *baixi* (variety show), which featured activities such as martial arts, sword-fighting display, and mimicking of animals, with music, song, dance, and movable props that resembled Chinese theatrical performances (ibid., 124).[13]

The sources of influence that led to the development of Chinese opera are diverse, including shamanistic ritual practices and folk performances such as weight lifting, tight-rope walking, acrobatics, mimicry, puppetry, and narrative singing. The precursors to Chinese opera as a dramatic and musical form—formal structure, tune construction, characterization—are generally acknowledged to be the *zaju* (variety play) of the Northern Song dynasty (960–1127), the *nanxi* (southern drama) of the Southern Song dynasty (1127–1279), and the related *chuanqi* (marvel tales) of the Ming dynasty (1368–1644) and *zaju* of the Yuan dynasty (1271–1368).[14]

The origins of regional stylistic differences in Chinese drama and borrowings between them may be traced back to these Song and Yuan dramas (Mackerras 1975, 14). During the Ming and Qing dynasties (1644–1911), economic and trade expansion, particularly in areas along the Yangzi

River, prompted the growth of regional dramas and *qiang* (tune system) as they diversified and developed widely (Mackerras 1972, 16–20).[15]

Closely related to Chinese opera, *qiang* combines the musical qualities of folk tunes, narrative forms, and instrumental styles of different regions to create musical styles identifiable with those regions (Yang 1981, 858–59). Some of the important *qiang* during the Ming and Qing dynasties include *haiyanqiang* in Zhejiang and Jiangxi provinces, *yiyangqiang,* which developed in Jiangxi and later spread to many parts of northern and southern China, *yuyaoqing* in Jiangsu and Anhui provinces, *kunshanqiang* in the Kunshan region of Jiangsu province, *bangziqiang* in Shanxi and Shaanxi provinces, and *pihuangqiang,* a combination of *xipi* (variant of *bangziqiang* that developed in the Hubei province) and *erhuang* in Yihuang county of Jiangxi province. Noteworthy among the major *qiang* is the *kunshanqiang,* which later developed into *kunqu,* or *kunju* (Kun opera), in the mid-sixteenth century, and *pihuangqiang,* which formed the basis of Peking opera in the late eighteenth century. Regional operas may share the same *qiang* or may combine characteristics of several *qiang* to develop new musical styles.[16]

Kun opera and Peking opera were two dominant forms of regional opera that somewhat transcended the "folk" or "local" facets of their regional origins in terms of how and where they were popularized, types of patronage, and social function. Kun opera was practiced and promoted by the literati, many of whom were also playwrights, and Peking opera had the royal patronage of the Qing court. Both operatic genres were gradually exalted as "high art" forms that extended beyond mere entertainment through processes of artistic refinement and literary sophistication: aesthetic theories were expounded through the publishing and performance of new plays, and repertoires were systematized (B. Yung 1989, 8).

At the same time, other forms of regional opera continued to proliferate as popular entertainment for the masses, performed mainly by itinerant troupes who "were very low in social status [and] were regarded by the law as slaves and suffered serious discrimination" (Mackerras 1983a, 98). The meanings and values of regional operas were shaped largely by the people associated with them. Similar distinctions may be discerned in Chinese operas performed in Singapore in terms of their regional distinctiveness but, perhaps more vividly, in relation to the performance practices of Chinese street opera.

Chinese opera in Singapore is performed by two groups of actors and musicians: the professionals (*zhiye*) and amateurs (*yeyu*). As the two primary operatic traditions in Singapore, their performance practices, organizational structure, ideology, history, and membership shape the aesthetics of Chinese opera and its associated notions of culture. For instance, professional opera troupes perform daily in the context of Chinese religious rituals, and consequently their performances are seen as mundane and functional. In this sense, culture is the practice of everyday life. Members of amateur opera troupes, on the other hand, perform several times a year for leisure and sometimes during nationwide events on a nonprofit basis; they are perceived as cultural bearers of Chinese opera as an art form. Culture, in this case, refers to the pursuit of artistic knowledge and skills. The significance of both the professional and amateur operatic traditions in constructing a framework for national culture emerges particularly through their performance of Chinese street opera.

PROFESSIONAL OPERA TROUPES

In Singapore, Chinese street opera is traditionally performed only by professional troupes. These are profit-oriented, full-time, itinerant groups of performers and musicians who perform twice a day for 200 to 250 days a year mainly on the outskirts of the main business, shopping, and tourist districts. The maintenance of a professional troupe depends exclusively on income earned through performance, and for most of its members, performance earnings are their main source of income. There are approximately thirty members in a professional troupe today, the majority of whom are middle-aged and above and have been involved in Chinese opera performance since they were teenagers. Generally, professional opera performers have very little, if any, formal education, in part because of their full-time commitment to Chinese opera from an early age.

Before the 1960s, professional troupes performed street opera as well as in indoor theatres, for both religious purposes and secular entertainment. Well-known troupes had approximately a hundred members and a huge following of fans, and an evening's performance would attract an audience of no less than a thousand people. With the gradual closure of opera theatres from the 1920s to 1960s, the number of professional opera troupes declined. The remaining ones either performed street opera and charged an entrance fee for their performances or solicited invitations to perform in temples for religious functions. Today, professional opera troupes do not perform in the secular context, and their only source of patronage is the religious institution that engages them for various forms of Chinese customary and religious activities.

AMATEUR OPERA TROUPES

In contrast to the professional troupes, amateur troupes are nonprofit organizations formed by opera enthusiasts who practice Chinese opera part time. They perform four to five times a year, usually in permanent indoor theatres and only occasionally in the street. Amateur troupes may be independent institutions or part of the cultural section of a larger association, for example, one that is based on regional or dialect affiliation, or a community club in a particular town.

Generally, each troupe has one to two hundred members who pay an annual subscription fee, but only an average of fifty members actively participate in daily administration, rehearsal, and performance. A significant proportion of their members are young, educated, and have full-time employment. As a result, rehearsals and training are usually held on weekday evenings and during weekends. Amateur troupes are wealthy and charitable social organizations, two important characteristics that traditionally distinguished them from the professionals. Indeed, they pride themselves as being educated and of a different social class than the professionals.

Chinese Street Opera and Cultural Nationalism

Since Chinese immigrants arrived on the island of Singapore in the early decades of the nineteenth century, Chinese opera has served as a form of entertainment as well as an important social and religious component for the Chinese masses. Professional Chinese opera troupes provided food and shelter for new immigrants during their initial period of arrival, and their makeshift stages even served as hiding places for victims of the Japanese occupation in Singapore during World War II (Wong et al. 1972, 6). Similarly, in the first half of the twentieth century, amateur Chinese opera troupes initiated and participated in fund-raising events to assist victims of wars and natural calamities in China, and constructed hospitals and schools for the Chinese community in Singapore (S. Tan 1996, 40–46).

The decline of Chinese street opera performance by professional troupes after the 1960s also marked the beginning of a new performance tradition—street opera performances by amateur opera troupes—in an explicit effort to preserve Chinese street opera as a cultural heritage in Singapore. Today, Chinese street opera continues to be performed daily by professional troupes and occasionally by amateur opera troupes in state-sponsored festivals. When amateur opera troupes began to perform Chinese street opera in the 1970s, they were creating a new form of performance practice in the amateur operatic tradition, built on a long-standing style that had hitherto been the sole domain of the professional troupes.

The new amateur Chinese street opera performances were organized and sponsored by national institutions, such as the National Arts Council, Singapore Tourism Board, and Chinese Opera Institute. Performances took place in open areas in the central business, shopping, and tourist districts and were often staged in conjunction with larger national festivals, such as the Chinese Cultural Festival, or as self-contained events, such as the annual "Traditional Theatre in the Park" series. Amateur Chinese street opera performances continue to be highly publicized occasions today, with ample funding that enables elaborate props, a huge cast of performers and musicians, specialized lighting and sound equipment, multilingual real-time projection of English synopsis and Chinese script, and relatively comfortable seating for the audience.

The professional and amateur operatic traditions are historically distinct from each other not only in their broader social requisites but also in terms of their group structure, organizational ideology, and performance practices. While performance opportunities for professional troupes vary according to changing patronage and social circumstances, the amateurs have maintained a relatively continuous presence through their performances in indoor contexts with support from wealthy patrons and membership enrollment. Since amateur opera troupes reinvented the Chinese street opera in the 1970s, however, there has been a discernable shift toward a comparative view of amateur and professional opera organizations framed against a backdrop of cultural nationalism.

Cultural nationalism aims to shape a national culture by identifying unique cultural attributes of a community. The process focuses on forging national sentiments primarily through cultural and artistic domains, such as language, clothing, food, and music (Turino 2000, 14–15). Its impact, however, rests on the relationship between such attributes and their effectiveness in the "moral regeneration" of the community (Hutchinson 1987, 16). In Singapore, the shaping of the morals and values of Singaporeans is a primary concern in the state's concept of nation-building: a key example is the introduction of the moral education program to the school curriculum in the 1980s (Ling 1989, 701–3; Vasil 1995, 73–76). "Asian" morals and values became defining traits of what a Singaporean identity should be, embedded in the cultural attributes of the Chinese, Malay, and Indian ethnic communities (Ang and Stratton 1995, 78; see also S. Wong 1988). Specifically, a Confucian framework emerged prominently in the state's discourse on national culture (Chua 1995, 147–68; Kuo 1996).

During the first two decades after Singapore's independence in 1965, cultural discourses were aimed primarily at achieving a multiethnic identity, maintained through private celebrations and public displays of dance, ritual, food, architecture, music, and other customs of the individual ethnic communities. From the mid-1980s, there was a significant emphasis in the state's conception of culture that transcended the disparate array of ethnic activities to the imagination of an overarching cultural ethos that is uniquely Singaporean, manifested in musical performances, heritage events, and other forms of social practices, such as the choreography of an exercise sequence known as the Great Singapore Workout. The performance practice of Chinese street opera in Singapore provides a framework with which to assess the changing social dynamics in a modernizing society, where cultural values and preferences are constantly negotiated through expressive forms.

In the state's framework of culture from the 1980s onwards, the "Asian" and the "ethnic" function as two primary barometers by which meanings and values of cultural practices are measured. In this way, Chinese opera, along with various other performing arts such as Indian classical music traditions, the Malay *kompang* and *hadrah* (frame drums), and traditional dances of the Eurasian communities, were seen as cultural heritage that needed systematic preservation and promotion (T. Koh 1989). Chinese street opera emerged as an appropriate symbol for the cultural ideal of a strong heritage in a rapidly modernizing social space because it embodied the imagery of a rural, simple, and rustic local tradition. At the same time, it signified an approach toward a cultural definition of national identity in contemporary Singapore.

Positing a cultural value on Chinese street opera throws into relief the dynamics between Chinese street opera performed every day by professional opera troupes and the envisioned "cultural" Chinese street opera. Amateur opera troupes were promoted by the state as representatives of Chinese street opera in Singapore and their performances redefined the structure and aesthetics of Chinese street opera from the 1970s onwards. Why were amateur organizations selected as practitioners of Chinese street opera when street opera performance was traditionally not part of their organizational practice? To rephrase the question, given that professional opera troupes perform Chinese street opera every day, why were they not chosen as the exemplars of the tradition? Answers to these questions allude to the role of the middle or elite class in the process of cultural nationalism (see Hutchinson 1987, 250–303; Turino 2000, 162–70).

In the state's imagination of a Singaporean national culture, the key components are education, creativity, globalization, technological advancement, and concern for local history, the synergies of which motivate nationalistic sentiments toward the country. In this framework, the structure, history, ideology, and performance practices of amateur opera troupes serve as an appropriate model of culture that the state wants Singaporeans to aspire toward: their members are educated, have stable occupations, are versed in a traditional art form and yet innovative, employ creative technologies in their performances, are known locally and abroad, and engage in artistic knowledge and practice as a leisurely and altruistic pursuit. As part of the middle class in Singapore, members of amateur Chinese opera troupes play a role in shaping a Singaporean culture through their history, structure, and performance of Chinese street opera.[17] They became cultural entrepreneurs at a particular point in Singapore's history and have continued in this role because their organizational structure and practices interconnect with the state's concept of a Singaporean national culture. Indeed, Chinese street opera performance by amateur troupes articulates a cultural framework that is applicable across ethnic boundaries and intersects with the state's pursuit of nationalism. Through continued innovations in creating an amateur Chinese street opera tradition, such as the adaptations of the Indian epic *Ramayana* into Chinese opera, more emphasis is placed on "universal" aesthetics of arts and culture than on issues associated with the Chinese ethnicity.

In the process of redefining the Chinese street opera tradition, two previously independent social organizations are contrasted with each other, and through such a comparison, various strands of meanings and values of Chinese opera and its practitioners emerge. Framed as a phenomenon that espouses "culture," Chinese street opera quickly became a marker of social identity that distinguishes the amateur from the professional. While amateurs are hailed as preservers of Chinese street opera as heritage and culture, professional troupes are devalued for being mundane and outdated, their members performing only to make a living out of it. Chinese opera performance thus becomes a way to distinguish social practices that are ascribed a "cultural" value from others that are not (Fiske 1992).

AMATEURISM AND CONFUCIANISM IN CHINESE OPERA

Emergent in the glorification of amateur Chinese opera troupes is the significance of Confucian attitudes in the cultivation of the self through the arts. Given the Confucian emphasis on education, a learned person engages in the arts for moralistic and altruistic purposes. The focus is less on technical specialization of a particular form but on achieving an aesthetic disposition and cultural celebration of that form and, most importantly, conveying such qualities to others (Cahill 1975; Levenson

1957). The social position of an amateur opera troupe is conspicuously marked using the adjective "amateur." Names of amateur opera troupes in Singapore use the Chinese reference *ru* to signify their amateur status; in conventional Chinese usage, *ru* connotes a scholarly stature and an association with Confucian philosophy. *Ru* is both aesthetically and socially expressive on organizational and individual levels.

In the broader social context, the Confucianist discourse is often invoked as the cultural underpinning that perpetuated the rapid economic successes in East Asia during the postwar period (Tu 1996). In Singapore, after attaining a satisfactory economic standard in the 1980s through rapid industrialization, Confucianism was appropriated as a state apparatus against perceived excesses in materialism and individualism as a consequence of "Westernization" through modernization, particularly among young people. To this end, the Confucian pantheon of ideas were introduced, which enhanced the importance of education, filial piety, loyalty and reciprocity in hierarchical relationships, and harmonious collectivism, values applicable to the multiethnic and multireligious context in Singapore.

Related to the institution of Confucianism was the reinstatement of "culture" in the 1980s, previously sidelined by the state's emphasis on economic, industrial, and political achievement. Rather than a mere set of ideas, Confucian ideals were made manifest through the "Asian" and "ethnic" traditions that also gained cultural currency in the 1980s, of which Chinese street opera is a case in point. In this context, Chinese street opera performance by amateur opera troupes becomes a means for the state to imbue its cultural ideology by associating what it defines as "culture" with specific character and behavioral traits of the amateur performer. "Amateurizing" Chinese street opera is therefore politically motivated. Interestingly, by framing amateur Chinese street opera under the rhetoric of "culture," the state's ideology of nationalism is depoliticized, naturalized, and, perhaps more importantly, translatable to all ethnicities to create a pan-Singaporean identity.[18]

Chinese street opera in contemporary Singapore may thus be seen as a microcosm of the changing social dynamics confronting a modernizing society. The current aesthetic distinctions between the professional and amateur performance traditions have been conditioned by shifting sociopolitical contexts in Singapore. Indeed, aesthetic discourses on Chinese street opera performance in Singapore today are not merely an espousal of artistic achievement but an indication of the state of cultural anxiety that continues to confront Singapore since its independence in 1965.

1 Chinese Opera in Singapore, 1840s–1960s

The history of Chinese opera in Singapore is inextricably linked to the social, cultural, and political circumstances of its Chinese communities. Changes in the practice of Chinese opera reflect broader changes in the society, first, of the Chinese immigrants and settlers during the nineteenth and early twentieth centuries, and later, of Singaporeans—predominantly but not limited to the Chinese community—in the process of nation-building after Singapore's independence in 1965.

Early Descriptions of Chinese Street Opera

As early as the fourteenth century, itinerant Chinese traders shuttling between China and Malaya began to form small communities in the Malayan region (Song 1967, 1–3; Cui 1994, 1–8).[1] It was only in the nineteenth century, however, that the Chinese population in the region increased tremendously. Early records on Chinese opera in Singapore date to around the mid-nineteenth century in travel dairies by visitors and official reports by foreign administrators.

On February 21, 1842, Lieutenant Charles Wilkes observed various ceremonies performed by the Chinese community in Singapore to celebrate the arrival of the Lunar New Year. Wilkes was the commander of the United States South Seas Exploring Expedition that arrived in Singapore between January 22 and February 19 that year (Bastin 1994, 46–53). He noted that the ceremonies consisted mainly of processions by groups of people carrying shrines, flags, and banners, among other objects, and were accompanied by the playing of cymbals and gongs, "on which every performer strove to strike with his utmost force, and if possible, oftener than his neighbour" (Wilkes 1984, 14). As part of these celebrations, there were numerous Chinese opera performances:

> Theatrical exhibitions were at the same time going forward in many places; open sheds were erected for this purpose, where the exhibition was entirely gratuitous. The actors, I was told, are paid by a general subscription, which also provides for the other expenses of the spectacle. These sheds are closed on three sides, but open on that which faces the street. The stage is raised about six feet above the street; the whole is richly decorated with silk hangings, and banners with many inscriptions, and illuminated with coloured lamps. The stage, which was by no means of large size, was occupied by a table and two chairs. The dialogue was in a kind of recitative, with an accompaniment performed by beating with two small sticks on the bottom of a copper kettle of the shape of a coffee-pot. The person who performed this duty appeared to direct all the spectacle, as prompter and leader of the orchestra. . . . The dresses of the actors were very rich, and the females were represented by young men or boys. The male characters were for the most part masked, but not the female; the former generally had long black and white beards. The principal part of the performance seemed to consist in attitudinizing, and appeared to interest the audience, as it did us, although according to our ideas it was not suited to the words or sentiment; for instance, during a pathetic part, whilst the actor was shedding tears, he would suddenly throw up one leg, and almost kick himself on the nose! The acting, upon the whole, was, to our notions, in a mock-heroic style; but this might have arisen from our not being able to comprehend the meaning, for the other spectators seemed greatly interested. (Wilkes 1984, 15–16)

In addition to Chinese New Year celebrations, Chinese opera performances were also central to religious festivities (*miaohui*) of the different Chinese communities in Singapore, as noted by Jonas Daniel Vaughan (1825–1891) in his book *The Manners and Customs of the Chinese,* first published in 1879. Vaughan lived in the Straits Settlements for forty-five years and held numerous official positions in Singapore: 1856–1861 as master attendant (harbor master), 1861–1866 as police magistrate, and thereafter as assistant resident. From 1869 until his death, he worked as a lawyer in Singapore. In his description of festivals celebrated by the Chinese communities in Singapore, he notes:

> In Singapore on the 26th day of the 10th month [of the lunar calendar] the Tay Chews [Chaozhou] carry their idol in procession from their cemetery at Tanglin to their temple in Philip Street to see the theatricals held

> there in his honor. . . . The Hokiens [Fujian] have a similar procession once in three years; the idol at their cemetery on the New Harbour road is carried in procession through the parts of the Town chiefly inhabited by Hokiens to the great Hokien temple in Teluk Ayer Street. . . . The procession is gorgeous in the extreme and costs the Hokien community a large sum of money. It is accompanied by coolies bearing flags, umbrellas, symbols, sedan chairs, and bands of music making the most horrible din. (Vaughan 1971, 49)[2]

The two temples Vaughan refers to are the Chaozhou Yuehai Qingmiao (Temple of the Canton Sea) established in 1820, and the Fujian Tian Fu Gong (Heavenly Fortune Palace) established in 1840, both of which are still active today.[3] Vaughan further describes a temporary performance space for Chinese opera in the Yuehai Qingmiao as part of his narrative on the religious activities of the Chinese communities in Singapore: "In the front of the temples is a large flagged square surrounded by a high wall, in which temporary stages are erected for theatrical performances; when of course the place is crowded by worshippers, who are attracted more by them, than the service of the gods. Chinese gods appear to be particularly fond of the drama. The wise say that these performances are often given to screen gamblers who play in adjoining houses, whilst the attention of the police is attracted to the crowd before the theatre" (Vaughan 1971, 52).

Performances such as those Wilkes and Vaughan observed are what is broadly known as *jiexi,* that is, street opera; characteristics of the street opera style of performance are the temporary performance space and the religious context. Thus, *jiexi* is also referred to as *choushenxi* (thanksgiving performance), and in many ways, *jiexi* is synonymous with *choushenxi,* the performance context being tied to its function. Traditionally, *choushenxi* are organized by temples and other social organizations such as clan associations, a village, or a group of stall owners in a market place, who pay professional Chinese opera troupes to perform as a way of offering thanks to their respective deities for protection and blessings. Count Fritz von Hochberg witnessed one such performance in a village in Singapore on February 20, 1908, which he described in *An Eastern Voyage,* published in 1910:[4]

> It was a lovely drive past all sorts of plantations, mainly cocoa-nut palms, which really are magnificent, and then in a large Chinese village where an open theatre was going on. We stopped to see it. The actors were just painting their faces, and mostly seemed to represent devils or such, but it was really interesting to see how ingeniously they painted their faces with black, white and red water-colours, and really succeeded in mak-

> ing marvelous unrecognizable masks of their faces, otherwise harmless enough. Then they proceeded with their dressing, and some had lovely old-gold embroidered costumes, some huge coloured wings and dragons' tails, crowns, etc., etc. The acting and singing was more a contorted sort of devil's dance in which the real Devil displayed much power with funny high jumps. None of the audience, though, paid the slightest attention to the acting. *We* were the theatre to them, and they did not take one eye off us. Especially my having sketched the face of the man who I thought painted himself best, interested them greatly. . . . (Wise 1996, 168)

Choushenxi were customarily held in conjunction with other social activities and entertainment including processions, gambling, or sale of food and goods such as beads, paper fans, toys, and other ornamental objects. When opium trading was not illegal in Singapore during the colonial period, it was also common to see the trading and smoking of opium underneath temporary opera stages (personal communication, Ng Jin Sim, August 21, 1997).[5] Such crowded contexts were therefore conducive to thieving, an example of which was an incident on April 13, 1888, at the Yuehai Qingmiao: "On the third day [of the third lunar month] at Yuehai Qingmiao's *choushenxi,* the audience was like human walls. It was extremely crowded with a mix of good and bad people. There was a person dressed elaborately and adorned with jewelry. Eyeing this person, a scheming thief gradually moved closer and snatched a necklace. The thief was caught by undercover police and brought to the station for interrogation" (*Lat Pau,* April 16, 1888, 5; translated from Chinese). A good example of how *choushenxi* served both religious and entertainment functions was an event in Chinatown on March 5, 1888: "On the evening of 23rd [of the first lunar month] in Chinatown's Dan Gui Yuan [Sweet-Scented Osmanthum Garden], Qing Bai Nian Ban [Celebrating a Hundred Years Troupe] performed an opera with a fireworks display to more than a thousand people who came to watch this innovative presentation, never before seen in Singapore. The troupe had previously advertised this event and indicated that the fireworks display would begin when the opera performance ended, which attracted many people. The opera began with singing accompanied by gongs and bamboo [and string] ensembles until 11:30 P.M. when the fireworks started" (*Lat Pau,* March 9, 1888, 2; translated from Chinese). The report continued with a description of the images created by the fireworks, which included shapes of butterflies, dragonflies, wheels, and small flowers such as plum blossoms, orchids, chrysanthemums, and bamboo. What is more intriguing was the creative presentation that followed: the report seems to suggest a simultaneous performance of various scenes by the opera troupe enhanced by the fireworks display, which included a battle in the sea and the imageries of two ritual plays—*Liyu Tiaolongmen* (*Carp Jumps over the Dragon Gate*) and *Liuguo Fengxiang* (*Minister of the Six States*).[6]

The informality of the audience at Chinese street opera performances was often noted by observers. George C. Morant, a British businessman who visited Singapore around 1905, noted the following scenario in his *Odds and Ends of Foreign Travel* published in 1913: "Members of the audience walked up one or other of the flights of steps at intervals and sat at the sides or on the edge of the stage with their legs hanging over, while children sat, squatted, or rolled about it at their pleasure, no notice whatever being taken of them by the actors."[7] In 1907, Arnold Wright and H. A. Cartwright watched a Chinese street opera performance along North Bridge Road (known locally as Xiaopo [Little Town]) and recorded the following observations in their *Twentieth Century Impressions of British Malaya* published in 1908: "There is also a Chinese theatre near at hand, where a seemingly interminable play goes on all night, and where it is amusing to observe the cool way in which the spectators will sometimes stroll across the stage right among the actors, to find some more convenient point of view or to exchange greetings with a friend."[8]

CHINESE OPERA AS SOCIAL ORGANIZATIONS

Chinese opera was also performed indoors in semipermanent and permanent spaces. In his description of Chinese drama in Singapore, Vaughan outlines the characteristics of Chinese opera theatres and different types of opera groups in the latter half of nineteenth-century Singapore:

> The theatres are simply large barns with a stage erected at one end; with a screen running across the stage about twenty feet from the front with two doors, for the exits and entrances of the actors. Rough seats are provided for the audience and charges of admission vary from twenty-five cents to half a dollar. During the performance the audience smoke and chat away at the top of their voices; when anything interesting is going on they sit very still and pay great attention to the stage. . . .
>
> There are theatres in Singapore occupied by Macao [Cantonese], Tay Chew [Chaozhou], and Hokkien [Fujian] actors. Besides these fixed companies there are itinerant companies who perform on hastily erected stages before audiences who stand in the open air unsheltered from wind and rain. (Vaughan 1971, 86)

The formation of "fixed companies" suggests that the demand for Chinese opera was sufficiently high to maintain opera companies during the mid-nineteenth century, supported by the Cantonese, Chaozhou, and Fujian communities, the three dominant Chinese communities in Singapore.

wurde auf Straße und Indoors gespielt

Note that the two groups of Chinese opera troupes in Vaughan's descriptions were distinguished by their organizational structure and performance space—one fixed and performing in permanent theatres, the other itinerant and performing on temporary stages. This may suggest a corresponding division in the functions of these troupes: the fixed companies in permanent theatres performed primarily for secular entertainment, and the itinerant group performed street opera for both secular and religious purposes. Such functional divisions were prevalent in the first half of the twentieth century with professional opera troupes, which may have indeed continued since the mid-nineteenth century as per Vaughan's observations and gradually subsided after the 1960s. What is important is the contrast between indoor and outdoor Chinese opera performance, which became a value-laden distinction in postindependence Singapore.

The formation of opera companies and building of theatres in Singapore during the latter half of the nineteenth century was underscored by a period of intense migration from China to Southeast Asia, motivated by the lifting of the migration ban and opening of ports after the Opium War (1839–1942), political instability, social unrest such as the Taiping Rebellion (1851–1864) and Boxer Rebellion (1898–1901), and other conflicts like the Sino-Japanese War (1894–1895). Chinese migration to the United States declined as a result of a series of immigration exclusion acts in the 1880s and shifted toward Southeast Asia, thus further increasing the Chinese population in Singapore.[9] According to a population census in 1881, 240 Chinese were listed as "Actors, Artists, Musicians" under the category "Professional Class" that includes vocations such as priests, barristers and attorneys, physicians, surgeons and dentists, pilots, engineers, and architects and surveyors (table 2). By 1921, this number had increased to 1,080 (Nathan 1921).[10]

The number of Chinese opera theatres built and refurbished in late nineteenth-century Singapore by wealthy Chinese is indicative of several social developments. First, the majority of these actors, artists, and musicians were likely to be involved in Chinese opera. Second, as a community of "Professional Class," Chinese opera performance was a full-time occupation, probably accorded a comparatively high level of respect in society (Pitt 1988, 58). Third, the rapid growth of the Chinese economy in Singapore and Singapore's position as an entrepôt during this period ensured an abundant patronage of opera troupes and performances.[11]

Chinese opera in nineteenth-century Singapore was performed primarily by all-male troupes. In his 1842 observations of Chinese street opera, Wilkes noted that "the females were represented by young men

Table 2. Registered "Actors, Artists, Musicians" in the 1881 Population Census

Ethnic Group	Male	Female	Total
Europeans/Americans	10	0	10
Eurasians	5	0	5
Malays/Natives of the Archipelago	14	3	17
Chinese	226	14	240
Tamils/Natives of India	12	1	13
Total	267	18	285

Source: Report on the Census of Singapore, 1881 (Talbot 1881).

or boys" (Wilkes 1984, 15–16). Vaughan also affirms that "[t]here are no female performers. Women are represented by young men who play their parts capitally deceiving the Chinese themselves. The writer has been at plays where some of the spectators have declared some of the performers to be women, but he has been assured by the proprietors of the theatre that women are not admitted into their companies" (Vaughan 1971, 85–86). From the 1880s onwards, however, female troupes were gradually formed in Singapore (Liu and Phillips 1988, 25). In 1887, Li Chung Chu, a Chinese official on a visit to Singapore, noted that in certain areas of Chinatown, "There are male and female theatrical troupes performing in the theatres. In 'Greater Town' [Dapo], there are 4 to 5 places for performances; in 'Lesser Town' [Xiaopo] there are only one or two. All of them perform Cantonese operas. Occasionally Fukien [Fujian] opera and Teochew [Chaozhou] opera are also staged. Only people of the same district flock to see the performance. The ticket fare is the cheapest; it is only three to four cents per head roughly equal to two to three candareen or fen of silver. Besides, there is only one type of ticket" (quoted in Archives and Oral History Department 1983, 20).[12] The presence of female theatrical troupes in the 1880s may be attributed to a significant increase in the number of female immigrants to Singapore at the turn of the twentieth century. From 1881 to 1890, 25,594 women migrated to Singapore; from 1891–1900, this number increased to 59,971 (Lim 1967, 99). This increase was in part because of social upheavals in China and also a result of policy changes in the Straits colonial administration that encouraged female immigration to obtain workers for tin mines and agriculture, and to curb negative behavior, such as clan rivalries among the male population in Singapore (ibid., 72–78).

CHINESE OPERA THEATRES

Along with the formation of theatre companies, many Chinese opera theatres were built in the late nineteenth and early twentieth centuries, located primarily within and around Singapore's Chinatown (table 3).[13]

Chinatown lies in the southwest region of the Singapore River and was constituted as a Chinese municipality in 1822 by Sir Stamford Raffles.[14] According to Li Chung Chu's description of Singapore in 1887, "There is a place known as Kereta Ayer [Kreta Ayer] in 'Greater Town' [*dapo*] where restaurants, theatres, and brothels are concentrated. It is the most populated area where filth and dirt are hidden. No place in Singapore can compare with it."[15] In other words, to an observer in 1887, Chinatown's landscape was broadly defined by three social organizations—restaurants, theatres, and brothels—all of which contributed to the social history of Chinese opera in Singapore.

Chinese opera theatres hosted performances of different operatic genres by both local and foreign troupes, and gradually came to be associated solely with specific operatic types. For example, Li Chun Yuan (Spring Pear Theatre) was known for its Cantonese opera performances, such that Smith Street and its nearby Temple and Trengganu Streets were popularly referred to as Xiyuanjie (Theatre Street), Xiyuan Houjie (Theatre Back Street), and Xiyuan Hengjie (Theatre Side Street) (Z. Wang 1997, 47–52). The Qing Wei Xin theatre (Celebrating Modernization) was also known for its Cantonese opera performances, while Qing Sheng Ping (Celebrating Peace) presented both Fujian and Peking operas (ibid., 53–58). Yi Yuan and Zhe Yuan were primarily Chaozhou opera theatres (Cui 1994, 94).[16]

Table 3. Chinese Opera Theatres in Singapore

Theatre	Location	Opera Genre	Period
Jing Chun Yuan	—	Cantonese	1890s–pre WWII
Yang Chun Yuan	—	Cantonese	1890s–pre WWII
Li Chun Yuan	Smith Street	Cantonese	1890s–1940s
Qing Wei Xin	Wayang Street	Cantonese	1890s–late 1930s
Qing Sheng Ping	Wayang Street	Fujian/Peking	1890s–late 1930s
Tianyan Dawutai	Eu Tong Sen Street	Cantonese	1927–1939
Tong Le Yuan	North Bridge Road & Rochor Road junction	Chaozhou/Hainan	1890s/1900s–1970s
Yi Yuan	Merchant Road	Chaozhou	1900s–early 1930s
Yong Le Yuan	North Bridge Road & Rochor Road junction	Chaozhou/Hainan	1890s/1900s–1970s
Zhe Yuan	New Market Road	Chaozhou	1900s–early 1930s

Source: Pitt (1988, 61–65); and Cui (1994, 93–95).

↳ hauptsächlich Kantonesische Oper

Chinatown and its immediate surroundings were defined by the locales in which different Chinese communities resided, a pattern carved out by Sir Stamford Raffles's constitution (Turnbull 1989, 20–21). A theatre's association with specific types of Chinese opera was largely attributed to the dominant Chinese ethnic communities residing within its vicinity. Cantonese lived mainly around Kreta Ayer, where Li Chun Yuan was located.[17] The Chaozhou community settled along the Singapore River, near Clarke Quay and Boat Quay, close to Yi Yuan and Zhe Yuan, while the Fujian community lived and worked mainly in the Telok Ayer area not far from Qing Sheng Ping (Cui 1994, 35–44; Z. Wang 1997, 5) (map 1).[18]

After Raffles marked out the land areas in Chinatown in the early nineteenth century, Chinatown was defined largely by the three largest Chinese communities in Singapore, namely Fujian, Chaozhou, and Cantonese (this pattern was only disrupted in the late 1960s when massive urbanization and resettlement programs were implemented). Just as these communities influenced the operatic genres performed in the theatres, these theatres were iconic of and, perhaps more importantly, continued to symbolize the identities of these communities in Singapore even after they were no longer used for Chinese opera. Consider the area known as Boat Quay, for example, where the Chaozhou community resided. An elderly interviewee who lived in that area when he first arrived in Singapore said, "Every year when opera shows were staged, we almost always invited those famous Teochew [Chaozhou] opera groups to come and perform at 'Chap bui kui khi' [Boat Quay]; all were Teochew opera shows. Almost seventy-five percent of the opera stages were built on the river, the remaining twenty-five percent were built on land" (Oral History Department 1990, 29). It is not surprising, therefore, to observe the dialect homogeneity of the audience attending opera performances in the late nineteenth century in Singapore's Chinatown, noted by Li Chung Chu in 1887, who remarked that "only people of the same district flock to see the performance" (quoted in Archives and Oral History Department 1983, 20). Thus, while the community residing around a particular theatre in a particular locale affected its musical identity, the performance itself also provided a context for the expression of group identity.

Vaughan's observations that Chinese theatre companies "occupied" different theatres indicated that opera troupes lived and performed regularly on a long-term basis in these theatres. Indeed, prior to 1895, Chinese theatres served as living quarters as well as performance spaces for the artists and their families. Health inspection records from the colonial office in 1895 reveal the deplorable conditions in these theatres: "As many

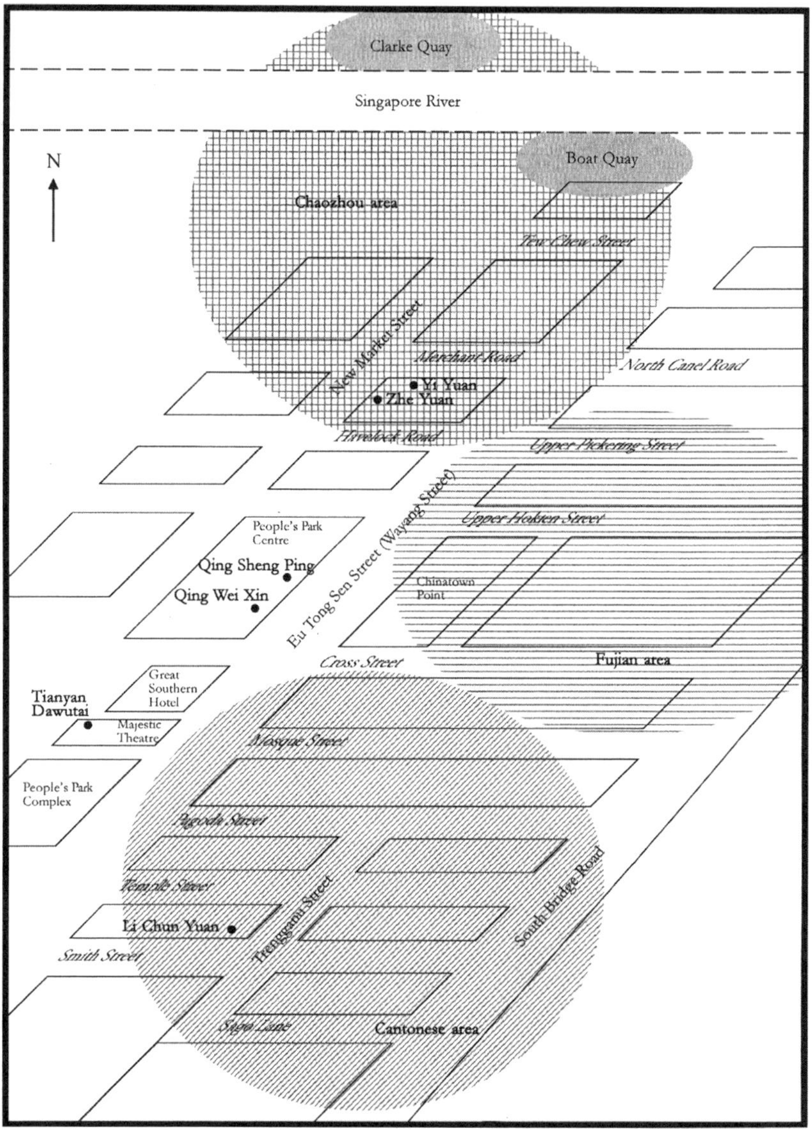

Map 1: Chinatown in Singapore, showing distribution of Chinese ethnic communities and Chinese opera theatres (adapted from Tang 1976, 141).

as 70 or 80 persons were found residing in one or two of the Chinese Theatres; wooden compartments having been erected for the convenience of a portion of the inmates while the remainder slept on the stage, in the galleries or anywhere where it was possible to lay down a mat. Refuse of all sorts was swept into convenient corners and allowed to remain and nuisances were committed in any part of the building. The building themselves had in several cases not been cleansed for years" (quoted in Liu and Phillips 1988, 28).

In 1895, new laws were instituted to restrict the use of theatres as living spaces, regulate their architectural specifications, safety, environmental conditions, and the administrative procedures that governed their uses (Pitt 1988, 61). As a result, many permanent theatres built in the 1880s were restructured (Tang 1976, 72–117; Liu and Phillips 1988, 28–35). Institutionalizing the practice of Chinese opera extended beyond forming fixed companies and restructuring theatres. In 1857, for example, the Cantonese community in Singapore formed the Li Yuan Tang (Theatre Hall), an association for Chinese opera artists, registered in November 26, 1906, as the Bahe Huiguan (Eight-Division Association) (Pitt 1988, 59). Like clan associations, Bahe Huiguan provided a locale for members' recreational activities and official meetings. A committee was further formed to oversee the general performance business and welfare of the members, and also served as an arbitrator in the event of disputes.[19]

One of the major changes in the reconstruction of theatres was the seat layout, from *chazuoshi* (teahouse style) with chairs and tables to seats arranged in rows (Liu and Phillips 1988, 28–31). Li Chun Yuan and Qing Wei Xin, for example, were converted from *chazuoshi* to evenly spaced rows of seats with different prices in the early twentieth century (Liu and Phillips 1988, 29–30). Such changes were attributed to the 1895 Theatre Ordinance (amended as the New Bylaws in 1917) passed by the British government to ensure that buildings used as public theatres adhered to specific safety and health standards (Liu and Phillips 1988, 27–29).[20] I suggest that another reason for the change in the seating concept was to increase the audience size, and consequently, the profit margin from ticket sales. Since the teahouse concept featured an open, informal arrangement with tables, chairs, and food, it required more space and thus seated fewer people than a hall consisting only of seats arranged in rows.

Li Chun Yuan, in the red light district at 36 Smith Street, was probably the most well-known theatre in the history of Chinese opera in Singapore. Chinese opera performances were held at Li Chun Yuan from the 1890s until it was converted into a cinema in the 1940s, and partially destroyed during World War II.[21] Before 1918, seats in Li Chun Yuan were *chazuoshi,* where audience members drank and ate as they watched Chinese opera; men and women were segregated, with men on the lower level and women watching from the upper level (Pitt 1988, 62; F. Wang 2004, 53–54).[22] After 1918, rows of seats replaced the *chazuoshi* and were divided into three categories: in the 1930s, regular seats cost forty cents; the next category, the "Concubine" seats, cost eighty cents; and the elite category, "Guangxu" (the Chinese emperor who reigned from 1875–1908), cost $1.20 (Z. Wang 1988, 147). Considering that an average Chinese laborer earned between fifty and seventy cents per day in 1938 (see Colonial Reports 1940, 42), a trip to a Chinese opera performance would have amounted to almost a day's wage for the majority of the Chinese populace. With the new seating layout, the practice of separating men and women in Chinese opera theatres was also abolished (Pitt 1988, 62).

Two methods were used to reserve seats, since entrance tickets did not indicate specific seat numbers. At Li Chun Yuan, audience members would place their handkerchiefs on the seats they wanted.[23] At other theatres such as Yi Yuan, the ushers would apply glue to the back of the tickets while guiding audience to their seats, and stick the tickets to the back of the seats; audience could also pay ushers an extra five cents to reserve seats for them in advance (Oral History Department 1990, 33; Z. Wang 1997, 74).

With the emergence and popularity of Chinese theatres, a gradual distinction surfaced between Chinese opera performed in indoor theatres and Chinese street opera. The new seating arrangements in theatres introduced a hierarchical division among the audience at opera performances, unlike the relatively heterogeneous audience space at street performances. In contrast to the informality of *chazuoshi,* rows of seats emphasized a clearer division between audience and the stage performance, thus reinforcing the formality of the event.

BROTHELS AND RESTAURANTS

Brothels and Chinese opera theatres were closely bound as social institutions, impacting each other in terms of patronage and performance schedule. For instance, Li Chun Yuan had wooden cubicles for patrons who attended opera performances with prostitutes; that the cubicle was occupied would be made known through flower decorations on the cubicle (Oral History Department 1990, 9). Chung Hon Kee, a Cantonese opera actor, notes that in the 1930s, the New World amusement park was the only venue that presented Chinese opera performances during the day. Its location near the red light district allowed prostitutes to patronize performances (National Archives Microfiche A000919/17). Prostitutes also played an important role in ritual events tied to Chinese opera, such as the three-night ritual September 8–10, 1890, in Chinatown: "On the evenings of 24th to 26th [of the seventh lunar month], Tong Jing Tang [Hall of Communal Respect] along Ma Jiao Jie [Horse Junction Street] held a *chaoyou* [ascension of spirits] ritual. Brothels and other establishments participated with elaborate decorations of lights, songs, and music, and Qing Bai Nian Ban [Celebrating Hundred Years Troupe] performed for three nights" (*Lat Pau*, September 11, 1890, 2; translated from Chinese).

Restaurants and teahouses were also popular places for Chinese opera performances and provided entertainment, food, and drinks to customers (Pang 1997, 34–35; F. Wang 2004, 41–42, 48–50). In these venues with limited space, the *qingchang* ("pure singing") style of presenting operatic excerpts, that is, singing without stage actions, was the primary form of performance. There were also full-scale performances of Chinese opera in restaurants and teahouses: on March 2, 1934, J. Douglas Graham observed two different types of Chinese opera at a restaurant during his stay in Singapore. The following excerpt was published around 1935 in his *My Wanderings in the Far East*:

> At night [we] dined with the Cowlings at a Chinese restaurant. This was a very big place. We were shown into a private room by two Chinese well known to the Cowlings, and who dined with us. Were waited on by three Chinese girls. After drinks—whiskey and beer—dinner was served. It was the weirdest I had ever had. There was bird's nest soup, sharks' fins, the skins of pig and duck, the latter two served with various sauces. At intervals one of the girls discoursed music, singing to a zither played with a bamboo hammer [*yangqin*]. All the songs were sung *piano* [softly] and sounded very sweet, only what the words indicated I haven't the slightest idea. I was informed they were love-songs.
>
> Then went up a lift to the top floor, where we found ourselves in a Chinese theatre. A play was being performed. The audience was 100% Chinese until we appeared. They sat in no regular order on little stools round the stage, with a constant movement. It was a most unusual and intriguing scene to me. Chinese men, naked to the waist, others in immaculate European clothes, mixed with their women kind, some carrying babies. This was the Cantonese theatre.
>
> Later, after partaking of a cup of coffee we descended to the next floor where there was a similar crowd, only a different style of play, peculiar to Shanghai, was being performed. It was most fascinating. The stage is really a platform, and has no wings, only a back-cloth. The stage hands move about the stage altering the scenery while the actors are performing, and they are always visible. In the Cantonese theatre the costumes were hung up at the side of the stage and taken down as wanted.[24]

I quote Graham's observations at length as they vividly portray the popularity of Chinese performing arts in large Chinese restaurants in early Singapore. Restaurants and teahouses served as patrons for Chinese opera by providing performance spaces for opera groups. The Nantian Dajiudian (Great Southern Hotel), for example, hosted both Peking opera and Cantonese opera performances in its restaurant and teahouse during the 1920s (Pang 1997, 34–35).[25]

As with early Chinese theatres such as Li Chun Yuan, seating arrangements in these restaurants was in the *chazuoshi* and was more casual than in theatres. There were usually two performances a day, one during afternoon teatime and the other for evening meals. Unlike the cost of purchasing a theatre ticket, customers paid only for the food and drinks, what was referred to as *chaqian* (tea money), except on occasions when they requested for specific operatic excerpts. While a pot of tea cost approximately ten cents, a song request was worth five dollars (ibid., 35).

According to the *Annual Report on the Social and Economic Progress of the People of the Straits Settlements, 1938,* wages in the Straits Settlements, which comprised Penang, Malacca, and Singapore, averaged fifty cents a day for men and forty cents a day for women, working in stores, factories, as rubber tappers, and in governmental departments; "Chinese agricultural labourers were mostly paid by results, earning from 50 to 70 cents a day" (Colonial Reports 1940, 42).[26] Considering that ticket prices at Li Chun Yuan during this period ranged between forty cents and $1.20 versus ten cents for a pot of tea at a restaurant where one could listen to Chinese opera, I suggest that restaurants and teahouses were more popular venues for the working class to enjoy Chinese opera performance. However, despite the relatively high costs required for song requests at Chinese restaurants and teahouses, requests were quite popular (Pang 1997, 35; see also F. Wang 2004, 42, 49–50). This suggests that Chinese opera performed in restaurants and teahouses offered a different mode of entertainment from that in theatres. While theatres offered primarily full-scale performances, viewing Chinese opera in restaurants and teahouses presented patrons opportunities to request for favorite excerpts, thereby personalizing their leisure.

FOREIGN CHINESE OPERA TROUPES IN SINGAPORE

Chinese opera troupes from China and Hong Kong frequently performed in Singapore and Malaya as well as other Southeast Asian countries such as Vietnam, Thailand, Indonesia, and the Philippines (Wu 1993, 479–83). It is difficult to ascertain when such visits began, but the formation of Li

Yuan Tang by Cantonese opera artists in 1857 suggests that Cantonese opera troupes from China may have already visited Singapore during that period (Cui 1994, 94).

The *Lat Pau,* Singapore's first Chinese newspaper, which circulated between 1887 and 1904, occasionally featured announcements of Chinese opera performances by visiting troupes. On Monday, October 5, 1891, an announcement placed by Zhen Fu Sheng Ban (Enhancing Luck Troupe) from Fuzhou, Fujian province, introduced three artists who would perform in Singapore, stating their names and role types, and singing praises for their skills (*Lat Pau,* October 5, 1891, 6; see also Pitt 1988, 59). Other troupes tried to attract their audience with advertisements vividly describing the plays they would perform, such as the announcement below by Fu Xiang Sheng Ban (Rising Luck and Fortune Troupe) from Beijing that performed Peking opera in Singapore's Qing Sheng Ping theatre along Eu Tong Sen Street (Wayang Street), for eleven days:

> PEKING OPERA TROUPE ARRIVES IN SINGAPORE
>
> We have invited top performers from Beijing and our group with more than ninety actors will perform many newly rehearsed plays, with traditional stories of the loyal court official and the filial son, and the confrontation between the Taiping and Imperial armies. The Taiping army has captured Jiujiang city, but Commander Hu managed to recapture the city; when the Taiping army entered Jiangxi province, they were repelled by Commander Zeng's troupe. Our realistic fighting scenes, amazing pyrotechnics, and stunts will make you believe that you are watching an actual invasion by the Taiping army. We will also present a newly composed play, *Yudeng Chutou* [*The Glowing Fishing Lamp*]. We will open on the 20th day of this 11th month [December 27, 1893] in a theatre in Singapore, and you are invited to come and enjoy our new shows.
>
> 15th day of the 11th month in the 19th year of Qing Dynasty's Emperor Guangxu, Fu Xiang Sheng Ban. (*Lat Pau,* December 25, 1893, 6)[27]

In 1908 and 1914, various groups of overseas Chinese communities invited the Cai Qing Yuan Muou Xiban (Cai Qing Yuan String-Puppet Theatre Troupe) from Quanzhou, Fujian province, to perform in Singapore, Penang (Malaysia), and the Philippines to high acclaim; the troupe performed for at least four months in the Philippines (Wu 1993, 481). From these and other accounts, we can surmise that there was an active Chinese opera scene in Singapore by the early twentieth century with performances by local and foreign troupes.

Chinese Opera, Local Identity, and Overseas Chinese Nationalism

By the 1890s, Chinese opera in Singapore had attained a prominent level of social significance with performances during celebrations related to events in China. The opera enjoyed the patronage of the upper-class Chinese community and their European acquaintances in Singapore, and was integral to fund-raising activities for disaster relief in China.[28]

Song Ong Siang (1871–1941), a prominent Straits Chinese in Singapore and author of *One Hundred Years' History of the Chinese in Singapore* (1923), recounts the following celebration in March 1889 to honor the marriage and accession of Emperor Guangxu to the throne:[29]

> The Chinese made the event a gala season, decorating and illuminating their houses, with theatrical performances in different parts of the town. Market Street was *en fête,* with masts erected on each side of the street, along and across which poles were suspended, bearing lamps and lanterns by hundreds, while a canopy of red and white cloth extended along the whole length of the street.
>
> These celebrations closed on the 23rd March, with a display of fireworks on Hong Lim Green [in Chinatown]. (Song 1967, 250–51)

A newspaper report of this celebration in *Lat Pau* details several locations with different musical performances by well-known troupes, including "Pu Qun Ying Ban [Popular Heroes Troupe] on Ma Che Jie [Horsecart Street], Qing Bai Nian Ban [Celebrating a Hundred Years Troupe] in Chinatown, Yushan Fengnu Ban [Jade Mountain Phoenix Female Troupe] in Shan Zai Ding [Small Hilltop]" and song performances by *geji* (women entertainers). The report further describes the elaborate decorations, which included poetry written for the occasion, put up by the Chinese community to celebrate Emperor Guangxu's marriage and transition from the reign of Empress Dowager Cixi, and eulogizes the continued loyalty of the overseas Chinese community to China (*Lat Pau*, March 8, 1889, 2; translated from Chinese). This loyalty to the emperor is also reflected in the labeling of the most expensive seats in the Li Chun Yuan theatre, at $1.20 per ticket, as "Guangxu" (Z. Wang 1988, 147).

In addition to public events, Chinese opera was also performed at private celebrations. Song describes one such celebration in 1891: "After the dismissal of the appeal of Yeo Kian Guan *versus* Seah Liang Seah, the Chinese showed their feelings of joy and satisfaction that a Court of law had upheld the honourable character of the late Seah Eu Chin, which had been impugned by the nature of the plaintiff's claim, by giving a *wayang* at Mr. Liang Seah's house to which Europeans were invited, and further, by the presentation of a silk scroll on which were set forth the virtues of the late Seah Eu Chin" (Song 1967, 262).[30] Chinese opera was also supported by wealthy Chinese through gifts presented to opera troupes. On September 4, 1905, a group of Chinese companies placed an announcement in the *Lat Pau* titled "List of Awardees" that detailed a register of gifts for the Nanyang Diyiban (South Seas First Troupe).[31] Such public recognition of Chinese opera reaffirms the relationship between Chinese opera and the upper-class Chinese community as theatre owners, troupe managers, patrons, and enthusiasts in the late nineteenth- and early twentieth-century Singapore.

Performances of Chinese opera in fund-raising events in response to incidents in China, particularly during the first half of the twentieth century, are important contexts to understand the intensity of nationalism among Southeast Asian *huaqiao* (literally "Chinese bridge"), or overseas Chinese.[32] The gradual decline of the Qing dynasty (1644–1911) in the second half of the nineteenth century and the concomitant impact of Western influence through trade, missionaries, and military strength sowed the seeds of nationalism in the Chinese diaspora (Pan 1999, 103). The role of Chinese opera in these events is indicative of its social significance to all segments of the Chinese population, framed by their responses to natural disasters and foreign threats in the motherland. Raising funds for China was an important means through which overseas Chinese expressed their nationalist sentiments. An example was a theatrical performance in 1909: "In aid of the Canton Flood Relief Fund and at the same time to spread the anti-opium movement, a company of wealthy Cantonese and Hokkien amateurs, which had toured the F.M.S. [Federated Malay States] and Penang, gave two performances in March at the Smith Street theatre hall [Li Chun Yuan] to crowded houses. The prices for seats ranged from $1 to $15, while fans and refreshments were sold, and bouquets, presented to the leading actors, were auctioned and realised fabulous prices" (Song 1967, 443). Standard ticket prices for Li Chun Yuan in the 1930s ranged between forty cents and $1.20.

The republican revolution led by Sun Yat-sen (1866–1925) received tremendous support from *huaqiao* in Southeast Asia (Wu 1993, 493–538). Indeed, in early twentieth-century Singapore, "[i]ncreasing numbers of Huaqiao came to feel that China's future lay in Sun Yat-sen's revolutionary cause" (Pan 1999, 205). Revolutionary currents began in the mid-1890s and culminated on October 10, 1911, in Wuchang, Hubei province, which ended the Qing imperial rule and established the Republic of China.[33] Singapore was an important center of revolutionary efforts among Southeast Asian Chinese communities in terms of media propaganda, activities of various individuals and clan associations, and monetary support (Wu 1993, 523–25). Chinese theatrical performances and other oral performance genres such as storytelling served as vehicles for spreading the propaganda of the revolution:

> The early days of November 1911 saw the Chinese in Singapore in a state of jubilation over the information that Peking was in the hands of a revolutionary party and that the Emperor and Prince Ching were prisoners. . . . The propaganda here was carried on through the medium of leaflets, vernacular newspapers and Chinese theatres, as well as in places like the People's Park [Chinatown] and coolie bangsals [workers' quarters], where itinerant Chinese orators denounced the tyranny of the Manchus over the Sons of Han. . . . Special performances were given in the Chinese theatre in Wayang Street [Eu Tong Sen Street] for the purpose of raising funds for the coffers of the revolutionary party, and speeches were made by representatives of the Hokkien, Teochew, Kwangtung [Cantonese] and Hylam [Hainan] sections. (Song 1967, 471–73)[34]

Nationalistic emotions among *huaqiao* were particularly fervent during military confrontations between China and Japan, initially in the Sino-Japanese War (1894–95), but especially after the massacre of Chiang Kai-shek's Northern Expedition Army in Jinan, capital of Shandong province, in May 1928 and during the Japanese occupation of China from 1937 to 1945 (Pan 1999, 103–5). *Huaqiao* responded primarily by boycotting Japanese goods and participating in fund-raising and resistance activities.[35] Activities surrounding the Shandong Relief Fund between 1928 and 1929, led by Tan Kah Kee (1874–1961), exemplified overseas Chinese nationalism across different social classes, which included wealthy individuals, commercial firm employees, factory workers, and prostitutes. "Other forms of fund-raising were experimented with, with considerable success. These included the staging of variety shows, theatrical performances and Teochew operas" (Yong 1987, 185–86).[36] The Chinese opera community and other theatrical groups also donated to the Shandong Relief Fund. For example, the Chew Wah Lim Club Teochew operas contributed $19,616, the Hoi Ting variety shows raised $12,000, and Chinese vernacular drama shows raised $5,762 (Yong 1987, 186).[37]

Chinese Opera in the "World"

Films were introduced to Singapore at the turn of the twentieth century beginning with open air cinemas that featured silent films (Cui 1994, 95). Many cinemas were built, one of the most prominent being Tianyan

Dawutai (Grand Heavenly Performance Stage) built in 1927 by Eu Tong Sen, established first as a Cantonese opera theatre and later converted to a cinema in 1939 (known today as the Majestic Theatre). The majority of theatres that had presented Chinese opera were converted to cinemas from the 1920s onwards, marking the beginning of a gradual decline of Chinese opera theatres in Singapore (Pitt 1988, 61–65).

Another factor that may have perpetuated the decline of Chinese opera theatres was the popularity of amusement parks in Singapore from the 1920s to early 1980s, modeled after similar entertainment establishments in Shanghai.[38] These amusement parks had numerous theatres that hosted various types of Chinese opera, Malay and English theatrical forms, the modern Chinese drama known as *huaju* (spoken drama), and performance by *gewutuan* (song-dance troupe).[39]

Amusement parks in Singapore provided alternative performance sites for Chinese opera and other dramatic forms from the 1920s to the early 1980s. These parks were referred to as *shijie* (world), and the three major ones were Xin Shijie (New World, built in 1923), Da Shijie (Great World, built in 1931), and Kuaile Shijie (Happy World, built in 1935).[40] They featured game rides, gambling parlors, cafés, restaurants, sports complexes, dance halls, cinemas, and theatres, and provided a central locus for entertainment. Proprietors at amusement parks engaged professional opera troupes on a contract basis and paid them allowances to perform without charging any rental fees for the performance space. Indeed, the emphasis in these "Worlds" was the numerous spaces for different types of theatrical performances, including *bangsawan* (Malay opera), *wayang peranakan* (Peranakan theatre), cabaret shows, and Chinese opera.[41]

Peking opera, Cantonese opera, Fujian opera, and Chaozhou opera constituted the majority of the performances at amusement parks, while other genres such as Hainan opera (*qiongju*) and Hakka opera (*hanju*) were performed less frequently.[42] Each amusement park had several venues for simultaneous performances of various operatic genres. The New World, for example, had two locations for Peking opera: Bajiao Ting (Octagon Pavilion) based on the teahouse style and an indoor theatre called Da Wutai (Great Stage) behind the pavilion (Pang 1997, 37–38); a space for Cantonese opera called Riguang Tai (Sunshine Stage), said to be the biggest theatre in the New World (see Chung Hon Kee, National Archives Microfiche A000919/17, 82–83); one for Fujian opera; and another indoor theatre called Bai Lao Hui (Community Assembly) that staged Chaozhou opera. Likewise, the Great World had a stage called Xiao Guang Han (Little Winter Space) for Peking opera, as well as the Guangdong Xiyuan (Cantonese Theatre), which was first used for Cantonese opera performances and later converted into a cinema that featured mainly old Cantonese films (Pitt 1988, 65–66).

To a certain degree, the amusement parks were associated with specific operatic genres. Chaozhou and Fujian operas were performed primarily at the Happy World, while Great World and New World were known mainly for Cantonese and Hainan operas. One reason for such associations was the proximity of the Chinese ethnic communities around the parks. Happy World, for instance, was situated in an area with large Chaozhou and Fujian communities and thus featured these two genres (Z. Wang 1988, 42). However, New World's Bai Lao Hui theatre was known for staging Chaozhou opera, even though it was not in a primarily Chaozhou area, and frequently presented one of the most popular local Chaozhou opera troupes, Lau Sai Thor Guan (Lao Sai Tao Yuan) Teochew Wayang (Old Honoring Peach). New World was located in the Jalan Besar area on the fringe of the Singapore's downtown, and the surrounding community was a cosmopolitan mix of Chinese, Indians, Malays, and Eurasians (Wong and Tan 2004, 281–85). Despite being located away from predominantly Chinese areas, its popularity for Chaozhou opera in particular and Chinese opera in general suggests that factors besides the neighborhood shaped performance opportunities and spatial distribution of Chinese opera in amusement parks: economic consideration was also a motivating factor.

Chinese opera performance was an important economic determinant in the management of the amusement parks. Proprietors would engage an opera troupe to perform in their parks with a certain amount of remuneration per day (Pitt 1988, 65–66). At Great World in the 1930s, proprietors paid from $70 to $100 a month per Chinese opera troupe (F. Wang 2004, 52). An average troupe had seventy members, so the pay for each member may have reached from $1 to $1.40 per month (this calculation does not take into account operating costs for the troupe). In comparison, a Chinese laborer earned between fifty and seventy cents a day in 1938, or $15 and $21 a month (Colonial Reports 1940, 42). However, a Chinese opera performer had few additional expenses since accommodation and food were paid for by the troupe.

While profits from the entrance fee to the park belonged to the proprietors, earnings from the sale of performance tickets belonged to the manager of the opera troupe. Park proprietors aimed to invite popular troupes to attract a large audience and increase their profit margins from the sale of entrance tickets to the park: new troupes coming into Singapore and well-known troupes that had established themselves in the region were given maximum opportunities to perform in amusement parks. Inviting a new troupe not only attracted audiences to the park but also provided a performance context for the troupe to be recognized in the new environment and, in the process, encouraged additional performance engagements for the troupe (Kew Bee Kee, National Archives Microfiche A000903/05, 11). Compared to the independently built theatres such as Li Chun Yuan, performing in amusement parks was more lucrative for opera troupes because of the remuneration and free performance space provided by the proprietor. Chang Tik Ying, a Cantonese opera performer, explains:

> In the 1930s, amusement parks were very popular among the opera troupes. Given a choice, we would rather stage our performances at these parks than in the theatres. Why? You had to pay rent to the owners of the theatres and there was no guarantee that you could recover the cost from your revenue. On the other hand, the owners of the amusement parks paid you to perform in the parks. The sum of money, of course, varied from troupe to troupe and depended on the locality of the park. At Great World, because it was farther away from the city, the owner paid between $70 and $100. Also, Cantonese troupes, which were much in demand, received higher payment. Indeed there were cases where the tenants of games stalls and shop owners refused to pay rent to the owners of the parks on the nights when there was no opera performance. (Liu and Phillips 1988, 41)

Whether a higher remuneration was for a well-known troupe or to make up for being further away from the city, such financial decisions suggest that Chinese opera played a central role in the operation of amusement parks. Giving a bigger payment to opera troupes to perform at a more distant amusement park indicates the high level of appeal that Chinese opera exuded to the general Chinese population.

Rental procedures further reveal the importance of Chinese opera performance in amusement parks. While free spaces were provided for opera performances, tenants of game and food stalls were required to pay daily rental fees, contingent upon the presence of an opera performance. As stated above, if there was no Chinese opera performance on a particular day, stall owners might refuse to give their day's rent. The reverse was also true: another Cantonese opera performer, Chung Hon Kee, said, "As long as there is a Cantonese opera performance, they will pay rent. Even if the stall is not opened, as long as there is a performance, they will pay rent" (National Archives Microfiche A000919/17, 112). Such practices were not exclusive to Cantonese opera, although the popularity of Cantonese opera over other genres implied that payments for Cantonese opera troupes were higher (Pitt 1988, 66).

Chinese opera performance was an influential factor in amusement parks. The absence of an opera performance would reduce the number of visitors and decrease entrance ticket sales, and prompt stall owners to refrain from paying rental fees (because of the lack of visitors), further reducing the proprietors' profit margin. The reverse held true. In the same way that a more established opera troupe would bring greater social prestige and economic returns to amusement parks, performing in the parks affirmed the status of the opera troupes through extended engagement with a consistent and sizable audience. Thus, for both amusement parks and opera troupes, Chinese opera performance mobilized increased participation, affected economic returns, and shaped social identities.

Broadly, Chinese opera in Singapore between 1920s and late 1970s differed from the decades after the 1880s when theatres flourished: the centrality of Chinese opera in the amusement parks shifted the dynamics between music performance and ethnic space. In the earlier period, the location of theatres and the type of Chinese opera performed were closely bound to the ethnic distribution of Chinese communities in and around Chinatown, carved out by colonial administrators in the 1820s. From the 1930s to 1960s, however, the spatial distribution of Chinese opera performances was largely influenced by the location and economic considerations of the amusement parks. In other words, amusements parks had displaced Chinatown as the locus for Chinese opera and became a center to redefine the meanings and values of being Chinese in Singapore.

The amusement park was a spatial symbol that signified a changing Singapore from the 1920s, combining Western cultures such as Shakespeare's plays and Asian traditions such as Chinese opera. The word "world" in the English names reflects cosmopolitan dynamics.[43] The rise of nationalism among overseas Chinese in the 1920s, particularly among the educated younger generation, prompted significant changes to the education of Chinese in Singapore: Mandarin replaced dialects as the medium of instruction, and, more importantly, following the May Fourth Movement of 1919, vernacular Chinese replaced classical Chinese, symbolizing a break from traditional ideas (Pan 1999, 206).[44] The intensity of nationalist sentiments toward China and emerging loyalty to their adopted homeland, Singapore, were manifested and reinforced in mass events and the rapid structuring of local Chinese schools, which strengthened the Chinese community to a degree sufficient to create concerns among the colonial powers (G. Wang 1989, 561; Cui 1994, 165–67). In short, modernizing currents in Chinese identities were pervasive during this period, which underscored the shifting contexts of Chinese opera performance.

The amusement park enacted such modernizing dynamics through an overarching concept of entertainment and by operating primarily under the economic forces of supply and demand. It refracted and diffused traditional Chinese ethnic divisions by staging simultaneous performances of different types of Chinese opera in one locale and encouraged social interaction by presenting multicultural performance traditions. Chinese opera in the amusement parks recontextualized Chineseness in Singapore from a traditional and colonial perspective of ethnic and dialect distinction, and a corresponding spatial division, to a broader framework based on modernity, plurality, and an overarching pan-Chinese identity.

Changing Contexts of Chinese Opera in Singapore

The proliferation of Chinese opera theatres between the 1880s and 1930s established indoor Chinese opera performances and introduced organizational shifts such as health and safety standards, seat hierarchy, and gender desegregation. Thus, in addition to offering a new performance space, these theatres shaped expectations and social behaviors.[45] Accompanying the popularity of theatres was the presence of wealthy merchants and upper-class Chinese communities who sponsored or owned Chinese opera theatres and troupes, which affirmed the social status of Chinese opera during that period. Equally important were groups of supporters and enthusiasts that developed around Chinese opera.

One such group was the *ergutuan* (women squadron), particularly though not exclusively associated with Cantonese opera and theatres such as Li Chun Yuan, Qing Sheng Ping, and Qing Wei Xin in Chinatown (Z. Wang 1988, 141–44; 2000, 92–95). *Ergutuan* were fan clubs of twenty to thirty wealthy women or prostitutes who supported male performers. They showered cash on their favorite performers, gave gold chains, jade pendants, watches, and *huapai* (flower baskets) with the performer's name marked out with banknotes, and lined them up outside the theatres where they performed.[46] Wealthy businessmen also supported popular female performers with cash gifts, gold and silver pendants, and after-show dinners (Z. Wang 1988, 142–43). *Ergutuan* and these male supporters were sufficiently prominent to constitute a unique social community in pre–World War II Singapore (Z. Wang 1988, 143). *Ergutuan,* in particular, regarded opera theatres as a locus for social gathering not unlike a clubhouse. Their presence and support affirmed the popularity of Cantonese opera in the early twentieth century and contributed to the so-called golden years (1946–48 and 1950–51) of Cantonese opera in Singapore (Liew Seng Hwa, National Archives Microfiche A000926/19, 145).[47]

Another important community that emerged through Chinese opera was the amateur opera organization. Some of the earliest public appearances by amateurs were the two performances in 1909 for the support the Canton Flood Relief Fund mentioned above (see Song 1967, 443). Like the *ergutuan,* amateur groups developed out of the social context that characterized the overseas Chinese community in late nineteenth- and early twentieth-century Singapore: increase in immigrant population, prosperity of the local economy and resulting wealth, heightened awareness of the relationship with China and Chinese identities. One major difference lies in their support and enthusiasm for Chinese opera through performance. Members of amateur groups were primarily wealthy and educated Chinese who performed Chinese opera for leisure. Their performance practices established a tradition that differentiated themselves from performers who formed opera troupes to make a living by performing Chinese opera, that is, the professional opera companies. By the early twentieth century, then, Chinese opera in Singapore may be distinguished in two ways: first, as street opera versus opera performed in indoor theatres, and second, performances by amateur versus professional opera troupes. Amateurs performed almost exclusively indoors, while professional troupes performed street opera and in indoor theatres.

The development of Peking opera in Singapore reflects the rapid growth of the Chinese communities in Singapore and the relationship between overseas Chinese and mainland China from the turn of the twentieth century until World War II. The series of performances by the Fu Xiang Sheng troupe in 1893–1894 described above was one of the earliest examples of Peking opera in Singapore, and for most of the following decades, Peking opera in Singapore was performed by visiting troupes from China and locally based groups made up of artists invited from China, especially from Shanghai and the Fujian province (F. Wang 2004, 34–46). Peking opera's historical support by the Qing court (1644–1911), its association with the Chinese capital (present-day Beijing), and its use of Mandarin, the language of education, status, power, and governance, probably resulted in its exalted position among the array of Chinese opera genres: in early twentieth-century Singapore, Peking opera was referred to as *guanyin* (official tune) or *zhengyin* (proper tune) (ibid., 72–75).[48]

Peking opera performances were primarily held indoors in teahouses and theatres: inaugural performances by visiting troupes usually took place in the Qing Sheng Ping theatre along Eu Tong Sen Street (Wayang Street) before proceeding to other theatres (ibid., 35). Unlike Chaozhou and Fujian operas that were performed both as street opera and in theatres, and thus attracted an audience from across different social classes,

Peking opera's exclusivity as an indoor, ticketed entertainment meant that the majority of its audience was relatively wealthy and, by implication, well educated and of high social stature.[49] In early twentieth-century Singapore, the Fujian ethnic communities were the largest and most affluent of the Chinese communities in Singapore, and they were pivotal in creating an audience base for Peking opera (ibid., 66–72; see also Cui 1994, 146–48). More importantly, it was from this comparatively well-educated and wealthy audience group that Peking opera amateur groups (*piaofang*) were gradually formed through the early to mid-twentieth century, which helped sustained the development of Peking opera as an amateur practice after the decline of professional troupes in postwar Singapore (F. Wang 2004, 88–106).

Visiting troupes from China, Hong Kong, and Taiwan continued to perform in Singapore until the 1940s when the war began. A few troupes such as the Lau Sai Thor Guan Teochew Wayang remained in Singapore (Cai 2003, 22–25); some, like the Lao Sanduo Ban (Old Sanduo) opera troupe, disbanded (Z. Wang 2000, 41–45), while others effected important changes in the local opera scene. Of particular significance was the impact of Taiwanese *gezaixi* on Fujian opera in Singapore. In 1930, Fenghuang Ban (Phoenix Troupe), a *gezaixi* troupe from Taiwan, performed in Singapore and Malaya with resounding success, and was emulated by other similar groups. *Gezaixi* was a relatively new operatic form established in the 1920s. Its use of folk tunes, popular songs, and the vernacular were among its reasons for success over the more classically based *gaojiaxi*, the dominant Fujian opera genre in Singapore before the 1930s. Many *gaojiaxi* troupes in Singapore and Malaya switched to perform *gezaixi* after the 1930s (Wong et al. 1972, 5; Z. Wang 1990, 83).

Chinese street opera, or *jiexi*, in early nineteenth-century Singapore was performed primarily as *choushenxi* (thanksgiving performance), a tradition that continued through the 1930s even when new performance opportunities emerged in indoor theatres and amusement parks. The increase in proceeds from permits given to *choushenxi* performances between 1915 and 1934 indicates that Chinese street opera in Singapore flourished in the early twentieth century when many troupes performed both *choushenxi* and in the amusement parks (Pitt 1988, 67).

At the beginning of the Japanese occupation of Singapore from 1942 to 1945, Chinese opera performances by local and foreign troupes declined but were later revived along with other arts and sports to encourage conditions of normalcy (Wong et al. 1972, 8; Pitt 1988, 67; Thio 1991, 106–7). The Japanese administration allowed public Chinese street opera performance for several related reasons. First, street opera performers, otherwise known as *xizi* (literally "show people"), were not considered a threat to the Japanese. Indeed, a popular saying was "*xizi juewucuo*" ("*xizi* can do no wrong") (Wong et al. 1972, 8; Liu and Phillips 1988, 46).[50] Second, the Japanese did not object to local religious practices and therefore did not ban *choushenxi* (Z. Wang 2000, 141). Third, after their initial distrust of the Chinese communities that culminated in the brutal *su qing* (or *sook ching*, purge and exterminate) campaigns against potential uprising, the Japanese encouraged Chinese opera performance to advocate their pro-Asian ideology, project a peaceful image, and appease the community (Pitt 1988, 67).[51] As a result of such positive reception of Chinese street opera troupes, many troupe quarters and makeshift stages became hiding places for political dissidents (Wong et al. 1972, 8).

The use of child performers in Chinese opera troupes came to the fore with the British administration around the 1950s. In May 1949, the government passed a law that prevented youths under seventeen years old to be employed as performers unless given permission by the labor departments (Pitt 1988, 68).[52] This was partially in reaction to the traditional practice of contracting children from poor families to live and work with Chinese opera troupes and undergo performance training by authoritarian troupe managers and teachers (Z. Wang 1990, 69–71, 78–81). The use of child performers was especially associated with Chaozhou opera troupes because their voices were deemed most suitable to match the shrill and bright sound quality of the lead string instrument, *erxian*, a two-stringed fiddle, that characterizes Chaozhou opera and music (Z. Wang 1990, 69; Phang 1998, 16–23). In their effort to protect the children, the British administration had proposed to ban Chaozhou opera performances in the 1950s, but this proposal was retracted on the condition that leading members of the Chaozhou Bayi Huiguan (Chaozhou Opera Association) attended all performances to ensure that no children were mistreated (Z. Wang 1990, 78–81; see also Cai 2003, 29).[53]

In the 1950s, the first film from China released in Singapore was *Liangshanbo yu Zuyingtai* (*The Butterfly Lovers*) in the style of Shanghai Yue opera, or *yueju* (Z. Wang 1992, 90–94). Numerous Chinese opera films produced in China were shown in Singapore in the following decade with tremendous success, the most famous being the Chaozhou opera films, *Chensan Wuniang* (*The Story of Chensan and Wuniang*) and *Su Liu Niang* (*The Story of Su Liu Niang*) in the mid-1960s (Wong et al. 1972, 8).[54] Such films reinvigorated the local Chinese opera scene, which had begun to decline in the early 1960s. By this time, Chinese theatres no longer served as performance spaces and Chinese opera troupes increasingly performed in the streets and amusement parks. Confrontations between Malaya and Indonesia over the establishment of the Federation of Malaysia in 1963 and political rifts between Singapore and Malaysia that manifested in tensions between the Chinese and Malay ethnic groups resulted in bombings in Singapore between September 1963 and May 1965, which led to a decrease in public performances (Wong et al. 1972, 8; Yeo and Lau 1991, 282).

Inspired by the successes of imported Chinese opera films, in May 1968 the state-run Radio and Television Singapore launched a weekly broadcast of Chinese opera performance by local professional and amateur opera troupes (Pitt 1988, 70; Z. Wang 1990, 71–72). During this transitional period of social disturbance and political upheaval leading to Singapore's independence in August 1965, performing for this new medium helped professional Chinese opera troupes maintain their business operations and encouraged the proliferation of amateur Chinese opera troupes.

2 *Chinese Street Opera and Professional Opera Troupes*

By the late 1960s, amusement parks started to lose their popularity in the face of competition from other forms of entertainment, such as television, radio, shopping malls, arcade games, as well as the government's curb on the illegal gambling that was rampant in the amusement parks (Rudolph 1996, 30–32). With the eventual closure of the parks, Chinese opera troupes lost yet another performance venue. The opera companies most dramatically affected were professional troupes that depended solely on Chinese opera performance for an income. When opera theatres and amusement parks ceased to function as performance spaces, these troupes turned exclusively to street opera performances (*jiexi*).

Based on visitors' accounts and newspaper reports of Chinese street opera scenes in nineteenth- and early twentieth-century Singapore, Chinese street opera during that period was primarily *choushenxi* (thanksgiving performance), as part of customary rituals or festivals to honor deities. Before the 1960s, although some troupes might perform street opera for secular purposes with ticket sales as they would have in indoor theatres, street opera was almost always *choushenxi* rather than purely secular entertainment. With the decline of theatres and amusements parks by the late 1960s, however, Chinese street opera served both religious and secular purposes: professional troupes continued to perform *choushenxi* under the patronage of Chinese temples or other religious communities, and also erected their own temporary stages in open areas and charged entrance fees for their performances. By the 1970s, Chinese street opera gradually lost its popularity as a form of social entertainment in the midst of a rapidly industrializing society. Secular street opera declined and performing *choushenxi* became the sole avenue of income for professional opera troupes. *Choushenxi*, performed by professional troupes, is now synonymous with Chinese street opera. Today, professional opera troupes perform Chinese street opera exclusively in the context of religious festivities, within temple grounds, or in temporarily sanctified open spaces.

Professional Chinese Street Opera Tradition

In Singapore, Chinese street opera performance by professional troupes comprises Fujian, Chaozhou, and Cantonese opera, with Fujian and Chaozhou operas being the dominant forms. All three opera genres were widely performed by local and visiting troupes during the first half of the twentieth century, particularly before the Japanese invasion in 1942, when professional Cantonese opera troupes were formed locally and many Fujian and Chaozhou opera troupes from China visited Singapore (Wong et al. 1972, 4–9).

FUJIAN OPERA IN SINGAPORE

In Singapore, Fujian opera (*fujianxi*) refers primarily to theatrical genres from the Minnan region in south Fujian province, with Zhangzhou and Xiamen as the main locus. The conventional use of the term "*fujianxi*" does not normally include north Fujian genres such as *fuzhouxi* (or *minju*) and *puxianxi* (or *xinghuaxi*), which are more commonly referred to with their specific genre names.[1] Thus, *fujianxi* in Singapore generally refers to different kinds of operatic traditions based on the Minnan vernacular.

1930 was a turning point in the development of Fujian opera in Singapore. Before 1930, Fujian opera troupes performed mainly *gaojiaxi*, a genre also developed in the Fujian Minnan areas.[2] From 1930 onwards, an influx of Fujian opera troupes introduced a new genre known as *gezaixi* to Singapore (Wong et al. 1972, 5; Z. Wang 1990, 83). *Gezaixi* became extremely popular with the Fujian community largely because of its colloquial language and catchy tunes, and local *gaojiaxi* troupes rapidly adopted and performed in the new form (Wong et al. 1972, 4–6). Developed in the 1920s, *gezaixi* is also known as *xiangju*, the former term associated with the genre's origins in Taiwan and the latter with its subsequent development in the Fujian Minnan region.[3] The tunes of *gezaixi* are based on the *lianquti* (string-of-tune "medley" form), using *qupai* (labeled tune) such as *qizidiao* (seven-syllable tune) and *kudiao* (crying tune), as well as *xiaodiao* (folk tunes) (Liu and Wang 1986,

393–431). The name "*gezaixi*" reveals the significance of folk tunes in its performance structure: in the Zhangzhou and Xiamen areas of Fujian province, *gezai* is the generic term for folk tunes. Thus, *gezaixi* literally means "folk-tune opera" (Wong et al. 1972, 5). In Singapore today, Fujian opera troupes primarily perform *gezaixi* with a handful of smaller troupes that specialize in *budaixi* (hand-puppet theatre) and *diaoxianxi* (string-puppet theatre) (figure 1).[4]

CHAOZHOU OPERA IN SINGAPORE

Chaozhou opera (*chaoju*) has roots in the *nanxi* (southern drama) of the Ming dynasty (1368–1644) (P. Lee 1982). It adopted characteristics of several popular *qiang* (tune systems) in Fujian and Guangdong provinces, such as *yiyangqiang* and *kunshanqiang* during the Ming dynasty, *bangziqiang* and *erhuangqiang* in the Qing dynasty (1644–1911), and local folk tunes and narrative songs.[5] The music of Chaozhou opera is based on a combination of *lianquti* (string-of-tune "medley" form) and *banqiangti* (tempo-variant form). The delivery of *qupai* uses four *diao* (modal systems) that characterize Chaozhou music in general: *qingsanliu* ("light third and sixth"), *zhongsanliu* ("heavy third and sixth"), *huo-*

*Figure 1: A performance of Fujian string-puppet theatre (*diaoxianxi *or* tixian muouxi*) (1997).*

sanwu ("lively third and fifth"), and *fanxian* (inverted mode) (Cai 2003, 71).[6] A characteristic trait of Chaozhou opera's vocal style is *bangsheng* (assisting voice), where multiple voices emphasize certain parts of a solo tune in unison, usually at the end of a phrase. *Bangsheng* is a unique stylistic feature of *yiyangqiang*, which further links Chaozhou opera to *yiyangqiang* (Yang 1981, 861; Zhang and Guo 1992, 479–80; Wu and Liu 1993, 288–91).[7]

Chaozhou opera troupes have performed in Singapore since the mid-nineteenth century. Lau Sai Thor Guan Teochew Wayang, arguably the oldest surviving troupe in Singapore, claims a history of 150 years in Singapore (and another forty to fifty years in China before that), which dates its arrival to the early 1850s (Cai 2003, 22). From the early 1900s until the Japanese occupation in 1942, many Chaozhou opera troupes from China performed in Singapore, Peninsular Malaysia, Thailand, Indonesia, Vietnam, and Sarawak (Wong et al. 1972, 7; Cui 1994, 95; Z. Wang 2000, 31).

Even though Chaozhou opera in Singapore was often performed indoors, it has been more closely linked to street performances and *choushenxi*. For example, in 1934, when the British government tried to confront social unrest caused by members of the Chinese secret societies, many of whom were associated with Chaozhou opera troupes, they proposed a ban on street opera (Pitt 1988, 67). Before the 1950s, *choushenxi* was dominated by Chaozhou opera troupes, even for ritual occasions organized by the Fujian community. Lau Sai Thor Guan was such a popular Chaozhou opera troupe for *choushenxi* that when Sin Sai Hong (New Honoring Phoenix) Hokkien Wayang started to perform Fujian *gezaixi* as *choushenxi* in 1954, Chaozhou opera fans referred to Sin Sai Hong as "Fujian Lau Sai Thor Guan" (Z. Wang 2000, 65).

CANTONESE OPERA IN SINGAPORE

Cantonese opera troupes from Canton and Hong Kong performed in Singapore before and after the republican revolution period in the early 1900s, but it was only after 1930 that professional Cantonese opera troupes were formed locally; before 1930, Cantonese opera was largely performed by amateur groups in Singapore (Cui 1994, 94; Wong et al. 1972, 6–7). Judging from the number of theatres known for Cantonese opera in the early twentieth century (such as Li Chun Yuan), the formation of *ergutuan* especially associated with Cantonese opera, and the relatively higher cost in engaging a Cantonese opera troupe to perform in the amusement parks, Cantonese opera was the most popular of the three main operatic genres in Singapore during the first half of the twentieth century.[8]

Writing in the 1950s, William Newell observed that of the four main types of Chinese opera performed in Malaya, namely Cantonese, Chaozhou, Fujian, and Hainanese, the "Cantonese and Teochiu [Chaozhou] players are predominantly professional, being employed full time by *wayang* managers; the Hokkien and Hainanese are predominantly amateurs, being employed for some particular occasion" (Newell 1961, 67). Notwithstanding Newell's definition of the terms "professional" and "amateur," Newell affirms the prominence of Cantonese and Chaozhou operas in mid-twentieth-century Singapore. Yet, despite its popularity and its perception as the most refined of the three types of Chinese opera prominent in Singapore, Cantonese opera is not as well represented within the purview of the Chinese street opera performance context because of the organizational practices of professional Cantonese opera troupes and the resulting high cost of engaging a troupe.

Unlike professional Chaozhou and Fujian opera troupes, Cantonese opera troupes in Malaya and present-day Singapore function more like companies. Two well-known Cantonese opera troupes in Singapore are Tin Ying (Heavenly Eagle) and Kong Fai (Exuberance).[9] These are not opera troupes per se but comprise several people who function as impresarios when Cantonese opera performances are required for *choushenxi:* they would engage Hong Kong performers for the lead roles and temporarily employ local performers for the minor roles. The companies remain relatively dormant for the rest of the year (W. Lai 1986, 27). Newell compares Cantonese to Chaozhou opera troupes in mid-twentieth-century Singapore and notes that Cantonese opera troupes focus on star performers in their advertisements in contrast to the more conventional emphasis on the troupe's name, as is the practice of Chaozhou opera troupes. He further adds, "Cantonese companies are continually reforming with changes in management and the amount of available financial support" (Newell 1961, 68). As a result, it is usually more expensive to engage a Cantonese opera troupe compared to Chaozhou and Fujian troupes.

Professional Chinese Opera Troupes

Professional Chinese opera troupes in Singapore are privately owned, profit-oriented companies whose income is derived solely from *choushenxi* performances. A professional opera troupe has an average of thirty members including a manager, stagehands, musicians, and performers. Approximately 20 percent are men who primarily serve as stagehands and musicians, with a few specializing in the standard roles of *jing* (painted face) and *chou* (clown), and the remaining members are women who take on the lead *sheng* (male) and *dan* (female) roles. The current troupe size is much smaller than it was before World War II, when each troupe had between one to two hundred members, or even compared to the 1950s and 1960s when troupes maintained seventy to eighty employees (Pitt 1988, 68; Cai 2003, 24).[10] During these periods, each troupe had several opera teachers, major performers with numerous supporting cast members, stagehands that included cooks, nannies, and barbers, and others in charge of stage props and costumes (personal communication, Johnnie Ng, July 28, 1997).

The average age of performers in professional opera troupes today is about fifty years old. In Lau Sai Thor Guan Teochew Wayang, the majority of members are between fifty and sixty-five and the youngest members are in their thirties (Cai 2003, 25). Most of these performers have gone through systematic training in Chinese opera with professional troupes. Goh Gek Lam (b. 1943), a *dan* performer with Lau Sai Thor Guan, began her opera training as a nine-year-old with Lau Chit Kee Hiang (Old One-Joss-Stick) Teochew Wayang, one of the earliest Chaozhou opera troupes to arrive from China in 1910, which remained in Singapore until it was disbanded in the 1970s (Wong et al. 1972, 7; Cui 1994, 95).[11] After seven years, the usual training period for opera performers, Goh was recognized as a fully trained performer and was able to seek employment with other troupes (personal communication, Goh Gek Lam, January 21, 1997) (figures 2 and 3).

Most professional troupes in the 1950s engaged teachers from China to teach various aspects of Chinese opera performance: one in charge of vocal training, another for dance and acrobatic movements, and another to train the musicians. Trainees lived and ate together in the troupe quarters (*xiguan*) for the entire period of training; they practiced various skills during the day and the more experienced trainees also performed in the evenings. They were only allowed to go home on special Chinese holidays and were fully under the charge of the troupe manager during the training period.[12] Traditionally, the ethos of professional Chinese opera apprenticeship presupposes a committed engagement with the performance tradition and, to a certain extent, to the troupe. Although the apprenticeship system continued as late as the 1980s, the turnover rate became extremely high. For instance, in 1986, Sing Yong Hoe Heng (New Peace and Properity) Teochew Wayang recruited about twenty new members in their teens and twenties who responded to an advertisement; after several years, only one of these new recruits remained (Z. Wang 2000, 56; Cai 2003, 31).

The process of full-time training in the professional opera tradition is known colloquially as *dapigu*, literally meaning "to beat the bottom,"

Figure 2: Goh Gek Lam (b. 1943) as a child performer, circa 1950s (photo courtesy of Goh Gek Lam).

*Figure 3: Goh Gek Lam as a young female character (*huadan*) (June 1998).*

a term used especially among Chaozhou opera troupes to emphasize the strict, under-the-cane training process through which performers were groomed as children. The term is also used to distinguish full-time members of professional troupes from part-time amateur performers. A typical response to discussions on the professional and amateur opera traditions in Singapore is "We are the *dapigu*. They [amateurs] just do it for enjoyment."[13]

There are fifteen to twenty professional Chinese opera troupes performing Chaozhou opera and Fujian *gezaixi* in Singapore today (see table 7 for a partial list). Several troupes are registered companies in both Singapore and Peninsular Malaysia, but they perform more frequently in Malaysia than in Singapore.[14] Before and shortly after Singapore's independence in 1965 when Chinese street opera was still a popular form of social entertainment, it was not uncommon for professional Chinese opera troupes in Singapore and Malaya to travel to and fro for performances.[15]

Professional opera troupes are usually engaged for twenty to twenty-five days a month to perform *choushenxi* for two to three days in several locations. There are usually two performances a day, one in the afternoon from 2 P.M. to 4 P.M., and another in the evening from 7:30 P.M. to 10:30 P.M. In the 1930s, evening performances lasted through the night and ended only the next morning at about 7 A.M., and in the 1950s and 1960s, evening performances lasted from 7 P.M. to midnight.[16] For secular shows, that is, non-*choushenxi* performances with ticket sales, a troupe performed in a particular location for at least ten days in order to complete an entire play. Generally, professional troupes have two different groups of performers, one that performs in the afternoon and evening, and the other involved only in evening performances. The former group includes mainly junior performers who take on minor roles, while the latter are experienced performers who are the "stars" of the troupe, popular with the audience for their specialized roles. These stars underwent stringent training in Chinese opera as teenagers when they were apprentices.

Performers of professional opera troupes have very little formal education because of their early commitment to full-time opera training. The *dapigu* system requires that apprentices stay in troupe quarters under the watchful eyes of the elders, shut off from the outside: "We were not allowed to go out at all; there was always someone looking after us. Even going to the coffee shop to buy food—someone else did it for us. I remember when I was younger, I was very nervous whenever I went to government places because I could not read or write" (personal communication, Goh Gek Lam, January 21, 1997). Goh further states that her knowledge of reading Chinese characters comes from her opera training when they were taught to read and memorize opera scripts. Today, not everyone in a professional opera troupe is a full-time employee in the sense that they work on stage the entire day. Goh is a housewife and performs mainly in the evenings. Ah Mui, a *xiaosheng* impersonator who often pairs up with Goh, works in an electronics assembly plant during the day. Johnnie Ng, the manager of Lau Sai Thor Guan, was originally in the construction business and now runs a retail shop that sells Chinese opera costumes, instruments, and other stage paraphernalia. Stage crews are all full-time employees, and some of them actually reside on the makeshift stage in order to look after the equipment. Broadly, because of their relatively low education level, professional opera performers who have additional jobs are generally blue-collar workers with jobs in the manufacturing sector or small retail business.

During my first few visits to the opera troupes in 1996, several performers thought that I wanted to be an opera performer. They told me that there were no prospects for a Chinese opera performer and that I would be better off looking for other jobs. The low social regard of a professional opera performer is summed up in the following statement by a lead *xiaosheng* impersonator in the Sin Sai Hong Hokkien Wayang who was in her fifties: "I work with a friend on some small businesses during the day. That's nothing to write about. Some things about being an opera performer are too embarrassing to reveal" (personal communication, December 18, 1996). I never probed further, but her response left a deep impression on me. Generally, professional opera performers have a low regard of their profession and of themselves, and are conscious of others' perceptions of them. Other performers concede that performing Chinese opera pays better than other jobs: "What other jobs pay you S$30 to $40 [US$18–$25] dollars for working three hours a night?" asks Goh. "And you don't really work for the whole three hours. Sometimes, you're only out there performing for less than one hour" (personal communication, Goh Gek Lam, January 21, 1997).[17] In contemporary Singapore, Chinese street opera performed by professional troupes is viewed as an outmoded form of entertainment and relegated to the realm of customary religious practices. Nonetheless, professional opera troupes continue to be patronized and supported by a regular community and constitute an integral social process in Singapore's Chinese communities.

Performance Genres

The majority of professional Chinese street opera performance is known as *daxi* (grand opera), that is, a full-scale performance of a complete play on a makeshift stage with musicians, actors, stage crews, lighting, backdrop, and props. In contrast to *daxi* are other performance genres that differ in size and performance styles.

Besides the more popular *daxi* genre, street performances of Chaozhou opera include two other performance styles: *qingchang* (pure singing) and *zouchang* (walk singing). *Qingchang* is also known as *chaoyin* (Chaozhou tune) and consists of a small group of musicians and singers who perform a complete play or excerpts of a play without any acting. *Chaoyin* is less expensive than *daxi* as it does not require a stage and is often engaged by smaller religious groups with limited funds or sometimes by wealthy individuals to perform simultaneously with *daxi*.[18] Two troupes that specialize in *chaoyin* performances in Singapore are Xin Yilixing Ban (New Happiness and Affluence Troupe) and Xin Tiancai Ban (New Rainbow Troupe) (figure 4). *Zouchang*, as the name implies, involves a group of performers who sing in market places and move from one stall to another, particularly during the Lunar New Year season. After a short performance at a stall, the stall owner usually gives the group a cash gift in a red envelope as a token of appreciation for their performance and as an offering of good wishes and blessings. The group usually consists of two singers, a percussionist, and a string player. The singers may play the *ban* (wooden clappers) or *xiaoluo* (small gong) as they sing, and the string player plays a small *yangqin* (hammered dulcimer) while the percussionist accompanies them on drums. A *zouchang* group may be formed as part of a larger *chaoyin* troupe or may simply be an informal group of performers with the aim of earning extra income.

In 1920s Singapore, before the introduction of *gezaixi*, Fujian *gaojiaxi* troupes were divided into three groups: *qizaiban* (seven-person troupe), *gaojia xiban* (*gaojia* opera troupe), and *shanglu laoxiban* ("upper-road" old troupe). *Qizaiban* were child apprentices aged between seven and fourteen years who perform *zhezixi* (excerpt plays) from the *gaojiaxi* repertoire with only seven performers. After age fourteen, these apprentices might continue to perform with the *gaojia xiban*, which commanded the highest fee and was the most popular performance style of the three categories. *Shanglu laoxiban* was made up of retired performers from *gaojia xiban* (Z. Wang 2000, 69).

Figure 4: A chaoyin *performance by Xin Yilixin Ban at Toa Payoh Lorong 4 market (photo by Low Eng Teong, 1998).*

Today, *gezaixi* is the most popular form of Fujian street opera, which sometimes also features two forms of puppet theatres: *budaixi* (cloth-puppet theatre or hand-puppet theatre; *potehi* in Fujian romanization) and *diaoxianxi* (string-puppet theatre; otherwise known as *muouxi* or *tixian muouxi*). In the discussion that follows, "Fujian opera" refers primarily to *gezaixi*. Full-scale *gezaixi* performance by troupes like Sin Sai Hong involves ten to fifteen performers, three to four musicians, and at least four stagehands. In contrast, smaller-scale performances may be presented by *qiyiban* (seven-artist troupe), with a stage only half the size of the regular stage used for *gezaixi*. In *qiyiban* performances, the seven performers are accompanied by one musician each for the percussion, string, and wind sections.[19]

PERFORMANCE CONTEXTS

Chinese opera plays an integral role in important religious events such as the birthday of deities, their ascension days, and the founding anniversaries of temples. Another important quasi-religious festivity that involves large-scale Chinese opera performances is the Yulan Festival, popularly known as the Hungry Ghost Festival. This festival lasts for approximately a month during the seventh month of the lunar calendar when it is believed that spirits are released to roam the earth. During this month, temples, business owners, clan associations, and dwellers of particular housing estates organize grand celebrations that include prayer rituals, dinner, auctions, and Chinese opera performance by professional troupes. The main purpose for the celebration is to appease and entertain the roaming spirits in return for protection and assurance of prosperity and peace. Thus, the front-row seats directly below the raised makeshift stage are reserved for spirits and are not to be occupied by human audience.[20] Other occasions in Singapore for which professional troupes are engaged include the propitiation of orphan souls, which uses mainly Chinese string-puppet theatre, and various thanksgiving rituals.

Collectively, Chinese temples are the most important patrons of professional opera troupes. Troupes perform at an average of ten different temples every month and often return to one temple in the same month for a different occasion. Different Chinese temples are emblematic of the diverse Chinese communities in Singapore and those with specific ethnic affiliations generally engage Chinese opera troupes of the same ethnic group. Table 4 lists five of the oldest and most important Chinese temples of the main Chinese communities in Singapore with the names of their respective patron deities.[21]

Table 4. Chinese Temples, Deities, and Ethnicity

Name	Location	Year	Ethnicity	Deity
Tian Fu Gong	Telok Ayer Street	1840	Fujian	Tianhou Shengmu
Yuehai Qingmiao	Phillip Street	1820	Chaozhou	Xuantian Shangdi
Haichun Fudeci	Telok Ayer Street	1854	Cantonese	Dabogong
Danrong Bage Dabogong	Anson Road	1861	Kejia	Dabogong
Tian Hou Gong (Qiongzhou Huiguan)	Beach Road	1857	Hainan	Tianhou Shengmu

Source: Juntaronanont and Mak (1994, 125–31).

Of these five temples, only Yuehai Qingmiao continues to engage professional Chaozhou opera troupes such as Lau Sai Thor Guan to perform during special occasions. Tian Fu Gong (Heavenly Blessings Temple) used to engage both Fujian *nanyin* and Fujian opera troupes several times a year, with indoor *nanyin* performances and outdoor opera performances along Telok Ayer Street.[22] Since the mid-1980s, however, Tian Fu Gong stopped sponsoring Chinese street opera but continued with *nanyin* performances mainly by the Siong Leng Musical Association (Lay 1998, 55–58). Haichun Fudeci (Coastal Luck and Virtue Temple) engages professional Cantonese opera troupes, and Danrong Bage Dabogong (Tanjong Pagar "God of the Earth" Temple) presents mainly *getai* (song-stage), a form of popular entertainment that features English and Mandarin popular songs as well as comic skits.[23] Supported by the Qiongzhou Huiguan (Hainan Association), Tian Hou Gong (Heavenly Goddess Temple) used to feature Hainan opera (*qiongju*), but today it continues to conduct religious rituals without any opera performances (Juntaronanont and Mak 1994, 177–81).[24] The correlation of temple ethnicity to Chinese opera genres is clearly delineated in temples such as Wuhemiao (Five-Consolidated Temple) at Toa Payoh Lorong Seven, where different temples within the larger compound feature their respective operatic genres on different occasions (ibid., 122).

RITUAL PLAYS

A troupe is usually engaged to perform on the day prior to the day of celebration, on the day itself, and often for an additional day after. Different plays are performed every day in the afternoons and evenings during this period. For a popular troupe such as Lau Sai Thor Guan, this requires seven to eight new plays every year for their performance repertoire (Cai 2003, 24). Since professional troupes perform primarily in religious contexts, ritual plays form an important part of their repertoire. More accurately, their entire performance is a ritual in that it is performed for deities. As Barbara Ward succinctly puts it, "[A]t the temple festivals [in Hong Kong], which take place annually (or biennially) on the so-called 'birthday' of the god to whom the temple is dedicated, the performances have a specifically religious rationale: they are given for the delectation of the god himself, a kind of birthday present" (Ward 1977, 194). Significantly, ritual plays are performed only by professional opera troupes as part of their role in Chinese religious practices and constitute a distinctive part of their social identity.

Ritual plays are specifically "rituals" in that the characters involved are immortals, gods, and deities such as the legendary Baxian (Eight Immortals) and Guanyin (the Goddess of Mercy). Ritual plays are collectively referred to as *banxianxi* (plays mimicking deities) and are categorized into *daxian* (big deities) and *xiaoxian* (small deities). When asked what ritual play would be performed on a particular day, the response is usually either "*ban daxian*" ("mimicking big deities") or "*ban xiaoxian*" ("mimicking small deities"). Ritual plays in the *xiaoxian* category are performed every afternoon and at least one *daxian* play is performed during each engagement period.

Similar categories of ritual plays are used for both Chaozhou and Fujian operas. In Fujian opera, the *xiaoxian* category includes *Baxian Heshou* (*Birthday Greetings from the Eight Immortals*) and *Xianji Songzi* (*Fairy Delivering the Deity*), and the *daxian* play is also known as *sanxian* (*Three Deities*), which celebrates the three legendary immortals, Fu (Fortune), Lu (Prosperity), and Shou (Longevity).[25] In addition to *Baxian Heshou* and *Xianji Songzi*, Chaozhou *xiaoxian* plays also include *Tiaojiaguan* (*Elevating Status*), *Li Shimin Jingpeng* (*Li Shimin Blesses the Stage*), and *Jingchenghui* (*Meeting in the Capital*), collectively known as *Wufulian* (*Sequence of Five Fortunes*). The Chaozhou *daxian* category comprises three plays: *Liuguo Fengxiang* (*Minister of the Six States*), *Liyu Tiaolongmen* (*Carp Jumps over the Dragon Gate*), and *Pantao Dahui* (*Meeting of the Heavenly Peaches*) (S. Yung 1997, 139–40).[26]

Chinese opera performance provides entertainment for humans and deities, but ritual plays are specifically for the deities. When a host temple honors its deity's birthday, it is auspicious to "invite" other deities to participate in the celebration, which is enacted through ritual plays. Through the performance of *xiaoxian* plays in the afternoon, the patron deity of the performing troupe is invited to sit with the host deity to whom the performance is dedicated and with whom the troupe's deity will celebrate the occasion by watching Chinese opera together. In the *Xianji Songzi* performance of the *xiaoxian* ritual play in both the Chaozhou and Fujian operatic traditions, two immortal characters (a male and a female) carry the troupe's deity down the stage accompanied by "bodyguards" to escort the deity to the central shrine where the host deity is placed. After paying respects to the host deity, the two immortals place the troupe's deity next to the host deity where it remains until it is escorted back to the stage during the evening performance (figure 5). The return of the troupe's deity may occur at anytime during the evening's performance, depending on the schedule of the host. The host delivers the troupe's deity respectfully onto the stage from the audience area, during which the performance may be interrupted by a change in musical accompaniment. A performer—preferably one dressed in red or any bright colors (but not one dressed in white)—would then be asked to receive the deity. The pause in performance for the deity's return demonstrates the importance of ritual practices in Chinese street opera.[27]

ATTENDING A PERFORMANCE

Working primarily with Lau Sai Thor Guan Teochew Wayang and Sin Sai Hong Hokkien Wayang, I followed their performances around Singapore between 1996 and 1998 to learn about the performance practices

Figure 5: A performer from Sin Sai Hong Hokkien Wayang receives the troupe's patron deity (photo by Low Eng Teong, 1997).

of professional opera troupes in contemporary Singapore. Since its arrival in Singapore around the 1850s, Lau Sai Thor Guan is probably the oldest extant Chaozhou opera troupe in Singapore today and certainly a household name in the Chinese street opera tradition in Singapore. The current manager and resident teacher, Johnnie Ng, began teaching and performing with the troupe around 1977 and formally took over its management in 1990 (personal communication, Johnnie Ng, July 28, 1997). From its formation in 1913 to 1936, Sin Sai Hong was known by various names and primarily performed Fujian *gaojiaxi*. Since 1936, the troupe adopted the performance of the popular Fujian *gezaixi* and has since been renowned as a leading *gezaixi* troupe in Malaysia and Singapore (Z. Wang 2000, 63–67). The troupe is currently managed by Chua Kian Hock who took over its management in the 1970s (personal communication, August 29, 1997).[28]

When I visited Lau Sai Thor Guan and Sin Sai Hong in the evenings, I usually set off for the performance site an hour before the performance began.[29] Very often, I spent some time driving around a particular housing estate, looking at my street directory, and wondering if I would ever find the troupe. The performance venue is usually a temple, parking lot, or an open ground. Many Chinese temples in urban Singapore are located in the heart of housing estates surrounded by high-rise apartments and shopping complexes; older temples are often in sparsely populated or industrial areas where very few people are likely to go in the evenings. Open areas reserved for communal celebrations are also located near housing estates for the convenience of people living in that vicinity.

The monthly performance schedule merely indicates the name of the town (or street) and the temple where the performance is held (figure 6). Performers and their fans are familiar with the location since they have performed or attended performances at that venue on many occasions. However, for someone who has not been exposed to this realm of social practice, locating the performance can be daunting. Fortunately, temples indicate that a celebratory event is taking place with rows of flags along sidewalks and strings of colored light bulbs suspended above. The flags often carry the temple's name and congratulatory messages such as *guotai pingan* (peace to the country) or *fengtiao yushun* (calm and tranquil environment). I would look out for these indicators and follow them; they line the main street where the temple is located and also the side streets that lead to the venue. The flags and lights usually stretch for more than 100 meters (328 feet) in all directions and are important directional devices because the event site is often not readily visible. Once I found these indicators, it usually took another five to ten minutes to arrive at the site.

STAGE SETUP

The stage may be constructed within the temple compound or immediately outside it. In either case, the front of the stage must face the temple and, in particular, the deity residing in the temple for whom the celebration is organized. Where space is limited, a temporary shrine area is constructed in a nearby parking lot or open ground. The shrine area is sheltered within an elongated structure made out of steel frames and covered with canvas, with the shrine at one end of the shelter and the rest of the area reserved for prayers, ritual enactment, or dining. The opera stage is usually a short distance away from the shelter, with its front facing the shrine (figure 7).[30]

润五月份	新赛凤福建剧团		21天	
初一至四	巴爷礼巴城隍庙		十三、十四	实龙岗北一巷
初五、六	汤申路九里洞		十五至十九	芽笼廿七巷A
初七	休息		二十	休息
初八、九	荷兰路大港内		廿一至三	班兰花园城隍庙
初十至十二	实龙岗北一巷		廿四至廿九	休息

Figure 6: Sin Sai Hong Hokkien Wayang's performance schedule during the leap fifth month of Wuyinnian (Year of the Tiger) (June 24–July 22, 1998).

Figure 7: A temporarily sanctified ritual space along Bishan Street 22: the opera stage (left) faces the altar (right) (1998).

The makeshift stage is a square of approximately 12 meters by 12 meters (40 feet by 40 feet) and is constructed out of timber poles, planks, and canvas. The platform is about 2 meters (6 feet) high, and hammocks are usually tied to poles underneath to allow troupe members to rest in between the afternoon and evening performances (figure 8). The canvas backdrop depicting different scenes divides the backstage and performance area, and also shields the backstage from the audience. Almost perpendicular to the backdrop on both sides of the stage are two painted wooden panels behind which the musicians sit. These wooden panels are doorways through which performers enter stage left and leave stage right.

The backstage is filled with makeup chests, props, backdrops, costume cupboards, and headgear (figure 9). Taking pride of place in the center of the backstage is the altar that houses the troupe's patron deity: Xuantian Shangdi (Supreme Divine Emperor of the Dark Heavens) and Taizi Ye (Crown Prince) for Chaozhou opera troupes and Tiandu Yuanshuai (Marshall Tiandu) for Fujian *gezaixi* troupes (figure 10).[31] Each performer has his or her personal makeup chest placed along the sides of the backstage in the same position wherever the troupe performs. Headgear is laid out neatly on a specially built structure, and costumes are taken out

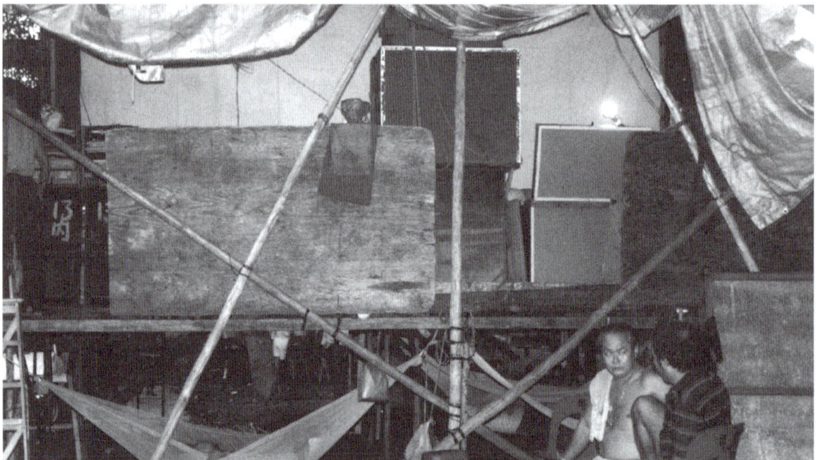

Figure 8: Members of Lau Sai Thor Guan Teochew Wayang taking a break (1998).

Figure 9: Performers of Lau Sai Thor Guan Teochew Wayang getting ready backstage (note the altar of the troupe's deity in the center) (photo by Low Eng Teong, 1998).

Figure 10: Chua Kian Hock, manager of Sin Sai Hong Hokkien Wayang, standing next to the altar of the troupe's patron deity, writing the title of the evening's performance on a display board (1996).

of the closets and hung outside during the performance for convenience. For every performance, there are at least five different backdrops that depict typical scenes in Chinese opera plays such as gardens, mountains, temples, and courts, each neatly rolled around a long pole connected to a pulley system. In addition, there is a huge curtain called a *damu* (large screen), richly embroidered with images of dragons, phoenixes, musical instruments, and the troupe's name, which is lowered during changes of backdrop and stage props.

MUSICAL INSTRUMENTS

The accompanying ensemble for both Chaozhou and Fujian opera follows the traditional divisions of *wuchang* (military section) and *wenchang* (civil section), with *wuchang* on stage left and *wenchang* on stage right. Lau Sai Thor Guan and Sin Sai Hong use only key instruments from the conventional Chaozhou and Fujian opera ensembles because of limited personnel; the following description is based on instruments used by these troupes.

For Chaozhou opera, *wenchang* consists of the *erxian* (two-stringed bowed fiddle), *yehu* ("coconut" fiddle), *suona* (shawm), and *yangqin* (hammered dulcimer). The Chaozhou *erxian* has a small cylindrical soundbox and produces a shrill, high-pitched tone characteristic of Chaozhou music. As a lead instrument, it is often known as *touxian* ("lead string"); the player (usually a man) is referred to as *toushou* ("lead hand") and directs the *wenchang* section. The *toushou's* playing position is a unique feature of classical Chaozhou music: he sits cross-legged with the instrument's soundbox on his left thigh and supports it with the ball of his right foot;[32] from his position, he has a good view of the entire *wenchang* and the performance area to his left (figures 11 and 12). The *yehu* is a two-stringed bowed fiddle that supports the *erxian* (usually through doubling at a lower octave) and is therefore also known as the *fuxian* (assisting fiddle). It has a sound box that consists of half a coconut shell covered with a thin piece of wooden board and has a lower-pitched tone that is also mellower than the *erxian*.[33] The *suona* is a double-reed, oboe-like instrument, and the *yangqin* is a dulcimer that is played using two thin bamboo hammers. A wind instrument known as *haotou* (natural horn) is used to start off the evening's performance. Made of brass in the shape of the letter "J," the *haotou* has a long neck and a flaring conical end and is blown to "chase away spirits that may cause disruption to the performance" (personal communication, Johnnie Ng, December 23, 1996) (figure 13).[34] Lau Sai Thor Guan usually has three *wenchang* musicians: a *toushou* who plays the *erxian* and *suona*, and one player each on the *yangqin* and *yehu*.

Figure 11: Wenchang *(civil) ensemble of Lau Sai Thor Guan Teochew Wayang:* yehu *("coconut" fiddle) in the front,* yangqin *(hammered dulcimer) in the middle, and* touxian *(or* erxian*; lead fiddle) at the far end (photo by Low Eng Teong, 1998).*

Figure 12: The toushou *(lead fiddle player) of Lau Sai Thor Guan Teochew Wayang has a good view of the performance on stage (photo by Low Eng Teong, 1998).*

Figure 13: The haotou *(natural horn) is blown to cleanse the performance space (December 1996).*

The *wuchang* consists of the *dagu* and *xiaogu* (large and small drums), *dabo* and *xiaobo* (large and small cymbals), *ban* (wooden clappers), *bangzi* (woodblock), *qinzi* (small knobbed gong), *quluo* ("tune" gong, usually played in pairs), and *shenbo* ("deep wave" large gong). The leader of the *wuchang* section plays the *ban, xiaogu,* and *bangzi* and sits facing the other percussionists with a full view of the performance on his right (figures 14 and 15). Two musicians play the *shenbo* and *quluo* suspended from a horizontal pole, and one alternates between the hand-held *qinzi* and *bo*.[35]

The *wenchang* that accompanies Sin Sai Hong's Fujian *gezaixi* performances consists of the *daguangxian* (large two-stringed bowed fiddle, also known as *erxian*), *kezixian* ("shell" fiddle: two-stringed bowed fiddle, also known as *yehu* or *banhu*), *erhu* (two-stringed bowed fiddle), *yangqin* (hammered dulcimer), *yueqin* (short-neck plucked lute), *suona* (shawm), electric keyboard, electric guitar, and saxophone. The Fujian *erxian* is different from its Chaozhou counterpart, with a large cylindrical sound box and a neck that widens toward the top. It produces a mellow tone with a nasal and melancholic quality characteristic of Fujian folk music; it is the principle accompanying instrument for the performance of *kudiao* (crying tune or bitter tune), one of the trademark *qupai* of *gezaixi*.[36] The *yueqin* is a two-stringed, moon-shaped, plucked lute, while the *banhu* is a short-neck bowed fiddle that produces a shrill tone (figures 16 and 17).

Sin Sai Hong's *wuchang* consists of the *zhangu* ("war" drum), *luo* (gong), *bangzi* (woodblock), *ban* (wooden clappers), and *bo* (cymbals). The *zhangu* is a barrel-shaped drum suspended vertically on a wooden frame and played with two wooden sticks. Two types of *luo* are used in Fujian opera: the *jingluo* ("capital" gong, borrowed from Peking opera) and *fengluo* ("phoenix" gong), both suspended vertically or sometimes laid horizontally on strings and played with a padded stick. Two musicians play the *wenchang* instruments in Sin Sai Hong, one plays the *erxian* and another plays the electric guitar, keyboard, or saxophone; the *wuchang* is often covered by one person (figure 18).[37]

PROCESSES OF TEACHING, LEARNING, AND PERFORMING

Afternoon performances are in effect practice sessions for junior members of the troupe when they take on roles usually assigned to the more experienced members who perform primarily in the evenings. If a *daxian* play is called for in the afternoon and there is not a sufficient number of performers to enact it, the evening casts may be called in for the ritual performance; in some cases, stage crews will don makeup and costumes to join in the ritual play.[38] After the show ends, many members remain

Figure 14: Wuchang *(military) ensemble of Lau Sai Thor Guan Teochew Wayang: (counterclockwise from right)* shenbo *(large gong),* dagu *(large drum);* bangzi *(woodblock),* xiaogu *(small drum),* bo *(cymbal) on table; a* xiaogu *(small drum) and* quluo *("tune" gong) hanging on left wall (another* quluo *in basket); a* xiaoluo *(small gong) and* qinzi *(small knobbed gong) on the wooden plank (June 1998).*

Figure 15: Johnnie Ng, manager of Lau Sai Thor Guan Teochew Wayang, as lead percussionist (June 1998).

Figure 16: Wenchang *instruments used in Fujian* gezaixi: *(right to left)* erhu *(two-stringed bowed fiddle),* erxian *(large bowed fiddle),* yueqin *(short-necked plucked lute), and* banhu *(two-stringed bowed fiddle) (1997).*

Figure 17: Wenchang *of Sin Sai Hong Hokkien Wayang with electric guitar and* banhu *(photo by Low Eng Teong, 1997).*

Figure 18: Wuchang *ensemble of Sin Sai Hong Hokkien Wayang with* zhangu *(barrel-shaped drum) in the front, two* luo *(gongs), and the percussionist playing the* bangzi *(woodblock) (photo by Low Eng Teong, 1997).*

on stage to eat, rest, or play a game of mahjong before the evening show.[39] In the evenings, performers arrive on stage at about 6:30 P.M. to prepare themselves for the performance at 7:30 P.M.: it takes about an hour to be fully geared up if the costume for a particular play is elaborate. While the performers put on their own makeup, they sometimes require help to adjust their headgear or heavy cloaks. If the troupe is putting on a new play that evening, it is not uncommon to see performers with scripts in their hands and perhaps even carrying a cassette recorder to prepare their parts backstage (figure 19).

Professional opera troupes in Singapore used to engage opera teachers from China, Taiwan, and Hong Kong in the 1950s and 1960s. Today, unlike amateur Chinese opera troupes, very few professional troupes can afford such a practice. Such was the case with Lau Sai Thor Guan, whose performers now learn new repertoire from Johnnie Ng, who sometimes also takes on the role of lead percussionist or *toushou* (playing the *erx-*

Figure 19: Goh Gek Lam reviews her part before going on stage (May 2004).

ian). He searches for new scripts from China, edits the text and music to suit the time constraint of three hours for evening performances, then records his rendition of the vocal parts for individual roles and distributes the recordings to the assigned performers with hand-copied scripts (Cai 2003, 24). It takes about ten days for an individual performer to become familiar with a new script, and three group rehearsals are needed before a new play is publicly performed; these usually take place on the stage between the afternoon and evening performances. Johnnie Ng decides on the play for the evening performance earlier that same afternoon: at about 3 P.M., performers (and ardent fans) call him to find out his decision. The host of the performance might request particular plays, although the absence of a performer specializing in a particular role or play might result in a different play being presented.

In 1936, when Sin Sai Hong switched from *gaojiaxi* to *gezaixi* performance, the troupe engaged a *gezaixi* instructor for a limited time to teach the new style (Z. Wang 1990, 83). Since then, however, the teaching and learning of plays in this family-run troupe depend mainly on the troupe manager and watching video recordings of *gezaixi* troupes from China and Taiwan. When Wei Mufa took over as troupe manager in the mid-1940s, he also took on the role of teaching stage movements (Z. Wang

2000, 68). Today, Wei's daughter, Madam Wei, is responsible for teaching, while her husband, Chua Kian Hock, manages the troupe. Sin Sai Hong's repertoire includes two types of plays: scripted and improvised. The majority of new scripts are transcribed by Madam Wei based on video recordings of *gezaixi,* particularly those performed by Taiwanese troupes. After selecting necessary scenes from the recordings to complete a three-hour performance, Madam Wei prepares scripts of the individual parts and has members learn their parts by watching the recording along with the scripts (personal communication, December 17, 1996).

For improvised plays, Madam Wei decides on the play for the evening's performance only about two hours before the performance, depending on available performers. After deciding on a play, she appoints specific roles to individual performers, many of whom already know the play by heart and need only refer to the *tigang* (topic outline) to refresh their memories. Should a performer take a new role, Madam Wei and the senior performers would offer tips on the character to be portrayed. The *tigang* is placed near the entrance to the performance area (on the stage left side) to allow performers a quick review of the scene before stepping onstage. The *tigang* is a large piece of paper on which information about the play is written: the title of the play is on the top of the page with a grid below containing scene numbers, characters, type of backdrop, and occasionally, the names of performers playing the characters (personal communication, August 6, 1997).

The performances of Fujian and Chaozhou operas reveal different modes of performance interactions depending on stylistic requirements, idiomatic practices, and individual expectations. The music of Fujian *gezaixi* consists of *qupai* to which different texts, *xiaodiao* (folk tunes), and contemporary pop songs may be added. Very often, performers do not know what tunes they will sing until they are actually on stage. Before they enter the performance area, they inform the percussionist with hand signals on the role and actions they will perform, each of which has different accompanying rhythms. For example, raising the index finger means that they will be singing to a tune (in contrast to merely having a dialogue), three fingers indicate the role of an official, a curved last finger represents a young female role, and an extended last finger tells the percussionist to provide an accompaniment for the role of a thief.[40] If a tune is not prearranged between the performer and the musicians, either the string player (on one of the two-stringed fiddles or electric guitar) or the performer may decide on the tune to be sung. Should the string player decide on a particular tune, he will play the opening strain of the tune to prompt the performer; conversely, the performer may begin by singing a few lines of the tune before the string player joins in. In the latter case, the string player may need to quickly transpose to the pitch of the performer, which may result in an unstable opening. Junior performers who are unsure of their parts may dance and mime the words of a tune sung by senior performers standing backstage.

Performers assist each other in various ways during the performance. In Lau Sai Thor Guan, "*dadianhua*" ("to make a telephone call") is a common way to help each other through a new play: backstage performers take turns shouting phrase prompts by standing close to the performers on stage with the script in hand. Most performers agree that a new play needs to be performed about three times in this manner before it is adequately memorized. The *bangsheng* (assisting sound) characteristic of Chaozhou opera (also known as *zhansheng* [stretching sound]), where phrase endings are punctuated by more than one singer, requires all performers to be alert at all times whether they are backstage or performing. Performers who are backstage retouching their makeup or changing costumes may collectively vocalize the last three words of certain phrases out loud.

WATCHING CHINESE STREET OPERA

The audience at a Chinese street opera performance is primarily middle-aged and elderly people, young children, and, at certain performance sites, foreign tourists. The host of the celebration provides plastic chairs, and audience members are free to choose where to sit.[41] The audience may be divided into two groups: those in the front rows pay more attention to the performance, but pockets of people scattered further away from the stage attend street opera primarily for social reasons. Audience size during an evening performance seldom exceeds fifty people; in an easily accessible site, this may increase to about eighty. Passing pedestrians may stop to marvel at the stage spectacle, and when performances are near construction sites, groups of foreign workers (for instance, from Sri Lanka, Bangladesh, Burma, or Thailand) may watch the performance as well. In tourist areas, it is not uncommon to see foreign tourists pose for pictures with the stage as a backdrop, or even ascend the ladder leading to the backstage to have their pictures taken with performers in costumes.

Members of the audience actively engage with the performance. On the evening of September 2, 1997, I attended a performance at Carpenter Street (near Boat Quay and Clarke Quay) by Lau Sai Thor Guan and overheard a conversation between two elderly people speaking in the Chaozhou vernacular. A *laosheng* (old male) character had just stepped on stage and strutted a few poses when they commented, "Ah Guang played a better *laosheng*. How can this performer take on the *laosheng* role?" Ah Guang specialized in the *laosheng* role but had left the troupe temporarily: the two men obviously preferred Ah Guang's performance to the one they were watching. Upon hearing the *laosheng* sing, one of them continued, "For a *laosheng*, you need a powerful voice. He doesn't have that kind of voice." The audience is not only critical of the opera but may also participate in the performance process, as at an evening performance by Sin Sai Hong on January 8, 1997. On stage, a master requested his servant to entertain him with a song. The servant hesitated and pretended not to know any songs. When a member of the audience shouted out a title, the master instructed the servant to sing that song, and as the servant began singing, the musicians joined in on the drums and electric guitar. In this instance, audience request merged seamlessly into the improvised performance of the troupe.

Such interactions with the audience are reminiscent of Sin Sai Hong's *gaojiaxi* performances before the 1930s, when time was allocated at the end of the evening's play for the audience to request specific *zhezixi* (excerpt plays); for each *zhezixi* performed, the audience member who made the request paid the performer(s) four dollars.[42] A related interplay with audience members within and outside the performance context involved performers who played female roles. Female impersonators in *huadan* (young female) roles attempted to attract more requests through acts of *chuanqing* (sending affections): they would point at a male member of the audience and cast a sensuous glance.[43] Seeing the *chuanqing* gestures, jealous bystanders would intercept by shouting "*shuai po*" ("break" or "shatter") to diffuse the affections sent by the *huadan*; in some cases, the interplay became a catalyst for fights. Audience interest in *huadan* impersonators extended beyond the performance; male fans might visit their favorite *huadan* backstage during the day at which time the *huadan* would dole out opium and cigarettes in exchange for money. This performance style that involved the audience prompted further actions that interplayed with the social, as wives and mothers of infatuated male fans argued and fought onstage (Z. Wang 2000, 70).

Chinese Opera and Group Identity

How familiar the audience is with the performers and repertoire of a particular Chinese opera troupe is indicative of the community that revolves around the professional Chinese street opera tradition. During evening performances, it is common for audience members to go backstage to socialize with performers. Many of them are long-time fans and attend street performances of their favorite troupes regularly.[44] Sin Sai Hong performers have photographs in different role types to give to fans who request for them, and all professional troupes prepare monthly performance schedules for distribution. New schedules for the upcoming month are usually given out during the evening performances at the end of the current month by the troupe manager and volunteers from the audience. There are fans who consolidate the performance schedules from different troupes of the same genre and rewrite these on a single page for printing and distribution. The new format becomes an overview of professional Chinese street opera performances in Singapore in a particular month (figure 20).

Not unlike the *ergutuan* (women squadron) associated with Cantonese opera in early twentieth-century Singapore, in the Chaozhou opera community, fans are collectively known as *shayu* ("sharks") and further distinguished according to the troupes they follow. Thus, fans of Lau Sai

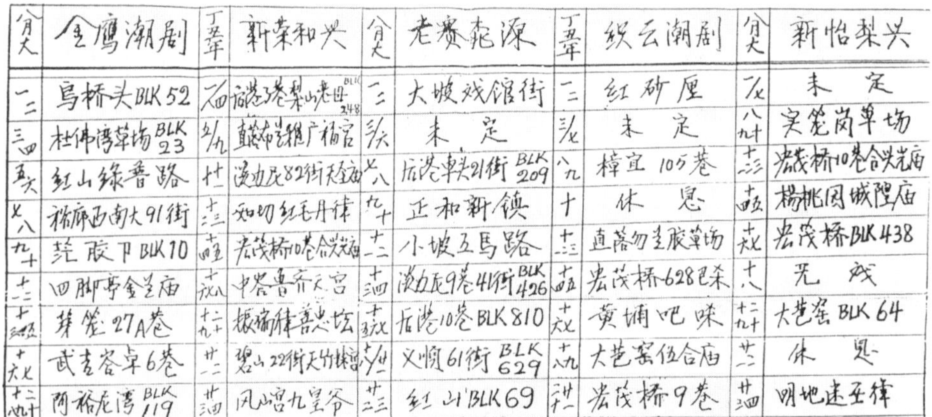

Figure 20: A schedule of Chaozhou opera performance by five troupes during the eighth month of Dingchounian (Year of the Ox) (September 2–October 1, 1997).

Thor Guan are "Sai Thor shayu" ("Sai Thor's sharks") and Sing Yong Hoe Heng's are "Yong Hoe shayu" ("Yong Hoe's sharks"). One group of *shayu* may be distinguished from another by their historical associations with a particular troupe, sense of support, and responses toward criticism hurled at their troupe; it is not uncommon for different groups of *shayu* to argue over the merits of their own troupes, especially when two troupes perform in close proximity (personal communication, Auntie Ng, December 12, 1997).[45] The phrase "*shayu guohai*" ("sharks crossing the ocean") is a metaphor for the distance fans would go to support their favorite troupe, and aptly portrays the enthusiastic support of Chaozhou opera fans.

Competitions between opera troupes have frequently led to animosity, such as the following incident reported in the *Lat Pau* on January 2, 1893. Qing Feng Nian (Celebrating Prosperous Year) and Qing Bai Nian (Celebrating Hundred Years) opera troupes had had tensions between them for several months, which were brought to the fore in December 1892 when both vied for a *huadan* (young female) impersonator and his *wusheng* (male warrior) companion when they visited Singapore. Both performers had negotiated a monthly salary of S$280 with Qing Feng Nian, but before this offer was confirmed, Qing Bai Nian intercepted with an offer of $320 with an initial payment of $20, which both performers immediately accepted. Upon hearing the news, Qing Feng Nian, the troupe that made the initial offer, swiftly ushered both performers and their luggage from their current lodgings to Qing Feng Nian's theatre, Yang Chun Yuan (Sunny Spring Theatre), increased their salary to $320, and quickly advertised their performance with the troupe on December 29, 1892. Meanwhile, Qing Bai Nian had announced its own performance with both performers on the same day, which caused public confusion. The performers eventually performed with Qing Feng Nian and Qing Bai Nian had to cancel its performance. Fearing retaliation from Qing Bai Nian, Qing Feng Nian requested police security during the performance (*Lat Pau*, January 2, 1893, 2).

The feud between Lau Sai Thor Guan and Sing Yong Hoe Heng is probably the most widely known in Singapore today.[46] Both troupes frequently tried to outdo each other with new stage effects, props, glamorous costumes, and acrobatics, especially on occasions when they performed at similar times and in close proximity to one another. Such competitive attitudes had a significant impact on performance styles, an example of which is the way the *xiaoxian* ritual, *Xianji Songzi* (*Fairy Delivering the Deity*), was performed, especially when both troupes enacted the ritual for their respective host deities: "When the two immortals escort the deity, there must be four accompanying soldiers (for each troupe). These four must be strong and fit; each holding one rod, very big rods. When they go down the stage, if anything happens, they will fight each other" (Chng Gek Huay, National Archives Microfiche A000860/18, 187).

Hostility between the two troupes is also manifested in the ritual play repertoire. *Liyu Tiaolongmen* (*Carp Jumps over the Dragon Gate*) is an important *daxian* ritual in the professional Chaozhou opera tradition, conventionally performed for sea-related communities such as fish farms and fishing villages in coastal areas and ship docks (S. Yung 1997, 171). Despite its 170-year history in Singapore, Sing Yong Hoe Heng does not perform this ritual. Instead, they perform another *daxian* play exclusive to the troupe known as *Pantao Duhui* (*Meeting of the Heavenly Peaches*) (ibid., 140). Colloquially termed "*Potao*" ("Breaking the Peach"), the enactment of this ritual involves the splitting of a *tao* (peach) and is said to symbolize the defeat of Lao Sai "Tao" Yuan (the Chinese name for Lau Sai Thor Guan; personal communication, Johnnie Ng, July 28, 1997).

For patrons of Chinese street opera, the process of engaging a troupe involves the interplay of social and musical considerations. A patron may be an individual, a group of individuals managing a temple, or an ad hoc group of people in a specific locale. Take, for example, a group of stall owners at a market place who form a committee to organize a thanksgiving ritual. Heading the committee is the *luzhu* (urn owner) who is responsible for the safekeeping of the urn that the group uses to pay respects to deities. In deciding on the opera troupe and genre to perform *choushenxi*, the committee considers various aspects such as the ethnic makeup of the committee, ethnic affiliation of the community it represents, deity's "preference" (if any), nature of the event, funds, and availability of opera troupes. At times, the choice may be directly related to the *luzhu's* ethnicity since the *luzhu* makes the final decision on every aspect of the celebration. More often, however, the decision is based on the consensus of the committee, availability of funds, and a concern for prestige.

The historical popularity of Chaozhou opera troupes in *choushenxi* performances has resulted in higher engagement fees relative to Fujian opera troupes: it costs between S$1,300 and $1,400 (US$812 to $875) to engage Chaozhou opera troupes and from S$900 to $1,000 (US$562 to $625) for Fujian opera troupes. Despite or perhaps because of the cost, putting on a Chaozhou opera performance affirms a certain level of credibility for the hosting group, particularly that of the *luzhu*. Similarly, inviting a popular troupe may be more expensive, but is likely to leave a better impression on guests than a less expensive and average troupe. Out of fairness, a committee with Chaozhou and Fujian members may agree to have Fujian opera for their Hungry Ghost Festival celebration and Chaozhou opera for the next event, such as the deity's birthday.[47] This "democratic" solution needs to be historicized and understood as an outgrowth of the strained relationship between the Chaozhou and Fujian communities in early twentieth-century Singapore when frequent fights occurred between the two groups (see Buckley 1984, 585–92; Lee 1978, 64–87; Song 1967, 402–4; Vaughan 1971, 95–104). Professional Chinese street opera performance manifests the intersection of music preferences, economics, social prestige, and ethnicity.

The profession of performing Chinese opera has traditionally occupied a low social position in China, especially when performers do it out of necessity rather than choice. In imperial China, opera performers were socially ranked as slaves, and laws prohibited them and their families from taking official examinations, the bureaucratic gateway to achieve status in Chinese society. Though such contempt applied to all actors from itinerant performers to those in private companies, a certain degree of social mobility was possible. One of the factors that enabled upward mobility was a shift from quasi-religious street performance for the masses to indoor performance for the wealthy and upper-class literati (Mackerras 1972, 42–44; see also 1983a).

The street-mass versus indoor-elite polarity emerged especially during the Ming period (1368–1644) when regional dramas developed that were closely associated with village festivities. This polarity may be attributed to the social and musical aspects of traditional Chinese street opera. The social facets of street opera performance—huge crowds, gambling, flirting, extortion, secret society meetings—were threats to the Confucian order, and governing officials imposed numerous controls (Mackerras 1972, 33–40). Many plays performed in street operas were secular dramas that deviated from idealized Confucian archetypes (ibid., 40); even Buddhist adventure plays, such as *Mulian Jiumu* (*Mulian Rescues His Mother*), were deemed unsuitable for the educated class. Writing about Ming dynasty *chuanqi* (marvel tales), Cyril Birch contends that the literati might visit public theatres but not village performances, and their preference was for *chuanqi* performed in private households (Birch 1995, 9–10).

In Singapore today, Chinese street opera performances by professional opera troupes fulfill a religious-customary function for the Chinese communities. The contextual shift from theatre and amusement parks in the late nineteenth and early twentieth centuries to secular street opera in the mid-twentieth century, and finally to street opera as *choushenxi* from the late 1960s, paralleled a change in perceptions toward the professional Chinese opera tradition—from a status of social adulation to a functional social role. Members of professional opera troupes lament their decline in performance standards in terms of stage props and size of the instrumental ensembles.[48] Their nonchalance regarding opera performed on the street is reflected in their desire to perform at indoor locations such as the Victoria Theatre.[49] Popular performers with professional troupes may even refuse to perform street opera: "as Johnnie Ng recalls, the then-famous Bao Zhu [a *xiaosheng* impersonator with Lau Sai Thor Guan] never performs street opera; she would only agree to perform in [indoor] theatres. Johnnie Ng says, 'that is where Bao Zhu's status differed'" (Z. Wang 2000, 21–22; translated from Chinese).

Notably, the historical association of professional Chaozhou opera troupes with street performance in Singapore prompted the Er Woo Amateur Musical and Dramatic Association (Yuyu Ruyueshe), the oldest amateur opera troupe in Singapore, to take up Hakka opera (*hanju*) instead of Chaozhou opera although their members were of Chaozhou ethnic descent:[50] "Early Chinese society looked down on professional opera troupes. Performers were *xizi;* to be friends with *xizi* would lower your status and to perform what they perform was shameful" (Z. Wang 2000, 36; translated from Chinese).

On June 16, 1998, I was backstage with Goh Gek Lam when Lau Sai Thor Guan performed at the Lorong Koo Chye Sheng Hong Temple. I noticed a few new performers and asked Goh about them, to which she replied, "It is like that these days: nobody stays long in this profession. It's funny—when you pay people to perform, nobody wants to perform for you. But there are so many people who would perform without pay, like the *rujia* [amateurs]."

3 *Amateur Chinese Opera and Confucianism*

Thursday, August 21, 1997, Singapore. I was sitting next to Goh Gek Lam while she touched up her makeup and waited for her turn to go on stage. That evening, Lau Sai Thor Guan Teochew Wayang performed on Bendemeer Road, in a historic area of Singapore's downtown that now hosts an increasing number of foreign tourists. I saw several new faces backstage, among whom was Tan Ooh Chye, a member of the Thau Yong Amateur Musical Association, playing the *erxian*. "He's a *rujia*," says Goh in the Chaozhou vernacular, as she nodded in Tan's direction. The Chinese character *ru* often appears in the names of amateur Chinese opera troupes in Singapore, especially the older, more established ones, but that was the first time I came across the use of the descriptive "*rujia*" to refer to an amateur performer.

Monday, December 22, 2003, Singapore. The Nanyang Pho Leng Hui Kuan (Nanyang Puning Huiguan), a clan association based on an affiliation with the city of Puning in southeast China, organized a banquet and an evening of entertainment to mark the winter solstice (*dongzhi*). Puning is in the Chaozhou-speaking region on the eastern part of the Guangdong province. It is not surprising, therefore, that a large portion of the entertainment was presented in the Chaozhou vernacular. The evening's program included martial arts demonstration, karaoke singing of Mandarin, Chaozhou, and Malay popular tunes, and performances of Chaozhou opera by the association's opera group, Puning Huiguan Chaoqu Xichangban (Puning Association Chaozhou Opera Singing Class), formed only months earlier in March 2003.

That evening's Chaozhou opera excerpts were presented in two styles: solo and group singing of popular operatic excerpts without movements (*qingchang*), and performances of excerpts by two actors in traditional costumes (*chaoju*). There were no live musicians accompanying the performances this evening and all excerpts were performed with recorded music. *Qingchang* is a common performance style in the Chinese opera tradition and is practiced by both professional and amateur opera troupes. This evening's performance, however, was unique to the amateur operatic tradition in that it was performed by a chorus of twenty-two men and women standing on stage and facing the audience.[1] Five men and six women sang the *sheng* (male) role and were dressed in white, long-sleeved shirts and trousers, and the remaining group of women sang the *dan* (female) part dressed in the colorful Chinese-style dress, *qipao* (commonly referred to in Cantonese as *cheongsam*).

One of the women who sang the *sheng* role was Tan Yang Ngor (b. 1962), a full-time mother to four children. She joined the association's opera group shortly after its formation in March 2003 and was quickly groomed for the role of *xiaosheng* (young male) because of her height and vocal quality. She often pairs up with Soh Ai Na, also a full-time mother of four children, who takes on the role of *huadan* (young female). This evening, in addition to participating in the group *qingchang,* they adorned full costume and makeup to perform the excerpt "Ai Ge" (Song of Love) from *Chunxiangzhuan* (*The Story of Chunxiang*) (figure 21).

Tan and Soh are amateur performers, and the association's Chaozhou opera group is one of more than twenty amateur Chinese opera organizations in Singapore. Amateur Chinese opera troupes are groups of musicians, performers, and administrators who perform Chinese opera on a voluntary and nonprofit basis, and primarily for leisure. The main distinction between amateur and professional Chinese opera troupes lies in their nonprofit versus profit orientations. Amateur troupes may be independent organizations or part of larger groups such as clan associations and community clubs. In many ways, independent amateur Chinese opera groups are similar to Chinese clan associations in their organizational structure, ideology, and sociocultural functions, and they may be understood as extensions of Chinese clan associations.

Figure 21: A qingchang *(pure singing) performance by the Puning Huiguan Chaoqu Xichangban, December 22, 2003. Tan Yang Ngor is in the front row, second from the right, and Soh Ai Na is the first person on the left end of the front row (photo courtesy of Tan Yang Ngor).*

Organization of Chinese Clan Associations

The Chinese community in early Singapore formed two major groups, one based on localized lineage according to blood, place of origin, dialect relations, and a common recent ancestry, and another on a nonlocalized system based on broader ties of kinship, region, language family, and remote ancestry (Yen 1981, 65). Various forms of kinship, locality, and surname were institutionalized as clan organizations, functioning as lineage systems transformed from the elaborate kinship patterns in China through immigration. In the late nineteenth and early twentieth centuries, clan organizations assisted immigrants to Singapore in aspects of food, lodging, dispute arbitration, funeral arrangements, ancestral and religious worship, and also promoted education and legalized marriage. The clan organizations played a central role as sociocultural institutions and frequently organized activities that involved Chinese opera performances, such as religious celebrations and thanksgiving rituals (Cui 1994, 57–80; S. Yung 1997, 193–222). Hierarchy was strictly observed in clan organizations, and seniority was determined by age, generation, status, and authority. Added to this was wealth, which constituted a central component in establishing leadership and social prestige in the colonial context (Yen 1981, 63).

The structure of clan associations consists of three broadly defined groups, with minor variations among organizations: (1) a standing committee that oversees the functioning of the clan organization, which comprises the clan leader, the deputy, and honorary secretary, treasurer, and auditor, (2) a managing committee that administers the organization's daily operations, and (3) the rank-and-file membership that forms the largest group (Yen 1981, 69). This organizational structure has remained relatively unchanged in the present, and it is in this structural domain that amateur Chinese opera troupes have emerged.

Strong allegiance to individual clan organizations was evident in the Chinese population in nineteenth-century Singapore, manifested in violent group confrontations.[2] It was only after the emergence of overseas Chinese nationalism in the 1880s and the relative weakening of dialect and regional identities that social tension between groups in the Chinese community in Singapore gradually subsided (Yen 1986, 202). In the booming economy of early twentieth-century Singapore, clan organizations gradually changed their emphasis to the importance of cultural and recreational activities, and several groups started their own music units, among which were Chinese opera groups. Wealthy Chinese individuals with interests in specific genres of Chinese music and opera also formed independent amateur music groups (Teo 1996). With the popularity of Chinese opera in Singapore at the turn of the twentieth century, it is important to note that amateur Chinese opera organizations developed concomitantly with the rise of overseas Chinese nationalism and economic prosperity.

Organization of Amateur Chinese Opera Troupes

Song Ong Siang's description of the March 1909 charity performances by Cantonese and Fujian amateur groups in Smith Street's Li Chun Yuan for the Canton Flood Relief Fund pinpoints two important characteristics that traditionally distinguish them from the professional opera groups: the participants were wealthy and their purpose was charity fund-raising (Song 1967, 443). Implicit in these traits was the voluntary and avocational nature of amateur groups, and, more importantly, a relatively high social status. Wealth enabled leadership power in clan organizations and society, which served as resources to motivate altruistic responses toward the local Chinese community and China.

Indeed, during the first half of the twentieth century, the organization of charitable events was one of the primary functions for Chinese voluntary organizations in general and amateur Chinese opera groups in particular. Many amateur Chinese music organizations initiated and participated in fund-raising events to assist victims of wars and natural calamities in China, and constructed hospitals and schools for the Chinese community in Singapore (S. Tan 1996, 40–46).[3] For example, the Er Woo Amateur Musical and Dramatic Association performed at a fund-raising event organized by the Chew Wah Lim Club in 1928 at the Qing Wei Xin theatre for the Shandong Relief Fund led by Tan Kah Kee (Yong 1987, 186; Z. Wang 2000, 33). In 1937, a group of prominent Chinese individuals, including a local war hero, Lim Bo Seng, formed the extant amateur Peking opera troupe, Ping Sheh (Singapore Amateur Beijing Opera Society), principally to raise funds for anti-Japanese campaigns in China through performances in the Great World, New World, and Happy World amusement parks and at Chinatown's Tianyan Dawutai (Pitt 1988, 67; Z. Wang 2000, 113).[4] The precursor to the current *nanyin* and *liyuanxi* troupe, Siong Leng Musical Association, comprised two music groups that gave street performances in the 1940s around the Tanjong Pagar area near Chinatown to raise funds for antiwar campaigns (personal communication, Wu Qiren, July 28, 1997). Thus, the social significance of the amateur in the practice of Chinese opera in Singapore needs to be contextualized as follows: (1) chronologically, at the turn of the twentieth century; (2) socially, when levels of economic prosperity and literacy were relatively high and continually rising; (3) culturally, as a diaspora with strong emotional and spiritual attachments to China; and (4) politically, in terms of nationalist sentiments toward China and, later, Singapore.[5]

While professional Chinese opera performances in Singapore declined from the late 1960s, amateur groups continued to perform Chinese opera in theatres and other indoor contexts, with support from wealthy patrons, their respective associations, and membership enrollments. The fact that amateur groups were able to maintain their Chinese opera activities was in part because of their organizational structure, ideology, practices, and access to various forms of public support.

Table 5 lists a selection of amateur Chinese opera troupes in Singapore with their year of establishment and operatic genre. New groups continue to form, but the twenty groups listed have made significant contributions to perpetuating interest in Chinese opera through regular practices, informal and formal performances, and lecture-demonstrations in schools.

Table 5. Amateur Chinese Opera Troupes in Singapore

Name of Group	Year	Genre
Er Woo Amateur Musical and Dramatic Association	1912	Hakka/Chaozhou
Lak Aik Amateur Musical and Drama Association	1929	Hakka/Chaozhou
Nanyang Khek Community Guild Opera Group	1929	Hakka/Chaozhou
Thau Yong Amateur Musical Association	1931	Hakka/Chaozhou
Ping Sheh (Singapore Amateur Beijing Opera Society)	1939	Peking
Siong Leng Musical Association	1941	Fujian
Kong Chow Wui Koon Music and Opera Troupe	1947	Cantonese
Tung On Wui Kun Cantonese Opera Troupe	1947	Cantonese
Tien Heng Kang Heng Nam Dramatic Association	1957	Hainan
Hyme Rhyme Sing Opera Club	1957	Hainan
Nan Hwa Amateur Musical and Dramatic Association	1963	Chaozhou
Kheng Lian Yew Dramatic Society	1965	Hainan
Chinese Theatre Circle	1981	Cantonese
Leling Beijing Opera Troupe	1981	Peking
Singapore Hainan Society Opera Group	1982	Hainan
Singapore Bukit Panjang Hokkien Konghuay Recreation Club	1986	Fujian
Kreta Ayer Cantonese Song and Opera Troupe	1989	Cantonese
Tian Yun Peking Opera Society	1992	Peking
Kit Yang Hway Kuan	1996	Chaozhou
Puning Huiguan Chaoqu Xichangban	2003	Chaozhou

Sources: J. Wong (1976, 32); Liu and Phillips (1988, 38); Directory of Associations in Singapore (1983, K101–14); National Arts Council (1996, 140–45).

Amateur Chinese opera troupes may be categorized into one of two types: independent groups formed by different communities and groups formed within larger social organizations. The Er Woo Amateur Musical and Dramatic Association is an example of the former, created by a group of businesspeople interested in Hakka opera (S. Chua 1992).[6] Opera troupes associated with a social organization are usually part of the cultural or recreational section of a larger guild, for example, those based on regional or dialect identity, such as the Singapore Bukit Panjang Hokkien Konghuay Recreation Club, Singapore Hainan Society, and Nanyang Khek Community Guild Opera Group.[7] In addition, some amateur opera troupes belong to community clubs specific to a particular area in Singapore, such as the Kreta Ayer Cantonese Song and Opera Troupe (or KACSOT), which was formed as part of the Kreta Ayer Community Centre (in Chinatown) in 1989.

Amateur opera troupes generally have about fifty core members who actively participate in Chinese opera performances. Several groups, such as the Hyme Rhyme Sing Opera Club, Siong Leng Musical Association, and Thau Yong Amateur Musical Association, have at least two hundred members, most of whom are sleeping/passive members, while only a quarter are either active members who participate in performances or core members who are involved in the general administrative and performance aspects of their group (S. Tan 1996, 16).[8] In this way, the structure of amateur Chinese opera troupes is similar to the three-tier model of early Chinese clan associations described above. Other groups such as the Singapore Bukit Panjang Hokkien Konghuay Recreation Club and the Puning Association Chaozhou Opera Singing Class have a smaller membership of about twenty to forty members who usually participate in every event. All members of amateur opera troupes, regardless of their level of participation, pay subscription fees to maintain affiliation with their groups.

Longer-standing amateur Chinese opera troupes formed before World War II and during the early years of Singapore's independence in the 1960s were generally initiated by members of the same Chinese language group. Examples of these are the Chaozhou opera groups, Er Woo Amateur Musical and Dramatic Association, Thau Yong Amateur Musical Association, and Nan Hwa Amateur Musical and Dramatic Association. In other words, amateur Chinese opera troupes also functioned as voluntary associations based on affiliations such as kinship or locality, where new immigrants from China might seek help and refuge upon their arrival in Singapore.

In postindependence Singapore, amateur opera troupes gradually become more inclusive in their membership. For example, Chaozhou opera groups that initially consisted of linguistically similar people from the Chaozhou region in China expanded to include the Fujian, Hainan, and Cantonese communities in the 1990s (S. Tan 1996, 16). Although these amateur groups used to be linguistically defined, today they define themselves artistically, in terms of individual interests and specialization in Chinese opera (personal communication, Tan Ooh Chye, July 25, 1997).

In her study of Chaozhou amateur music and opera groups in Singapore, Tan Sock Lay notes that 68 percent of the members are between twenty-six and forty-five years old, while only 7 percent are between fifty-six and sixty-five (Tan 1996, 17–18). Likewise, at the Singapore Bukit Panjang Hokkien Konghuay Recreation Club, the youngest member is about fifteen years old and the oldest is fifty-five, with the majority in their twenties and thirties (personal communication, Sim Siew Tin, October 6, 1997). Generally, there is an even mix of men and women in amateur opera troupes, and the majority of them are less than forty years old, which is relatively young compared to members of professional opera troupes, where the average age is fifty years with a majority between fifty and sixty-five years.

The literacy level of members of amateur Chinese opera troupes is generally quite high; most, if not all, have had a certain level of formal education. For example, 57 percent of Chaozhou opera group members have secondary school education (junior high school), and junior college (high school) and university graduates constitute 18 percent and 11 percent respectively (S. Tan 1996, 19). Before the 1950s, when formal education had not been systematically implemented in Singapore, the equivalent to a high literacy level was wealth and occupation. In her study of Ping Sheh, Pang Chai Ping notes, "In terms of social class, many of the members of Ping Sheh during the 1930s and 1940s were wealthy merchants and business proprietors, while members of other smaller amateur Peking opera group are generally salaried workers" (Pang 1997, 56; translated from Chinese).

Pang further notes that in the 1930s, membership in Peking opera groups was a high-class leisure activity that also served as an icon of self-identity (Pang 1997, 57; see also F. Wang 2004, 72–75). Indeed, since the early twentieth century, amateur Chinese opera troupes have served as a locus for the middle and upper classes in their pursuit of leisure and social recognition. For instance, Tan Yang Ngor and Soh Ai Na of the Puning Association Chaozhou Opera Singing Class are independently wealthy, upper-middle-class full-time mothers who practice Chaozhou opera for leisure.

Members of amateur Chinese opera troupes generally have white-collar professions such as teaching, administration, sales, account management, and other managerial positions. For example, Tan Ooh Chye, a musician and Chinese opera composer of the Thau Yong Amateur Musical Association, worked in a bank and later became head of the arts management division at the Nanyang Academy of Fine Arts. Sim Siew Tin, the administrative secretary of the Singapore Bukit Panjang Hokkien Konghuay Recreation Club, teaches in the mornings and attends to matters relating to her Fujian *xiangju* group in the afternoons and evenings.

Amateur Chinese opera troupes are registered with the Registry of Societies as nonprofit associations.[9] Each group has a committee that administers its operational aspects, such as membership matters, general training schedule, fund-raising, performance engagements, and the recruitment of overseas instructors and musicians. For all large-scale public concerts, a separate organizing committee is formed to conceptualize and prepare for these performances. These committees normally consist of the following units: (1) an administrative group, which includes a committee chairperson, secretary, treasurer, librarian, production manager, and other personnel responsible for the design and publication of the performance brochure, fund-raising, publicity, and ticketing matters; (2) an artistic group, which usually includes the artistic directors, scriptwriter and composer, choreographer, costume designer, lead musician, and others in charge of casting, lighting, and prop design; (3) the backstage crew, which includes makeup assistants and personnel in charge of preparing costumes, changing props, and projecting slides of text translations; (4) musicians, who are acknowledged separately from the performers because they are generally not members of the group they accompany. Instead, the accompanying ensemble is usually made up of freelance musicians, musicians from professional opera troupes, and others who play in Chinese instrumental ensembles.

All activities and rehearsals take place in the clubhouses (*jushe*) of individual troupes. These spaces are usually equipped with training spaces, kitchen, administrative offices, restrooms, and a lounge area equipped with television, video player, and sound systems. The clubhouse serves both as a training space and a locus for social activities. Group members usually arrive early in the evenings before their scheduled activities to have dinner, watch television programs, or listen to music together (S. Tan 1996, 24). Members who are fans of particular opera performers may also use the clubhouse for informal gatherings where they watch videos of their favorite performers or exchange write-ups on them from newspapers and entertainment magazines (personal communication, Sim Siew Tin, June 23, 1998).

Such social interactions at opera clubs are not unlike those which took place in Cantonese opera clubs in San Francisco in the 1970s: "Music making per se is not always the predominant concern of some of the present-day associations. General socializing and mahjong occupy the time of many of the members. For those who no longer live in Chinatown, the club is useful as a stopping-off place, before or after shopping or appointments, and as a generally convenient place to relax with friends" (Riddle 1983, 198–99). In addition to social activities, some amateur groups carry out regular private religious rituals in honor of their patron deity. Thau Yong Amateur Musical Association and Nan Hwa Amateur Musical and Dramatic Association organize annual large-scale rituals to pay respects to their patron deity as well as smaller, private rituals every month. Every year, on or around the twenty-seventh day of the eighth lunar month, members of Er Woo celebrate the birthday of their patron deity, Confucius, with a particular ritual sequence followed by a grand dinner (S. Tan 1996, 28–29).

Chinese opera performance remains the core activity of amateur Chinese opera troupes, and every group has regular practice schedules.

Generally, members have not had any systematic training in Chinese opera prior to joining a group, although many of them had an interest in this performance tradition as youths. After joining a group, members then go through scheduled periods of training, either with senior members of the group or, in the case of some groups, with opera teachers engaged from mainland China, Hong Kong, or Taiwan.

As the majority of amateur group members have full-time occupation, training and rehearsals are generally held during weekday evenings and also on weekends. However, when performances fall in the evening during the weekdays, it is not unusual for members to take leave from work in order to prepare for it. Table 6 summarizes the Chinese opera activities at the Singapore Bukit Panjang Hokkien Konghuay Recreation Club during a typical week.

A typical practice session in the evening begins at 7:30 P.M. and lasts approximately two to three hours. A senior member of the group usually undertakes the responsibility of ensuring the smooth running of the session. Coaching in practice sessions covers various aspects of Chinese opera performance, such as basic movements, vocal style, and memorization of scripts. For a large-scale performance, an amateur group may engage overseas personnel to assist them, which may include directors, musicians, vocal teachers, or instructors for stage movements. Fees for these overseas instructors are borne by members who benefit directly from them as participants in the training sessions. In other words, members who perform on stage for a particular event would be required to pay a predetermined fee in addition to their annual subscription to the organization (personal communication, Sim Siew Tin, June 23, 1998).

During weekly practice sessions at the Puning Association Chaozhou Opera Singing Class, the primary focus is on singing (figure 22).[10] The group has approximately twenty members and each pays S$50 (US$31) for a term of twelve lessons. Each practice session is led by an instructor

Table 6. Timetable of Activities at the Singapore Bukit Panjang Hokkien Konghuay Fujian Recreation Club

Day	Time	Type of Activity
Monday	7:30 P.M.–10:00 P.M.	Performance rehearsal
Tuesday	7:30 P.M.–10:00 P.M.	Training of basic skills
Thursday	7:30 P.M.–10:00 P.M.	Performance rehearsal
Saturday	2:00 P.M.–5:00 P.M.	Training of new members
	7:30 P.M.–10:00 P.M.	Performance rehearsal

Source: Personal communication with Sim Siew Tin (June 23, 1998).

Figure 22: Members of the Puning Huiguan Chaoqu Xichangban attending a vocal practice session (May 2004).

who teaches by rote and through the use of music notation. Members repeat each phrase after the instructor, paying attention to proper intonation, technical nuances, breathing, and ornamentation. Depending on the instructor's preference, he or she may use an *erhu* (two-stringed bowed fiddle) or a *yangqin* (hammered dulcimer) as accompaniment at these sessions, or simply sing a cappella. Individual students are sometimes invited to stand in front of the class to sing solo, after which both instructor and students offer comments and suggestions for improvement. The instructor explains the programmatic content of the excerpts and how this relates to specific vocal gestures, and encourages members to record each session to aid them in their practice at home.[11]

Amateur Chinese Opera Performances

Amateur Chinese opera troupes generally present small-scale and large-scale performances. Small-scale performances take place once or twice a month in schools and community clubs where excerpts of plays are presented; in schools, performances are often accompanied by lecture-demonstrations. Small-scale performances are often part of customary festivals such as Chinese New Year celebrations or Mid-Autumn Festival, or presented during national events such as Chinese Cultural Month or Senior Citizens' Week. For remuneration, amateur opera troupes such as the Singapore Bukit Panjang Hokkien Konghuay Recreation Club charge between S$800 and $1,200 (US$500 and $750) for each performance, depending on the occasion (performance during festive occasions are more expensive) and the length of performance (personal communication, Sim Siew Tin, June 23, 1998).

Large-scale performances are usually part of the group's anniversary celebrations and fund-raising events, and they include annual or biannual concerts during which tickets are sold to the public. An organizing committee is formed to oversee the substantial planning and preparation necessary. A significant amount of money needs to be raised to put up large-scale performances, as performance expenses may range between S$10,000 and $30,000 (US$6,250 and $18,750) for a two or three-day event (personal communication, Tan Ooh Chye, July 25, 1997). A large part of the initial capital is obtained through fund-raising, support from art and cultural institutions such as the National Arts Council, and private sponsorships from wealthy members of the group as well as from other individuals and voluntary associations.

For both large and small-scale performances, members generally receive only a nominal fee for their participation, primarily to cover transportation expenses, commonly referred to as *chemafei* (car-horse fee). Those involved in performing for a festive occasion, such as the Mid-Autumn Festival or Chinese New Year, receive additional remuneration for their efforts. Musicians playing in the orchestra, such as for the Singapore Bukit Panjang Hokkien Konghuay Recreation Club, are paid individually because they are not members of the group but guest performers. In other words, remuneration constitutes a distinguishing feature between members and nonmembers of the group. Members of amateur Chinese opera troupes pay to perform; invited musicians and performers are paid to perform. Remuneration, or rather a lack of it, constitutes an important component in the organizational ideology of amateur Chinese opera troupes that allows them to become credible and trusted entrepreneurs of culture in modern Singapore.

Large-scale public performances are usually held on weekend evenings from about 8 P.M. to 11 P.M., and sometimes there is a matinee on Sunday afternoon from 3 P.M. to 6 P.M.. A portion of the tickets for these public performances is usually given free to registered group members, while the remaining tickets go on sale to the public. Tickets are usually priced within the range of S$3 to $25 (US$1.80 and $15), and sometimes up to S$50 or $100 (US$31 or $63) in cases where the proceeds go to charity. Very often, these public performances are widely advertised on television, radio, and newspapers, and they are held in large air-conditioned theatres.

Public performances of Chinese opera by amateur opera troupes are formal events, with elaborate staging that is not seen in performances by professional troupes. Lights in the concert hall are dimmed just before the performance begins; the only lighted area is the performance stage and the two side panels on which the Chinese script and English translations of the evening's play are projected. The props are elaborately constructed and constitute a central visual aspect of the performance. With a large stage—at least twice the size of the makeshift stages used by the professionals—there is sufficient room for different types of two- or three-dimensional stage props and scenery, such as structures of palaces, temples, and hills.

The orchestra generally has at least five musicians each in the *wenchang* (civil) and *wuchang* (military) sections. The musical instruments used in amateur performances are similar to those used by professional troupes, except that the amateur troupes have a larger orchestra in which melodic parts are played by at least two of the same type of instruments. With the financial ability to engage a larger pool of musicians, amateur Chinese opera troupes are also able to incorporate a larger variety of instruments than professional troupes.

The cast of performers is also relatively large, ranging between twenty and thirty people. The senior and most experienced members of the group often take the lead roles, while junior members take on lesser roles such as accompanying servants and military personnel. In addition, temporary casts may also take on accompanying roles. These temporary performers are usually full-time students who, after witnessing a lecture-demonstration by a particular amateur troupe in school, for example, develop an interest in joining the group as an occasional member. Very often some performers, particularly those who take on lesser roles, also double as stage crews or sing in the backstage chorus.

Large-scale performances generally attract a huge audience, which may range from three hundred in smaller theatres to eight hundred in larger ones (Moey 1995, 42). If the event is in support of a charity, it is not unusual that a full-house audience attends the performance. The audience includes families and friends of the performers and members of the opera group and other similar performing organizations as well as the public. It is also not uncommon to find senior citizens' groups from community clubs that arrange special outings for their members. Very often, especially during charity performances, guests of honor and their entourages are present to grace the event. Generally, audience members show support for the performance by applauding whenever an actor executes a brilliant movement, and some proceed to the backstage during intermission to visit the performers or await their favorite performers after the evening's performance to request an autograph or a photograph with them.

With a large cast of performers and musicians, supported by special lighting effects and sound system, individual wireless microphones, and elaborate props, amateur opera performances exhibit a spectacle of colorful costumes and grand battle scenes amid individual displays of vocal artistry. This is in stark contrast to Chinese street opera performances by professional opera troupes. In addition to the clarity of voice projection, the audience of an amateur opera performance is able to follow the plot of the play by reading projected text translations; differences in the Cantonese, Fujian, Chaozhou, Hakka, and Hainan vernaculars thus cease to be a barrier in the reception of amateur Chinese opera. These factors, combined with the meticulous planning, wide publicity, centralized performance locations, and organized presentation, contribute to the accessibility and overall success of amateur opera performances. Through such performance practices, amateur Chinese opera troupes have acquired social recognition as bearers of cultural heritage in Singapore. This position in society is also due to their links to Confucianism.

Confucian Ideology and the Amateur in Singapore

In his book *Organizational Culture and Leadership,* Edgar Schein defines organizational culture as a set of "basic assumptions and beliefs that are shared by members of an organization, that operate unconsciously, and that define in a basic 'taken for granted' fashion an organization's view of itself and its environment" (Schein 1985, 6). For amateur Chinese opera troupes in Singapore, Confucian ideology underscores much of their organizational history, structure, and process. To be sure, they are also shaped by other frameworks of an organization, such as language and community, but I emphasize the Confucian aspect because of its historical significance in the concept of being an "amateur" in Chinese performing arts, and because of its pivotal role in the conceptualizing of a national culture in Singapore.

A basic premise of the Confucian ideology as it relates to the arts is that it accords a superior status to a person who "attends to the spiritual things and not to his livelihood" (Lin 1966, 191). Thus, although both amateurs and professionals perform Chinese opera, members of amateur Chinese opera troupes are socially superior because they perform it for leisure while professionals perform it for a living. Commenting on the aesthetics of painting in Song dynasty China (960–1279), James Cahill notes, "Literati painting theory is based upon, and completely in harmony with, the Confucian ideals of the arts. . . . As a worthy activity for the literatus who wishes to 'seek delight in the arts' and to manifest his mind, painting is now a means of self-cultivation; and the products of this activity, as embodiments of the admirable qualities of cultivated individuals, serve a Confucian end in conveying those qualities to others" (Cahill 1975, 92). Viewed thus, artistic pursuit is only a means and is only as worthy as its function in conveying the Confucian ethos to others. Members of amateur Chinese opera troupes pay to perform for themselves and to edify others through charitable and cultural events. Professional opera troupes, on the other hand, perform solely for functional reasons, both socially, in terms of Chinese customary and religious rituals, and personally, to make a living. The amateur Chinese opera organization, therefore, fulfils the dual function of social altruism and spiritual enlightenment through the arts.

Within the remit of Confucian ideology, technical achievement is dialectically linked to the embodiment of specific traits. Cahill further writes, "A man of wide learning, refinement, and noble character will, if he adds to these attributes a moderate degree of acquired technical ability, produce paintings of a superior kind" (Cahill 1975, 91). From the strictly technical perspective of Chinese opera performance, members of professional opera troupes may be more proficient than the amateurs because they have been trained for this profession since they were teenagers. Amateurs, on the other hand, receive basic training only when they join their organizations, generally at a later age than the professionals. Yet, as social organizations, amateur Chinese opera troupes are deemed better than the professional troupes. Such a value judgment is predicated solely on the "amateur" ethos and thoroughly informed by the Confucian ideology.

The Confucian emphasis on education and the importance of art for the purpose of refining the mind and soul are manifested in the structures and practices of the amateur opera troupe. Amateur organizations exemplify the ideal Confucian literati: they foreground education as a central premise of their organizational membership and engage in the practice of Chinese music and opera as a pursuit of leisure and edification. Amateur opera troupes perpetuate the emphasis on education by early Chinese clan associations and magnify this tradition by foregrounding the Confucian ethos and by actualizing this ethos through teaching Chinese opera in schools and other public forums. With the Confucian emphasis on the aesthetic and symbolic aspects of artistic practices in ascribing social values, one might say that amateur Chinese opera troupes attain their superior social status in Singapore despite, or perhaps because of, their moderate technical knowledge.

The social position of an amateur Chinese opera organization is conspicuously marked using the adjective "amateur" in its name. In Singapore, the Chinese equivalent for "amateur" in such organizational names is *ru*. Er Woo Amateur Musical and Dramatic Association, for example, in Chinese is called Yuyu Ruyueshe: Er Woo (Yuyu) Amateur (Ru-) Musical and Dramatic Association (-yueshe). In its conventional usage, *ru* connotes scholarly stature and an association with the Confucian philosophy. In Singapore's Chinese opera tradition, being an amateur signifies a learned individual or organization that embodies Confucianism.

Recalling Goh Gek Lam's description of Tan Ooh Chye at the beginning of this chapter, an amateur performer is often referred as *rujia*, specifically referring to an educated person or one associated with Confucian teachings. The terms *ruyueshe* (amateur music association) or *rujushe* (amateur opera association) are often found in the names of amateur Chinese opera troupes. *Ruyueshe* is condensed from the phrase *rujia yueshe*, which refers to *ruya de yeyu juyue zuzhi* ("literary and elegant amateur opera and music organization) (S. Tan 1996, 8). *Ru* as used in amateur Chinese opera in Singapore is expressive in both the social ("literary") and aesthetic ("elegant") sense. Indeed, the amateur prides him/herself on being educated and of a distinct social class.

Perhaps the epitome of the confluence between Confucianism and the concept of the "amateur" is having Confucius as the patron deity of an amateur opera troupe, as is the case with the Er Woo Amateur Musical and Dramatic Association. The two banners framing the portrait of Confucius in the troupe's premises sums up the Confucian ethos of amateur Chinese opera troupes. In figure 23, the right banner, "Yuyu Cun Zhengya," may be read as "Yuyu [the troupe] promotes righteous entertainment" or perhaps more broadly as "Vernacular entertainment [yuyu] embodies classic elegance." The left banner, "Ruyue Qi Wenming," may be understood as "Ruyue [the troupe] inspires civilization" or "Confucian music [ruyue] engenders cultural enlightenment." Although not all amateur opera troupes in Singapore pay respects to Confucius as the patron deity, the impact of Confucian ideologies on their social organization remains significant. What are the Confucian characteristics espoused through the practices of the amateur opera troupe and how do these traits function as a means of social differentiation?

Figure 23: Portrait of Confucius at the Er Woo Amateur Musical and Dramatic Association; photo taken during a ritual to mark his birthday (1997).

CONFUCIANISM, THE INDIVIDUAL, AND THE ORGANIZATION

An amateur performer engages in Chinese opera as an avocation, motivated by personal interests with the intention of self-edification. Insofar as the amateur performs to express individual interests, Chinese opera becomes a means for self-development and thus functions as a kind of "rational recreation" through the devotion of leisure to personal improvement (Kift 1996, 182). Technical expertise is neither expected nor required, and a suitable level of technical proficiency serves only as a means to enable the amateur to fulfill a role in both performance and social terms. To recall Cahill's description of the Confucian rhetoric about Chinese painting quoted above, an amateur music performance embodies "the admirable qualities of cultivated individuals [that] serve a Confucian end in conveying those qualities to others" (Cahill 1975, 92).

Amateurs practice Chinese opera as a community. Unlike performances by professional troupes where the focus tends to be more on individual star performers, amateur troupes generally learn, practice, and perform Chinese opera as a group. Such teaching and learning is significantly different from that of the professional opera performers, who generally learn new scripts individually in their own time and only rehearse intermittently as a group before and/or after each day's performance. In addition to the staging of particular scenes and *qingchang* by individual pairs, an amateur Chinese opera performance often includes a chorus-style presentation of specific arias to showcase members who may otherwise not be ready or willing to perform individually.

During training and rehearsals, amateur performers emphasize aesthetic issues such as clear enunciation, suitable vocal effects, precise lead-in between instrumental and vocal sections, and eloquent and convincing movements. The focus is more on presenting a persuasive performance through communal interaction than on the technical artistry of individual performers. Indeed, by extending their technical proficiency as a means of educating and relating to others, the amateur performer fosters "a community of spirit" (Cahill 1975, 87).

The not-for-profit status of amateur opera troupes and the process of paying to perform foreground a sense of "passion," a "real" feeling for what they do, and create the authentic ethos of a "raw" and "uninhibited" enthusiasm. As I noted in the previous chapter, professional opera performers comment with irony that the young would rather perform with amateurs without pay than be paid to perform with the professionals. While new trainees in professional opera troupes are an anomaly in Singapore today, amateur troupes are enjoying a constant rise in new membership. This scenario may be understood from a Confucian perspective that accords higher respect to those who attend practices for personal enlightenment than to those who focus merely on their livelihood.

In Singapore, Chinese opera performance is respected as an avocation but not as a vocation. I suggest that for the amateur, performing Chinese opera is a celebration of social status more than an achievement of technical expertise. Cahill's description of this Confucian ideal in Chinese painting is informative: "the scholar who was equipped with only a moderate technical facility in painting, but who had practiced the self-cultivation and acquired the classical education of the ideal literatus, was . . . considered to be better prepared to produce worth-while paintings than the professional who had concentrated upon learning the technique of the art" (Cahill 1975, 100). The Confucian framework of an amateur thus values the broader humanistic edification of the performer, as well as, if not more than, technical excellence. Viewed in this way, the social significance of amateur Chinese opera troupes lies not merely in performing Chinese opera, but also in the values espoused through their performances.

As individuals, members of amateur Chinese opera troupes may or may not be consciously aware of the interface between Confucianism and the amateur organization. However, just being a member of the organization predisposes them to be active participants in the perpetuation of the Confucian pantheon of values. To begin with, the amateur and non-profit nature of such organizations constitutes a set of unspoken criteria that influences membership characteristics. For example, a prospective member understands that making a living through music performance in an amateur Chinese opera troupe is not possible, both structurally (this is not what the organization is about) and ethically (the organization is bound by its ideology not to make profits through its activities). Therefore, to sustain membership in such an organization, the prospective member needs to have a minimum level of economic sufficiency.[12] As a part of an amateur organization, he/she then functions within its established organizational structures and practices, thus further promoting the organizational ethos.

An amateur performer or performing group functions in three broad categories, namely, avocation, transmission of knowledge and values, and social status. As a practitioner, the amateur is motivated, first and foremost, by self-interest in an art form and practices it for recreational and aesthetic purposes.[13] To this end, amateurs do not receive remuneration and instead, pay to perform. An amateur learns by joining an organization and is taught by professionally trained artists and their peers. For the most part, an amateur performance is for private consumption, whether it takes place in the public or private arenas, and more importantly still, for purposes of educating, sharing knowledge, and building broader interests in the art form. In order to fulfill these functions, amateur performers usually are part of a respectable social class with occupations to sustain them comfortably and sufficient leisure time to practice Chinese opera.

In many ways, the characteristics of amateurs described above are applicable to amateur musicians in Afghanistan (Baily 1979), amateur participants in Noh theatre in Japan (I. Johnson 1982), and avocational performers of Kun opera in China (Mark 1990). Viewed in this way, the concept of "amateur" is not exclusive to a Confucian interpretative framework. Indeed, the significance of the amateur performer is constituted differently in varying musical, social, and historical traditions. In Herat, Afghanistan, the primary distinction between amateur and professional musicians is in their status differences in Afghan society, informed by Islamic notions of music (Baily 1979, 46–47). In contrast, amateur and professional Noh performers in Japan work interdependently to sustain the theatrical tradition: professionals support themselves largely through teaching amateurs, who promote Noh in terms of finance, individual motivation, communal practice, and performance activities (I. Johnson 1982, 115–17). Historically, amateurs have played an important role in the development of Chinese theatre such as Kun opera as dramatists, performers, and financial sponsors (Mark 1990, 97–99). Colin Mackerras notes that the rise of the amateur performer in Peking opera in nineteenth-century China helped elevate the social status of the Chinese opera performer (Mackerras 1975, 79–80).[14]

Amateur Chinese opera organizations in Singapore are characterized by several factors: the historical position of Confucian ideology in Chinese performing arts, the social significance of the amateur status, their organizational and performance practices, and individual characteristics of group members. These organizational traits are foreground as they merge with changing ideology in Singapore after its independence in 1965 to shape new discourses of culture and identity. Specifically, the positioning of Confucianism as an organizational framework for amateur Chinese opera troupes in Singapore is further enhanced, as it simultaneously feeds into the role Confucianism plays within the broader social and cultural context of Singapore.

Economic successes in East Asia in the decades after World War II catapulted Confucianism forward as a model for Asian capitalism (see Tu et al. 1992; Tu 1996). In Singapore, Confucianism was first highlighted as an Asian inoculation against excessive Westernization, framed in terms of positive work ethics. From the late 1970s, by way of extending Confucianism beyond its fundamental Chineseness, Confucianism was folded into a rhetoric of "Asian values," which shapes the state's conception of local cultures. As a historically rooted and widely recognized social practice, Chinese street opera was a fine example of local culture in Singapore. However, in the state's ongoing discourse on a national culture that signifies meritocracy, modernity, and heritage, a Chinese street opera tradition invented by amateur opera troupes in the 1970s—invented in the sense that amateurs were not historically associated with the street opera performance style—was the preferred cultural icon over that performed by professional troupes. Once the exclusive domain of professional opera troupes in Singapore, Chinese street opera is now appropriated by the amateurs. Within the framework of national culture in contemporary Singapore, amateurs have replaced the professionals in Chinese street opera performance.

At the winter solstice celebration on December 22, 2003, at the Puning Association, *Jingchenghui* (*Meeting in the Capital*) was the first Chinese opera excerpt performed. *Jingchenghui* is often performed as an independent play, but it also belongs to the *xiaoxian* (small deities) ritual repertoire of the Chaozhou operatic tradition and is thus also a ritual play (*banxianxi*). The Puning Association traditionally invited Lau Sai Thor Guan Teochew Wayang, the professional company, to perform at their annual winter solstice event, and Lau Sai Thor Guan always begins a day's work with a ritual play, as is the conventional practice of professional opera troupes. After the Puning Association's amateur Chaozhou opera group formed in March 2003, however, it has taken over Lau Sai Thor Guan's role in performing Chinese opera at the solstice celebration. As an amateur troupe, it now performs ritual plays, once one of the distinguishing practices of the professionals.

4 *Reinstating Patronage and Tradition*

CHINESE TEMPLES AND THE REVIVAL OF CHINESE STREET OPERA

During the weekend of May 15 and 16, 2004, *Lianhe Zaobao,* the main Chinese newspaper in Singapore, published several feature articles on Chinese street opera and temple celebrations. These articles coincided with a 105-day birthday celebration of Qingxi Xianyou Bozhu (Deity of the Virtuous and Blessed) at the Lorong Koo Chye Sheng Hong Temple, which began on May 16, 2004.[1] The main events in this celebration were the *choushenxi* performances by professional Chinese opera troupes. One of these articles, titled "Busy Atmosphere of Temple Festivals Sees Resurgence" (*Lianhe Zaobao,* May 16, 2004), describes how different Chinese temples in Singapore are reviving temple festivals (*miaohui*) to honor their deities, mark special religious occasions, and to commemorate customary events such as the Lunar New Year or Mid-Autumn Festival.

A temple festival, which includes food and game stalls, arts and crafts exhibitions, and Chinese street opera as the main attraction, was a focal event in traditional Chinese villages in Singapore before the 1960s. Beginning in the 1990s, Lorong Koo Chye Sheng Hong Temple started to gain prominence for its annual temple festival, for which the main focus was the daily Chinese opera performances by professional troupes. As Barbara Ward cogently states in her study of temple festivals in Hong Kong, "If the operas are the highlight of the fair, the festival in its turn highlights the operas" (Ward 1985, 185). In light of the scarcity of temple festivals and the concomitant decline of professional Chinese opera performances in the previous two to three decades in Singapore, Lorong Koo Chye Sheng Hong Temple's annual festival is a remarkable contribution to the maintenance of the professional operatic tradition in Singapore.

Chinese Opera and the Temple Festival

In the 1920s and 1930s, the Lorong Koo Chye Sheng Hong Temple held the usual two-day temple festival to honor its deity's birthday, similar to what I have described in chapter 2. The period of celebration increased to a month in the 1960s, and from the early 1990s onwards, these birthday celebrations consistently lasted over a month: from 42 days in 1992 to 79 days in 1996 and 1997, peaking at 109 days in 1998, 101 days in 1999 and 2000, 80 days in 2003, 105 days in 2004, and 80 days in 2005. Within a decade, the temple festival at the temple between May and August every year became a distinctive event for Chinese opera performances by professional Chinese opera troupes in Singapore, justly described as an opera gala.

In 1997, the temple celebrated the eightieth anniversary of the shrine of its deity and the official opening of its new premises at 15 Arumugam Road, Paya Lebar. The deity, Qingxi Xianyou Bozhu, has its roots in the Cheng Huang Miao (City-God Temple) located in Anxi county, Fujian province, China. The deity was brought to Singapore in 1918 by two men from the temple in Anxi county to raise funds from Anxi immigrants in Singapore for the reconstruction of the original temple. Upon completion of the fund-raising activities, the deity reportedly requested to remain in Singapore (*Lianhe Zaobao*, November 30, 1997). According to legend, the deity also enjoyed watching Chinese opera (*Lianhe Zaobao*, May 15, 2004).

A shrine for the deity was first housed in the premises of a Chinese puppet troupe, Lao Quanan Zhangzhongban (Old Quanan Fujian Hand Puppet Troupe), on Craig Road, not far from Chinatown. A few years later, the shrine was relocated to a temple in an area known as Fengli Shan (Pineapple Hill) in present-day Hougang (in the mideastern part of Singapore). At Fengli Shan an increasing number of villagers visited the shrine, especially on the deity's birthday. In 1938, both the shrine and the community at Fengli Shan were relocated to a village known as Lorong Koo Chye (Chives Way). A temple was built to house the shrine and thus began the history of the Lorong Koo Chye Sheng Hong Temple. The temple was refurbished in 1956 as the number of worshippers continued to grow. Numerous religious activities were organized, and during this period both Chaozhou and Fujian opera troupes were invited to perform for the deity's birthday.

In 1978, because of massive urbanization and industrialization in Singapore, the government acquired the piece of land at Lorong Koo Chye where the shrine was located. A committee in charge of constructing a new temple was set up to raise funds for a new building. In 1986, the shrine was moved to a temporary site at its present location in Arumugam Road while awaiting the completion of the new temple in its present form in 1988 (*Lianhe Zaobao*, November 30, 1997).

HOSTING THE OPERA GALA

Each year, a committee is formed to organize the temple festival to celebrate the birthday of its deity, which falls on the twenty-eighth day of the fifth month of the lunar calendar. Flyers listing the opera troupes participating in the festival are distributed to temple devotees and guests and are displayed in enlarged format at the temple grounds shortly before the first day of the festival. The announcement for the 2005 festival begins, "In conjunction with the celebration of Qing Xi Xian You Bo Zhu (City God) birthday, our temple has engaged the following Opera Troupes to perform traditional drama shows from 16.5.2005 to 3.8.2005, a total of 80 days. Apart from 4.7.2005, which is engaged by temple, devotees sponsor the remaining 79 days."[2] Following this paragraph is a list of professional Chinese opera troupes with the dates of their performances. Except for the performance on the actual birthday itself (in 2005, it was on July 4), which is sponsored by the temple, temple devotees pay for all other performances.[3]

Temple devotees sponsor Chinese opera performances for several reasons: first, to express their gratitude to the deity for providing them guidance and protection through the year; second, to pray for continuous blessing in the following year; and third, to maintain a favorable relationship within the temple culture and to celebrate themselves among existing and/or new members of the temple (personal communication, Tan Chiew Hai, August 6, 1997).[4]

As the temple flourished through the years, more devotees requested to sponsor Chinese opera performances. To accommodate its devotees, the festival committee decided that it would allow more Chinese opera performances to constitute the pre- and post-birthday celebration periods. The temple does not restrict the number of performances, nor does it limit the number of sponsors. The number of performances is determined by the number of suitable days available and is dependent on two factors. First, the committee has to take into consideration the celebratory events organized by the temple next door. For example, in 1997, Chinese opera performances began on the ninth day of the fourth month (May 15, 1997) at the Lorong Koo Chye Sheng Hong Temple so as not to clash with Chinese opera performances held by its neighboring temple prior to that date. Second, the temple committee has to ensure that the post-birthday performances do not stretch into the seventh month of the lunar calendar, the month of the hungry ghost, during which, according to Chinese beliefs, spirits roam the human realm. During the seventh month, Chinese opera performances are prevalent throughout Singapore to entertain and placate these spirits. Since Chinese opera performances at the Lorong Koo Chye Sheng Hong Temple are solely for the purpose of honoring its deity's birthday, it is crucial that these celebratory performances do not extend into the seventh month.[5]

Sponsorship requests are fulfilled as early as a year prior to the festival. Five days after the end of the performance series at the temple in 1997, seventy sponsors had already registered to pay for the 1998 series, which amounted to about seventy performances (personal communication, Tan Chiew Hai, August 6, 1997). Such enthusiasm, as temple organizers would proudly assert, is not unusual for a temple such as the Lorong Koo Chye Sheng Hong Temple. From the mid-1990s, the number of sponsors has consistently outnumbered the possible number of performances for that year, and their sponsorship had to be postponed to the following year. On rare occasions, these prospective patrons might agree to cosponsor a performance, and the committee would then be able to accommodate them in the current year. As soon as sponsorship monies are in place to pay for the predetermined number of performances, the committee contacts various professional Chaozhou and Fujian opera troupes and invites them to perform at the temple. The committee negotiates available performance dates and payment with the opera troupes, and as soon as the performance schedule is prepared, the committee allocates the performances to the patrons according to the number of performances the patron agreed to sponsor. After the performances, the patrons pay the sum of money involved in engaging the troupe to the committee, who then pays the troupe.

The committee thus serves as a mediator between individual patrons and the opera troupes. Individuals do not generally inquire about the cost involved in sponsoring a troupe before they register their names: their primary concern is to ensure an opportunity to sponsor a performance. Occasionally, a patron may request to sponsor specifically Chaozhou or Fujian opera, or, less often, they may ask for a specific troupe. In such cases, the committee tries to satisfy their requests as it is important to maintain goodwill between the patrons and the temple. Broadly, the committee decides on four factors related to Chinese opera performance: (1) which troupes to engage, (2) payment for the troupes, (3) performance schedule (in collaboration with the troupes concerned), and (4) sponsors for performances (except when special requests are made). Among the decisions the committee has to make, selecting and paying the troupes raise intriguing questions. On what basis does the committee decide on which troupes to engage? How does the committee decide on the amount to pay the troupes? What do opera troupes consider when invited to perform at the temple?

Chinese Opera and Temple Identity

The opera gala at the Lorong Koo Chye Sheng Hong Temple features primarily Fujian and Chaozhou operas. The origin of the temple is in Anxi county in the southern part of Fujian province, where the majority of the population speak the Minnan vernacular (also known as the Taiwanese language), simply known as the Fujian dialect in Singapore. Despite its roots in south Fujian province, the temple deity served the needs of both the Fujian and Chaozhou communities when it established itself in Singapore in the early twentieth century (*Lianhe Zaobao*, November 30, 1997). Thus, in addition to Fujian opera, Chaozhou opera has also historically been included in temple events.

ENGAGING AN OPERA TROUPE

The festival organizing committee has a list of the major Chaozhou and Fujian opera troupes in Singapore and writes to invite them to perform at the temple. When approached by the committee, opera troupes submit their available times to the committee if they are interested in participating in the opera gala. The committee then determines the number of performances to be allocated to each troupe.[6] The committee and opera troupes attempt to keep the same set of dates every year so that these performances at the temple become a standard engagement for both parties. The foremost concern is to ensure that there will be a troupe to perform on the birthday of the deity before filling in the rest of the performance schedule.[7]

The process in which Lorong Koo Chye Sheng Hong Temple engages professional Chinese opera troupes is indicative of the historical and social identities of the temple and its community, which involve three criteria: the relative number of Fujian opera and Chaozhou opera troupes, remuneration, and status ranking of troupes.

In the four years from 1997 to 2000, a total of fifty-five professional Chinese opera troupes performed at the temple. Of these, two were foreign Fujian opera troupes from Xiamen (1999) and Taiwan (2000) and the rest were from Singapore and Malaysia. Of the fifty-three troupes from Singapore and Malaysia, thirty-nine troupes performed Fujian opera (74 percent) and fourteen performed Chaozhou opera (26 percent). As the sample of professional Chinese opera troupes in table 7 shows, there are more Fujian opera troupes than Chaozhou opera troupes in Singapore, which may be a contributing factor to the majority presence of Fujian opera at the temple. However, this temple has origins in Fujian province and a history among the Fujian community in Singapore. The troupes it has invited from China and Taiwan have all been Fujian opera troupes. The predominance of Fujian opera at the temple is a conscious display of the temple's provenance, social history, and demographics.

Remuneration for opera troupes range from S$1,200 to $1,500 (US$750 to $938) per day, for two performances each day, and payments are made according to a ranking system set by the festival committee.[8] Category 1 receives approximately $1,200, category 2 receives $1,300, and category 3 receives between $1,400 and $1,500. Broadly speaking, these categories are based on the status of the troupes in Singapore and the size of the audience they are able to attract. Based on my observations at the Lorong Koo Chye Sheng Hong Temple between 1996 and 1998, category 3 troupes attract more than one thousand people per night, while troupes in category 1 draw in about five to six hundred. In all cases, however, the audience size at the opera gala far exceeds the number of people attending evening performances by professional opera troupes during their daily engagements elsewhere. Figure 24 shows an announcement of the 1997 temple festival, and table 7 shows the thirteen opera troupes in the different categories, including a breakdown of these categories.

As I mentioned above, remuneration depends on the troupe's status and its ability to attract an audience: the more well-known the troupe, the bigger its audience and the higher its remuneration. Of the nine Fujian opera troupes that performed at the temple in 1997, six were classed category 1 (lowest remuneration) and two in category 3 (highest remuneration).[9] The Chaozhou opera troupes were more evenly distributed across the categories. Despite (or perhaps because of) the larger number of Fujian opera troupes compared to Chaozhou opera troupes in Singapore, this figure affirms the general perception that Fujian opera has a lower

韮菜芭城隍庙

庆祝"清溪显佑伯主圣诞"

[通告]

本庙订于1997年5月15日(农历丁丑年四月初九日)起至1997年8月1日(历丁丑年六月廿八日)止,为庆祝"清溪显佑伯主圣诞"礼聘闽、潮剧团公演七十九天连宵助兴,除农历五月廿八日一天由本庙聘请外,其馀七十八天均由善信商翁喜敬答谢.

	演出日期	剧团	
农历四月	初九、初十	四季春闽剧团	2 天
	十一、十二、十三	玉珠凤闽剧团	3 天
	十四、十五、十六、十七	新宝凤闽剧团	4 天
	十八、十九、廿、廿一	新月凰闽剧团	4 天
	廿二、廿三、廿四	新赛凤闽剧团	3 天
	廿五、廿六、廿七、廿八、廿九	双明凤闽剧团	5 天
农历五月	初一、初二	新燕玲歌剧团	2 天
	初三、初四、初五、初六		
	初七、初八、初九、初十	筱麒麟闽剧团	8 天
	十一、十二、十三、十四、		
	十五、十六、十七、十八、		
	十九、廿、廿一	南艺闽剧团	11天
	廿二、廿三、廿四	老赛桃潮剧团	3 天
	廿五、廿六、廿七、廿八	金鹰潮剧团	4 天
	廿九、卅、六月初一	新赛凤闽剧团	3 天
农历六月	初二、初三、初四、初五、		
	初六、初七、初八	筱麒麟闽剧团	7 天
	初九、初十	新荣和潮剧团	2 天
	十一、十二、十三、十四、十五	新燕玲歌剧团	5 天
	十六、十七	新宝凤闽剧团	2 天
	十八、十九、廿、廿一、		
	廿二、廿三、廿四、廿五	四季春闽剧团	8 天
	廿六、廿七、廿八	织云潮剧团	3 天

附启 : 农历五月廿八日聘混元道坛启建清醮一天,庇祝风调雨顺,国泰民安.
注 : 本庙并无派人出外捐缘,敬请垂注.
巴士川行 : 24, 70, 76, 84, 135, 152, 154, 8, 22, 61, 65, 66.

韮菜芭城隍庙庆委会 启
巴耶礼峇阿鲁姆甘路门牌15号 (芽笼警局后面)
15, Arumugam Road, Singapore 409960 Tel : 7443187

Figure 24: List of professional Chinese opera troupes performing at Lorong Koo Chye Sheng Hong Temple in 1997.

status and is therefore less expensive to engage than Chaozhou opera. However, the only Chaozhou opera troupe in category 3, Lau Sai Thor Guan Teochew Wayang, was paid only a category 1 fee of $1,200 per day in 1997. This conforms to the general practice of paying Chaozhou opera troupes less than Fujian opera troupes at the Lorong Koo Chye Sheng Hong Temple because of its Fujian roots (personal communication, Tan Chiew Hai, August 6, 1997; Johnnie Ng, December 2, 1997).

Thus, because Fujian identity is centrally constituted in the social history of Lorong Koo Chye Sheng Hong Temple, performing Chinese opera at the temple inverts the common notion that Fujian opera has lower socioaesthetic value than Chaozhou opera. In the hierarchy of Chinese opera based on socioaesthetic values, there is a consensus among performers and audience in the professional Chinese opera tradition in Singapore that Cantonese opera ranks the highest, followed by Chaozhou opera, and then Fujian opera. Such hierarchical distinctions are prevalent

Table 7. Categorization of Opera Troupes at the Lorong Koo Chye Sheng Hong Temple (1997)

Troupe	Operatic Type	Category
1. See Quee Choon Opera	Fujian	1
2. Gek Choo Hong Troupe	Fujian	1
3. Sin Poh Hong Troupe	Fujian	1
4. Sin Guat Hong Wayang	Fujian	1
5. Sin Sai Hong Hokkien Wayang	Fujian	2
6. Shuangmingfeng Minjutuan	Fujian	1
7. Sin Yen Ling Hokkien Wayang	Fujian	1
8. Hokkien Sio Kee Lin Troupe	Fujian	3
9. Hokkien Lam Geh Troupe	Fujian	3
10. Lau Sai Thor Guan Teochew Wayang	Chaozhou	3
11. Kim Eng Teochew Opera	Chaozhou	2
12. Sin Yong Hoe Heng Teochew Wayang	Chaozhou	1
13. Chek Hoon Teochew Wayang	Chaozhou	2

Category	Fujian	Chaozhou
3	2	1
2	1	2
1	6	1
Total	9	4

Source: Personal communication with Tan Chiew Hai (August 6, 1997).

in the professional Chinese opera context, more so than in the amateur circles in Singapore. Professional Chaozhou opera performers note that Cantonese opera has the most elegant costumes and makeup, refined *qiang* and music systems, and graceful movements. Chaozhou opera emulates some of these traits from Cantonese opera and is respected for its adherence to traditional practices, stringent training of performers, and complex *qiang* system. Fujian opera ranks the lowest of the three operatic types in Singapore for its improvisatory nature; use of folk songs, popular tunes, and modern instruments, such as synthesizer and electric guitar; and the relatively poor skills (or lack thereof) of its performers, which critics claim is a consequence of the genre's reliance on improvisation. However, as the 1997 opera gala at the temple shows, the relationship between ethnicity and socioaesthetic values of Chinese opera in Singapore is tenuous, and draws its meanings and values only through specific contexts.

PERFORMING AT THE OPERA GALA

Noticing the prestige accorded to Chinese opera at the Lorong Koo Chye Sheng Hong Temple, I asked members of Lau Sai Thor Guan Teochew

Wayang and Sin Sai Hong Hokkien Wayang what it means for them to perform at the temple, in contrast to performing in other religious contexts. "Performing there is good because the place is good. There are seats for the audience and canvas shelter with fans. The stage is big and they sell food during the performance," says a member of Lau Sai Thor Guan (personal communication, July 28, 1997). Indeed, the comfortable space provided for watching opera performance in the temple is an important factor in drawing an audience of at least six hundred people each evening, which far surpasses the small crowd of about thirty to fifty people that opera troupes generally attract elsewhere.

A *xiaosheng* (young male) impersonator from the Sin Sai Hong Hokkien Wayang hailed the opera gala as the annual highlight for the troupe: "This is when we perform new shows and put on new costumes because it's like a competition between the troupes. We perform every day, one troupe after another, so the audience is comparing us with one another. We perform our best during this time" (personal communication, July 4, 1997). When performing at the Lorong Koo Chye Sheng Hong Temple, Sin Sai Hong will usually engage more temporary performers. Very often, the older children of troupe members will be asked to take the roles of servants or soldiers. Likewise, new costumes and props will be used for performances at the temple. The main aim is to create a grand spectacle with special lighting and sound effects, elaborate costumes adorned with intricate paraphernalia, and a strong cast of performers, with the performance of at least one new play and the reenactment of favorite plays. The resulting performances are refreshingly different from the more mundane daily performances throughout the rest of the year. Plays performed during the opera gala are generally characterized by elaborate military scenes and comical settings. While the former type requires well-coordinated martial arts movements that often invoke plenty of interest and applause, the latter features slapstick scenes that induce laughter among the audience and performers.

Wednesday to Friday, May 28–30, and Thursday to Saturday, July 3–5, 1997, Lorong Koo Chye Sheng Hong Temple. Sin Sai Hong performed at the opera gala over two periods of three days each this year. The stage was done up more elaborately than usual: baskets of flowers lined the front of the stage, each given by a fan or a group of fans; banners hung in front and below the stage, with congratulatory inscriptions to the troupe for a successful performance. Names of sponsors were displayed on a banner placed just below the stage and in front of the audience. The huge curtain (*damu*) that shields the performance area from the audience and used during scene changes was brand new, given by fans whose names and areas where they are from were displayed on a register hung on the wooden panel on the stage left side behind which the percussion ensemble sits (figure 25). Examining the register, I could not help but be amazed: to gather sixty fans of Sin Sai Hong from at least seven different areas in Singapore required a fair amount of planning, and to consolidate resources in order to make a huge curtain that costs approximately S$3,500 (US$2,188) is surely an affirmation of their support for the troupe.

During performances, after a favorite performer finished a scene and returned backstage, fans would enter the supposedly "out of bounds" area that leads to the backstage to request to have photographs taken with the performer. All performers would oblige their fans by posing for and with them, after which they returned to the stage to get ready for the next scene (figure 26). Having followed Sin Sai Hong Hokkien Wayang for almost a year prior to their 1997 performance at Lorong Koo Chye Sheng Hong Temple, I had not seen such enthusiasm from their fans in other locations. This suggests that it is the context of the opera gala at Lorong Koo Chye Sheng Hong Temple that generated such behavior among the troupe's supporters, which affirms the role of the temple in elevating the aura of professional Chinese opera performance and reception in Singapore.

Although the temple committee does not decide on the plays to be performed, Lau Sai Thor Guan and Sin Sai Hong tend to arrange military and comic plays during the opera gala to enhance the festive atmosphere, with the primary aim of attracting and pleasing their audiences. One of the most popular comic plays in Lau Sai Thor Guan's repertoire is *Yijin Ronggui* (*A Glorious Homecoming*). On June 28, 1997, Lau Sai Thor Guan was performing its last show at Lorong Koo Chye Sheng Hong Temple and had arranged to perform *Yijin Ronggui*. Unfortunately, the actress who usually plays a lead role had had a bad fall the day before and was admitted to the hospital. Usually the troupe would perform a different play that did not require this actress in such circumstances. However, it was considered important for this occasion to keep *Yijin Ronggui* on the program, even though this meant substituting a performer who was unfamiliar with the role (personal communication, Auntie Ng, June 28, 1997).[10]

Professional opera troupes recognize the temple's inclination toward Fujian opera. Goh Gek Lam of Lau Sai Thor Guan affirms that "for the Fujian troupes, this is a kind of competition. There are many Fujian troupes performing there and many Fujian people watching them" (personal communication, Goh Gek Lam, March 28, 2000). Especially since the 1990s after the Lorong Koo Chye Sheng Hong Temple had established

*Figure 25: List of donors who gave a new curtain (*damu*) to Sin Sai Hong Hokkien Wayang for their performance at Lorong Koo Chye Sheng Hong Temple in 1997.*

Figure 26: Fans of Sin Sai Hong Hokkien Wayang taking pictures of their favorite performers at the opera gala (1997).

itself in the new location, the increased number of Chinese opera performances and the increased number of opera troupes has turned the opera gala at the temple into a kind of "focused gathering" (see Goffman 1961), an event in which both Fujian and Chaozhou operas take center stage. Here, Chinese opera performance is not merely an adjunct to customary celebrations of the deity's birthday but is the core feature to attract temple devotees and guests and to glorify the temple's religious devotion. In this process, Lorong Koo Chye Sheng Hong Temple has become an arena for professional Chinese opera troupes to offer their best to the operatic tradition in Singapore and, more broadly, in the Southeast and East Asian region. Through casual conversations among opera troupes, temple festival organizers, and audience members, there is a general understanding that a troupe must be of a credible standard to be invited to perform at the temple. Conversely, performing at the temple boosts the reputation of a troupe.

Whether or not the temple consciously set out to be known for producing professional Chinese opera performance, the temple's festival committee and audience at the opera gala do acknowledge that since the 1990s, it has become a place to attend outstanding Chinese opera performances. Several reasons contribute to such a status for the temple in the Chinese opera community in Singapore: (1) the primary focus of the birthday celebration of the deity is the performance of Chinese opera; (2) the consecutive opera performances for several months showcase numerous troupes; (3) the whole performance event is organized, constructed, and promoted as a communal, social, and even secular event. As the focal point in the temple, Chinese opera performance is no longer solely associated with religious rituals and for the entertainment of deities and spirits, but also as a secular form of entertainment for the general public. This last point is particularly evident in the temple's production of performances by Fujian opera troupes from China and Taiwan since 1993.[11] Tickets were sold for these performances, each troupe performed an average of twenty shows at the temple, and proceeds were donated to specific community organizations, the Singapore Kidney Foundation, and other social and charitable groups (Lorong Koo Chye Sheng Hong Temple 1999; 2000). Thus, through Chinese opera, the temple has been able to continue its customary birthday celebrations to honor its deity, maintain its community service, and transform itself into a theatrical space and a producer of professional Chinese opera performance in Singapore (see *Lianhe Zaobao*, May 25, 2004).

In Singapore today, there are rarely performances by professional opera troupes for consecutive months in the same locality, a performance schedule that existed as recently as the 1960s in amusement parks and in the streets under temporary shelters, as I described in chapter 1. The opera gala at the Lorong Koo Chye Sheng Hong Temple is a performance context that not only conjures a particular historical period of Chinese opera activity in Singapore but, at the same time, redefines the concept of Chinese street opera in contemporary Singapore.

Attending the Opera Gala

The Lorong Koo Chye Sheng Hong Temple is located next to the Pan-Island Expressway along Arumugam Road, at the junction of Paya Lebar Road and Ubi Avenue Two. The temple is situated within an industrial area: the backyard is visible from Ubi Avenue Two, but it is otherwise rather secluded. During the opera gala season, a huge signboard is placed at the entrance on Paya Lebar Road leading into Arumugam Road to announce the birthday celebration of the temple's deity (figure 27). Along Arumugam Road, flags are hung on lampposts with the name and logo of the temple imprinted on them, together with congratulatory messages such as *fengtiao yushun* (calm and tranquil environment), *guotai pingan* (peace to the country), and *hejing pingan* (peace to the community).

Figure 27: Large sign announcing the birthday celebration at Lorong Koo Chye Sheng Hong Temple (1997).

The opera stage is located to the right of the main gateway, along one end of the temple (figure 28). The entire area for the stage and the audience is about the size of two basketball courts. When additional space is needed, the audience may extend to the left side of the gateway, opposite the stage. A temporary shelter made of canvas and supported by steel frames covers the audience and performance spaces. Directly in front of the main gateway are prayer rooms and sacred spaces where shrines are placed. Numerous signs are placed on structural steel poles reminding the audience that reservation of seats is not allowed and that seating is first-come, first-served. These signs give an indication of the large crowd that is expected to attend the performances, especially in the evenings. A passageway leading to the lavatories separates the shrine rooms from a three-story administrative block. Next to the passageway is a shop selling incense, paper money, joss sticks, and other materials for prayers and offerings. Huge containers of *fushui* (blessed water)—Chinese tea, barley water, coffee, and black tea—are placed along the passageway for visitors to the temple during the opera gala season. Located next to the shop is the administrative office.

From about 7 P.M. to just before the performance begins at 8 P.M., crowds of people stream in, most of them in groups who spread themselves around the area to reserve seats for others who come later. Some

Figure 28: Watching the opera gala at Lorong Koo Chye Sheng Hong Temple (photo by Low Eng Teong, 1997).

arrive with their children, taking this as a family outing, and others come alone and try to get the best seat to watch the performance. Many ignore the instructions not to reserve seats. Women stuff pieces of tissue paper in holes in the seat as a sign that the seats are taken, and men place objects such as umbrellas across the seats next to them for their friends. When the temple is exceptionally crowded and the "reserved" seats are the few seats left, people looking for seats remove the objects and sit down, despite protest from those who are trying to save those seats. These actions of reserving seats and occupying reserved seats suggest that the majority of the temple crowds in the evenings are there to watch Chinese opera, not attending the performance because it happens to be there while they carry out their religious practices. Many of them burn incense and offer some prayers while they are at the temple, but their main focus is the opera performance.

As with Chinese street opera elsewhere, the audience moves around the area freely during performance to take a drink provided by the temple, buy food from the various stalls lining one side of the temple, or look at religious artifacts, cassette tapes, video recordings of previous performances at the temple, and other curiosities at the stalls by the entrance of the temple. Many also go to the out-of-bounds area to speak and take photographs with their favorite performers. Here at Lorong Koo Chye Sheng Hong Temple, audience members are more attentive and excited about the opera performance on stage. They offer generous applause whenever the performers display complex movements and laugh out loud whenever a comic scene is enacted, behavior that is markedly different from what I had observed in other performance locations when I traveled with Lau Sai Thor Guan Teochew Wayang and Sin Sai Hong Hokkien Wayang.

AN EVENING AT THE OPERA GALA

Saturday, June 28, 1997. I sat next to Auntie Ng at Lorong Koo Chye Sheng Hong Temple that evening, waiting to watch Lau Sai Thor Guan Teochew Wayang perform *Yijin Ronggui,* its last show for the opera gala this season. It was very crowded, so we could only find seats at a corner, close to the shrine area. Sitting with Auntie that evening was an enriching experience, as she is knowledgeable about the performance practices of Lau Sai Thor Guan and Chaozhou opera in Singapore in general. For the past decade since her husband, Johnnie Ng, took over the troupe as its sole proprietor and teacher, Auntie has accompanied him every evening when he visits or performs with the troupe. She usually sits in the audience and watches the performance while Johnnie Ng plays the drum or lead fiddle on stage, or is finalizing business deals with temple organizers.

She also distributes monthly performance schedules of the troupe to the audience and therefore knows many regular fans and supporters.

That Saturday evening, two men had each donated a sum of money to the troupe and had requested a *Tiaojiaguan* (Elevating Status) ritual to be performed before the actual show. Their names were written on a rectangular piece of paper and hung from the top of the stage. It was also indicated on the paper that they were giving the money to the entire troupe, and the full amount in dollar notes was pasted onto the paper itself: one gave S$2,000 (US$1,250) and the other S$250 (US$156). The amount would be shared equally between troupe members (figure 29).[12]

At the opera gala, a troupe would generally perform twice a day, not unlike an engagement at other temples, and ritual plays may be performed during the day or evening depending upon the request of the temple. Besides the regular ritual plays from the genres of *daxian* (big deities) and *xiaoxian* (small deities), the more unusual ritual *Tiaojiaguan* is performed frequently during the opera gala and almost exclusively during the evening performances. *Tiaojiaguan* is a play presented by one performer to express gratitude to individuals, groups, or institutions that have sponsored the opera troupe in terms of cash gifts. Names of these sponsors are written on a piece of red paper with actual dollar notes stuck

Figure 29: A Tiaojiaguan *(Elevating Status) ritual at the opera gala performed by Lau Sai Thor Guan Teochew Wayang, with two banners displaying the names of the donors and congratulatory messages, with the donation attached (June 1997).*

to it and hung at the top of the stage for maximum view. The performer goes through choreographed movements and displays several banners to the audience with messages of congratulations, praise, and gratitude to the donor. Given the public nature of the opera gala, the predominance of *Tiaojiaguan* during this event is perhaps not surprising. With opera troupes giving their best during the opera gala and attracting huge crowds, it is a suitable environment to celebrate oneself and be made known to the public for affluence and generosity. Yet I realized that evening that *Tiaojiaguan* is more than a mere status celebration.

While the *Tiaojiaguan* ritual was being performed that evening, Auntie directed my attention toward the man who had given the troupe $2,000, seated about five seats away from us. I recall vividly his look of pride and satisfaction as he stared intently at the performer carrying out the ritual. Auntie Ng said that he is a very wealthy man and an ardent supporter of the troupe. I asked her why some donors request the *Tiaojiaguan* ritual to be performed whenever they donate cash gifts, while others prefer to donate it under more private circumstances. Auntie's reply revealed a spiritual side of Chinese opera that I had not heard nor read before.

Requesting a *Tiaojiaguan* ritual is more than a conspicuous celebration of oneself. It is a process of being glorified, congratulated, and, more importantly, blessed in the context of an opera performance. Words of blessings for peace and prosperity for the individual and his or her family are written on the red paper when the ritual is being performed. Phrases such as *hejing gaosheng* (prosperity to the community) and *hejing pingan* (peace to the community) are used for individuals and their families, while *heshe gaosheng* (prosperity to the institution) is used to bless institutional supporters of the troupe.

Why be blessed through a Chinese opera performance? Auntie gave the following example: thirty to forty years ago, when opera troupes performed, ate, lived, and slept as a large family unit, members of the public would always ask for a share of the rice cooked for the troupe, referred to as *xifan* (literally, "opera rice" or "troupe rice"). She maintains, "These people believed that if their children eat some of this rice, they will prosper and be blessed as they grow up." Even in Singapore today, when troupes do not live together and communal cooking and eating are no longer practiced, members of the public sometimes buy their own sacks of rice, take it to the troupe, and request that it be blessed by the troupe's deity. Such is the recognition of the spiritual power of Chinese opera performance in general, and of the troupe's deity in particular, which is manifested upon the performers especially during ritual performances.[13] Being blessed by such power, especially in an intense, out-of-the-ordinary context such as the opera gala, is seen as a privilege in tangible and material terms and is also spiritually compelling (personal communication, Auntie Ng, June 28, 1997).

That evening, a member of the audience told me of the following two events that supposedly happened at the opera gala, which further supports the compelling nature of Chinese opera performances. During a performance by a Fujian opera troupe, a popular *xiaosheng* performer came on the stage as a poor vegetable seller, carrying real stalks of vegetables. As he sang and acted, members of the audience rushed up to the stage and stuffed cash into his pocket to buy a stalk of vegetable from him. At a Chaozhou opera performance, a female performer played an old woman begging for money. Her acting was very realistic, and she actually cried. She said, "Ladies and gentlemen, please be kind," and held out a bowl. Audience members rushed up and put money into the bowl (personal communication, June 28, 1997).[14]

We may interpret these anecdotes in different ways. First, skilled performers are so realistic and compelling that members of the audience are moved. Second, audience members respond to their favorite performer, especially in a context of the opera gala, as a public announcement of their support and perhaps identification with the character and performer, in other words, an expression of the self. Third, the audience wishes to partake in the spiritual blessings accorded to opera performers by their deities through the sharing of their possessions and donating money to them. However we may understand these practices, it is clear that the confluence of the temple's history and community with the professional Chinese opera tradition in Singapore has created a context that is more than the sum of its parts. Chinese opera performance at Lorong Koo Chye Sheng Hong Temple positively sets itself apart from Chinese street opera performances in other contexts. The division between "pragmatic" performances for rituals and "aesthetic" presentations for artistic entertainment and reflection are blurred in the context of the opera gala at the temple, a performance space that makes things happen—standards and perceptions are changed, new behaviors and status are created, affirmed, and transcended (cf. Waterman 1990, 213; Stokes 1994, 5).[15]

Opera Gala as Context

The opera gala at Lorong Koo Chye Sheng Hong Temple constructs a performance context that not only maintains the traditional practices of Chinese opera in religious and customary celebrations but also produces unique social practices that are less often expressed in other contexts.

First, the context itself is unique in the Chinese opera culture in Singapore. Bringing together professional opera troupes and arranging consecutive performances creates a highly charged atmosphere in terms of performing and viewing Chinese opera. It centralizes professional Chinese street opera performance and positions the deity's birthday as an important event during the calendar year for the temple, opera troupes, and for fans of Chinese opera. At the same time, the event creates a performance space in which opera troupes exhibit their nicest costumes and newest stage props, and perform to the best of their abilities to present a grand spectacle and set a performance standard that is perhaps not possible elsewhere.

Second, the audience acknowledges, and perhaps even expects, a high standard of performance during the opera gala. In this way, their presence enhances the performance level at the gala. With an extraordinary crowd attending the gala, it is a suitable context to express their support for particular troupes or performers, celebrate themselves in front of others by donating and requesting certain rituals, critique the standard of opera performance, and maintain and widen social contacts. Erving Goffman's concept of "focused gathering" is a useful interpretation of the opera gala: he describes an assembly of persons engaged in a common flow of activity and relating to each other in terms of that flow (Goffman 1961, 9–10). Clifford Geertz applied Goffman's concept to his interpretation of the Balinese cockfight and said such gatherings "take their form from the situation that evokes them" (Geertz 1973, 424). The size of the audience at the opera gala far surpasses any group attending a regular street opera performance. In other words, the opera gala probably attracts people who do not attend street performances regularly. Among the audience members are those who pool their resources and buy gifts for their favorite troupes only at the opera gala in the forms of flower baskets, banners, and stage curtains.

Third, the annual opera gala at the Lorong Koo Chye Sheng Hong Temple recaptures a particular period in the history of Chinese opera in Singapore. Chinese street opera was presented in opera areas, with games and food stalls and attended by huge crowds, until the 1960s. Today, Lorong Koo Chye Sheng Hong Temple is the only space in Singapore that features this social tradition. The event affirms the social position of professional Chinese street opera troupes and their performances in Singapore. While the opera gala is based on the traditional practice of engaging Chinese opera troupes as part of religious and customary celebrations, it also creates new dimensions in Chinese opera performance in Singapore. In this context, functional practices of ritual become aesthetic performances of theatre, and boundaries between the two domains are diminished.[16] The total structure of the performance event, in terms of the program, type of troupes involved, and the performance space to name a few aspects, requires (albeit unspoken) a high level of performance standard from the troupes that is not seen elsewhere.

Broadly speaking, then, the annual opera gala constitutes an important ritual in the performance calendar of professional opera troupes in Singapore today. It is a performance context that affirms the existence and the central role that professional Chinese opera troupes continue to play in a modern society. Viewing the opera gala from the perspective of the usual notion of Chinese street opera in Singapore, in other words, professional opera troupes being paid to perform on a temporary stage in a religious setting, it is no different from the everyday contexts that frame opera performances by professional troupes. In other ways, however, the opera gala is a unique and important social phenomenon in contemporary Singapore, not only to professional opera troupes but also to their supporters. The opera gala is the only context that is supported by, as its success further encourages, patronage from individual members of the temple. While the conventional two- to three-day street opera performances are sponsored by the religious institution as a group, the opera gala at Lorong Koo Chye Sheng Hong Temple creates opportunities for private sponsorships of Chinese opera in Singapore.

With the large number of sponsorships from its devotees, the temple has sufficient funds to provide a larger-than-usual stage and a sheltered space for the audience equipped with fans, lights, air conditioning, and chairs. In addition, the temple provides free drinks and engages food hawkers to set up their stalls during the evening performances. These amenities, which are not part of the usual street opera performances in Singapore today, provide a comparatively comfortable setting for both the performers and audience, which heightens the experience of watching Chinese opera.

In this way, while the opera gala is rooted in the tradition of Chinese street opera, it approaches a "concert" performance not unlike that presented by amateur groups and other foreign opera companies in theatres. The opera gala is an event structured by the generally acknowledged purpose of Chinese street opera in Singapore, that is, to provide entertainment for the temple's patron deity on its birthday with opera performances by professional troupes. However, the event exceeds what one normally expects from a Chinese street opera performance and transgresses the negative notions generally associated with it.

Indeed, the opera gala constructs a performance context that contradicts such perceptions of professional Chinese opera troupes in Singapore.

While the usual street opera performances by professional troupes last an average of three days in one particular locale attended by twenty to thirty people, the opera gala features several months of opera performances attended by no less than five hundred people every evening. Moreover, while the usual street opera performance can be apathetic and lacking artistic qualities, opera gala performances are otherwise, with actors displaying their utmost dedication to opera performance and their audience expressing approval in watching them. The opera gala circumscribes a particular time and space in the calendar year when professional opera troupes reaffirm their status in Singapore, or even rejuvenate their performance standards and presentation. In the process, the event critiques the notion that professional Chinese opera is a stagnant, even dying tradition in Singapore.

5 *Tourism and Cultural Authenticity in Chinese Opera*

> Why not experience a completely different arts performance while you're in Singapore? A wayang is a Chinese opera, performed in Mandarin or one of the numerous Chinese dialects. Performed on a make-shift stage at a street corner in a suburb, wayangs are typically held in the months of August and September during the Hungry Ghost Festival or during temple celebrations. With elaborate costumes and props, a wayang is a unique experience you'll never forget!

Accompanying the above invitation by the Singapore Tourism Board on its "Uniquely Singapore" Web site are two pictures: one of a Chinese opera performer striking a generic pose, and the other of three foreign tourists watching two performers while having a meal (www.visitsingapore.com).

It is likely that the latter photo was taken at the Chinese Opera Teahouse, which was opened in 1998 and operated by the Chinese Theatre Circle.[1] Between 1996 and 1998, visitors to Clarke Quay in Singapore, an upscale area that has been important to Singapore's Chinese immigrants since the early nineteenth century, were treated to a dose of "Traditional Chinese Street Opera" performed several times a week by the Chinese Theatre Circle. Given that Chinese opera performances in teahouses were prevalent in Singapore during the first half of the twentieth century, it is intriguing that the Chinese Theatre Circle describes its teahouse as the "first of its kind in Singapore" (www.ctcopera.com.sg/teahouse.html). It is equally interesting that the Traditional Chinese Street Opera event was performed and supported by institutions that are not usually associated with professional Chinese street opera performances in Singapore. Understanding Chinese opera in the context of tourism requires us to reconsider the multiple meanings of authenticity, especially when it impacts the meanings and values of local cultures.[2] The Traditional Chinese Street Opera event is a fine example to explore such issues.

Clarke Quay is a historical site along the Singapore River, near Chinatown. In the last two decades or so, it has been reconstructed into a bustling area with pubs, restaurants, cafés, and antique shops, among many other attractions, mainly for tourists and middle- to upper-class Singaporeans. The Traditional Chinese Street Opera series at Clarke Quay began on August 1, 1996, and was performed by the Chinese Theatre Circle twice a week on Thursday and Friday evenings "to bring Cantonese opera to both Singaporeans and tourists" (*Straits Times*, July 30, 1996).[3] This performance situates itself in traditional concepts of Chinese street opera and, at the same time, helps shape and define new meanings and values of Chinese street opera in Singapore. At Clarke Quay, the concept of Chinese street opera is recontextualized and redefined within a framework of cultural tourism, where tourism develops the cultural resources that it feeds on (see Picard 1996).

Clarke Quay as a Modern Historical Site

Clarke Quay was one of two major sites (the other is Boat Quay; see map 1) for the import and export of goods such as rice, gambier, and pepper in the nineteenth and twentieth centuries. Cargo ships docked at the bay area (now known as Marina Bay) and smaller vessels would then carry the goods on the Singapore River to Boat Quay and Clarke Quay. Chaozhou and Fujian people formed the dominant communities in this area. In fact, Clarke Quay was (and still is) known colloquially in the Chaozhou dialect as "Cha Jung Tau" (Chai Chuan Tou in *pinyin*), which literally means "harbour [or jetty] for ships carrying firewood" (Oral History Department 1990, 30). The area is named after Singapore's second governor, Sir Andrew Clarke. A special feature along both Clarke Quay and Boat Quay are the rows of two-story houses that originally housed immigrant laborers who worked along the river. Some of these houses were also used as godowns, warehouses for storing goods. These laborers were known as "coolies" and the houses were referred to as "coolie quarters" or "ducking beds" (ibid., 31).[4] Today, these coolie quarters have been renovated and refurbished, and most have been leased out as pubs, cafés, and restaurants. Both Clarke Quay and Boat Quay historically were important locales for Chinese opera performances, especially for Chaozhou operas (ibid., 29–34), in addition to other street entertainment such as storytelling (Z. Wang 1990, 190–98).

Today, Clarke Quay refers specifically to the area surrounded by Clarke Quay, North Boat Quay, and River Valley Road (map 2). Two main thoroughfares cut across the area, perpendicular to each other: Clarke Street (half of which is locally renamed Carnival Street) and Read Street (half of which is renamed Satay Club). At the end of Clarke Street and in the middle of North Boat Quay is Gas Lamp Square, where the Chinese Theatre Circle presents its weekly Traditional Chinese Street Opera.

In the Clarke Quay visitor's brochure, the area is packaged and marketed as a "riverside festival village." Carnival Street, for example, has a merry-go-round at one end and a pavilion known as the Gazebo at the other end (located in Central Square in the middle of Clarke Quay), which sometimes features music performances. Along the street, there are outdoor game stalls not unlike those found in the amusement parks of the first half of the twentieth century. In addition, huge pushcarts display souvenirs, paintings, and other local artifacts for sale. The section of road between the merry-go-round and Central Square is renamed "Carnival Street," to reflect its carnivalesque atmosphere. On official street maps, however, the whole street is known as Clarke Street. There are foreign food joints such as Hooters, local food venues such as Hawkers Alley, and numerous shops selling antiques, handicrafts, and designer apparel. Musically, there are pubs that feature blues, jazz, and rock music, as well as discotheques and Cantonese opera performances.

One of the significant details in the entire spectacle at Clarke Quay is the emphasis on traditional and historical features of old Singapore. The site itself, an important area in the history of the Singapore Chinese community, is a juxtaposition of historical reality, nostalgic sentiments, and contemporary popular culture, the conversion of the historic "coolie quarters" into modern amenities being a case in point. Along North Boat Quay, for example, some shops are modeled on historical interior architecture, and restaurants are built on large traditional wooden boats called *tongkang*, or bum boats, which are replicas of traditional Chinese sailing ships used by Chinese immigrants to Singapore. The Chinese opera stage itself, a simplified version of the traditional makeshift stage still used by professional Chinese opera troupes today, symbolizes the persistence of a traditional Chinese cultural form, reinterpreted in order to ensure its continuity in a changing contemporary context (figure 30).

Perhaps the foremost tribute to old Singapore is the Clarke Quay Adventure at the junction of Carnival Street and Satay Club. The en-

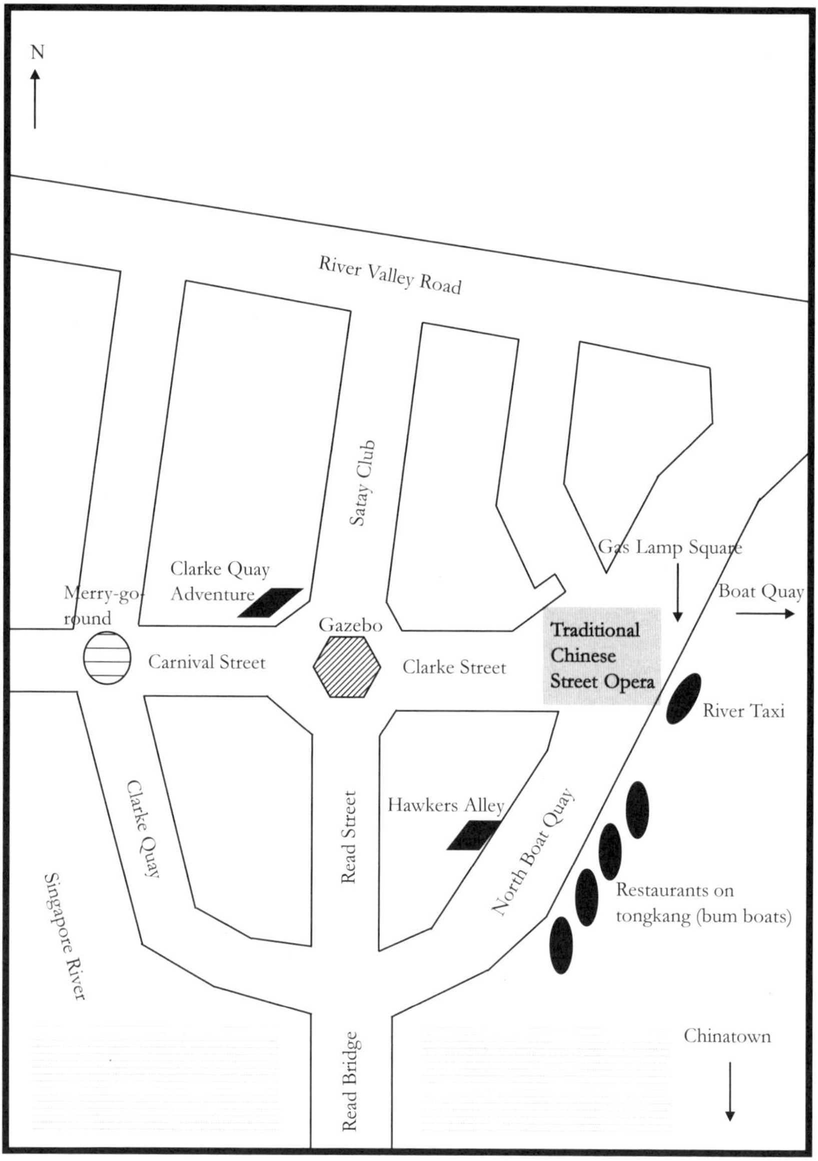

Map 2: Clarke Quay, Singapore.

Figure 30: Clarke Quay with Chinese opera stage at Gas Lamp Square (November 1997).

trance to the building that houses Clarke Quay Adventure is similar to that of other buildings. However, the inside is decorated with replicas of historical items, such as old radio sets, wine bottles, and pictures. The highlight of the adventure is a ride on a boat-like carrier on flowing water that runs through the building. The ride begins with the image of Singapore as a forested fishing village and journeys through the entire history of Singapore until modern times, depicted aurally and visually using life-size figures of human, animals, and other artifacts.[5]

GAS LAMP SQUARE, CARNIVAL STREET, AND CLARKE STREET

The Chinese opera stage is in Gas Lamp Square, which is strategically located in the middle of North Boat Quay. It is visible to people walking along the street or coming from the Boat Quay area further south of the river. It can also be seen from the major road junction between River Valley Road and New Bridge Road. Tourists and Singaporeans traveling between Clarke Quay and Boat Quay on river taxis (half-covered wooden boats propelled by an engine) embark and disembark right behind the Chinese opera stage. In other words, the stage is positioned conspicuously as a major attraction in Clarke Quay. The street leading from the Gas Lamp Square through the center of Clarke Quay to the other end of the area is significant because it constitutes a central space for public performances and entertainment.

As shown in map 2, Carnival Street/Clarke Street is one of two central avenues in Clarke Quay, the other being Satay Club/Read Street. The use of the space along Carnival Street/Clarke Street is an important strategy in defining Clarke Quay culture, that is, the construction of Clarke Quay as a festival village. This space is framed by a major entrance/exit point near the merry-go-round and an embarkation/disembarkation point at the other end near the river, where the stage is situated, a distance of approximately 200 meters (650 feet). Visitors entering the Clarke Quay area from the entrance near the merry-go-round will experience different forms of entertainment as they walk straight ahead along Carnival Street toward the river. Lining the streets are outdoor booths for various types of games, arcade games in indoor halls, and large wooden pushcarts selling food, drinks, and souvenirs. At Central Square where the Gazebo is located, there are cafés and restaurants and ample outdoor seating for alfresco dining around the pavilion, where music performances by local groups and comic acts by buskers are presented. Further on, Clarke Street continues to be dotted with stalls selling local crafts. Whenever there is a Chinese opera performance, it would be audible just past the Gazebo. As one approaches the source of the music, Clarke Street opens into Gas Lamp Square, a junction that is often crowded with people eating and drinking, tourists queuing up for the river cruises, browsing shoppers, and people standing in front of the opera stage.

The merry-go-round, the Gazebo, and the Chinese opera stage demarcate a space that includes different forms of entertainment. The lane stretching from the entrance at the merry-go-round to the opera stage is a microcosm of the entire Clarke Quay. It constitutes a continuum of public entertainment from the western merry-go-round to performances in a bandstand and a Chinese opera performance near the river. The modern Clarke Quay has been reconceptualized as a riverside festival village that embodies Asia and the West, high and popular cultures, the exotic and familiar, traditional and modern.

Gas Lamp Square is located in the center of the North Boat Quay thoroughfare, the only avenue running parallel to the river. It is named after the gas lamps that used to line the paths in Clarke Quay; the original gas lamps can still be seen along the streets of Clarke Quay. While these lamps used to be lighted manually, they are now electronically controlled. The square, which is closer to the shape of a pentagon, is approximately the size of a basketball court and the opera stage takes up about half of it.

The opera stage faces the Wild West Tavern, whose outdoor seating extends into Gas Lamp Square. The space between the stage and the perimeter of this outdoor seating section is approximately 9 meters by 6 meters (30 feet by 20 feet), and is used by the audience and by the ensemble accompanying the opera performance. Excess audience space may extend into the outdoor seating areas of the Wild West Tavern or other nearby eateries, where diners have their meals and drinks and watch Chinese opera at the same time (figure 31).

The stage is about 9 meters by 5 meters (30 feet by 16 feet). The framework is constructed out of timber poles and planks, and it is covered on the sides and the top with large pieces of canvas. The stage is significantly smaller than the usual makeshift stage used by professional opera troupes for their daily street performances. In addition, the stage at Clarke Quay is only large enough for a performance area and therefore does not have a backstage, although two partially covered areas house the sound system, stage props, and costumes. These two areas are concealed from the audience by two whitewashed wooden planks, each about 2 meters (6 feet) wide. They have the following inscription:

CLARKE QUAY
SINGAPORE

TRADITIONAL CHINESE STREET OPERA
EVERY WEDNESDAY, THURSDAY, & FRIDAY
TIME: 7:45 PM—8:30 PM
CHINESE THEATRE CIRCLE
presents

The panel on the audience's right is written in English while the panel on the left is written in Chinese. The Chinese version is slightly different. The Chinese Theatre Circle performs solely Cantonese opera, so the announcement reads "*jietou yueju*," literally meaning "street Cantonese opera." Below the word "presents" is an empty space for the projection of the synopsis of the play in English or Chinese.

Two small walkways on either side of the stage lead to boats known as river taxis. At specific times during the day, groups of tourists can be seen along the walkways, either embarking on or disembarking from their cruises on the Singapore River. Standing immediately behind the stage is one of the main gateway structures (the only gateway via the river) to Clarke Quay. Visitors arriving at Clarke Quay by river during opera performances often join the audience before proceeding to other attractions. Thus, Gas Lamp Square is a strategic location for a cultural show—it is the river gateway to Clarke Quay, positioned in the middle of the North Boat Quay thoroughfare (which stretches along the river), and it is part of the Carnival Street/Clarke Street entertainment locus. Whenever there is a performance, an average of eighty people gather at

Figure 31: Diners at Clarke Quay watching a performance at Gas Lamp Square (November 1997).

Gas Lamp Square to watch Chinese opera, drawing the largest crowd of any outdoor performances at Clarke Quay.

"Traditional Chinese Street Opera"

Friday, November 21, 1997. At about 5:15 P.M., the stagehand arranged chairs and stage props. He set up two tables on either side of the stage, in front of the white wooden panels, on which slide projectors would be placed during performances. He placed three white plastic chairs in between the tables, parallel to the stage, and positioned two long bamboo poles on them to cordon off an area for the orchestra. At 6 P.M., the spotlights on the stage were turned on and gave a warm glow to the stage, with the darkening sky and setting sun as the backdrop. At 6:30 P.M., one performer arrived and started to put on her makeup. Her mirror and cosmetics were placed on one of the tables for the slide projector. Visitors walking along Gas Lamp Square sometimes stopped to watch her put on her elaborate makeup. The opportunity to see someone put on the elaborate Chinese opera makeup is a deliberate arrangement by the Chinese Theatre Circle. While some curious onlookers may take a photograph of the demonstration, others merely glance and walk on (figure 32).

Figure 32: A makeup demonstration at Clarke Quay's Traditional Chinese Street Opera (November 1997).

Then the sound system was prepared and speakers erected in front of the stage. The stagehand brought musical instruments in on a trolley and arranged them on the stage. For this performance, I realized that the three white plastic chairs and bamboo poles used to demarcate the orchestral space had been removed. The orchestra was to be positioned on the stage that evening. I wondered if it was because of the rainy weather. During my previous visits, the orchestra was invariably placed in front of and below the stage, not unlike the orchestra accompanying a Western opera or Broadway musical in an orchestra pit. When below the stage, the *wenchang* and *wuchang* of the ensemble sat together. When positioned on stage, the ensemble was always divided, as is the custom at other venues, with *wenchang* on the right and *wuchang* on the left of the stage.

At about 6:45 P.M., the musicians arrived and began to set up and tune their instruments. There were five musicians in the *wenchang* playing the *gaohu* (treble two-stringed bowed fiddle), *zhonghu* (mid-range two-stringed bowed fiddle), *yangqin* (hammered dulcimer), *yueqin* (moon-shaped, short-necked plucked lute), and the *guan* (vertical double-reed instrument). The *wuchang* had three musicians: a lead percussionist playing several woodblocks and the *zhangu* (barrel-shaped war drum), and two musicians playing different types of *bo* (cymbals) and *luo* (gongs).[6]

After the afternoon drizzle and as the sun set in Clarke Quay, the number of people walking along North Boat Quay gradually increased. The lighted-up stage, with props, musical instruments, performers putting on their makeup, and musicians and stagehands making final preparations for the performance, attracted a lot of attention from visitors walking by. At about 7:30, a crowd of about forty people stood in front of the stage waiting for the show to begin. The instrumental prelude started off the performance at about 7:50, and at this time, the crowd numbered about seventy people. After the prelude, Leslie Wong, chairman of the Chinese Theatre Circle, gave a speech on the stage in English:

> Good evening ladies and gentlemen, welcome to Clarke Quay Festival Village. The Chinese street opera is brought to you by Clarke Quay Singapore, with the support of the Singapore Tourist Promotion Board, and performed by the Chinese Theatre Circle. It is customary to precede the show with a piece of music. The music you've just heard is a very popular piece called "The Sorrow of Two Stars." You notice that the orchestra is put on the stage this evening, and traditionally, this is the layout of the orchestra of a Chinese opera stage: the percussion on your left and the string and wind instruments on your right.
>
> The Chinese street opera was a very popular street entertainment. It used to be a common sight in old Clarke Quay, especially during religious festivals. And with much bustling activities during festivals in this area, Clarke Quay thus became known as the Festival Quay. In the past, families gathered in front of the opera stage with their own wooden benches to watch the shows. The audience would also peep behind backstage to watch the performers put on their elaborate makeup. The face colors and costumes adorned by the performers symbolize different types of characters and personalities.
>
> The opera tonight is performed by the Chinese Theatre Circle, Singapore's premier Cantonese opera group, a professional arts company. Established in 1981, its aim is to preserve and promote Chinese opera, drama, dance, and music. Since then, it has put [on] over one thousand shows in Singapore and overseas. It is certainly the most widely traveled troupe in Singapore, having performed in fifteen countries spanning across five continents, countries including Australia, Belgium, Canada, China, Egypt, England, Germany, Italy, Japan, Malaysia, New Zealand, Romania, Scotland, Turkey, and United States of America. It has also participated in the prestigious Edinburgh Festival. The troupe has won many honors and awards throughout the years, including the most recent "Excellence for Singapore" award from the Singapore government. The Chinese Theatre Circle is also responsible for organizing the annual Chinese Opera Festival in Singapore. It is usually held in the month of March.
>
> In an effort to keep the age-old tradition alive, Clarke Quay is holding regular opera shows here at Gas Lamp Square, on every Wednesday,

> Thursday, and Friday, at 7:45 P.M. You are welcome to take photographs of the performance. You may if you wish come as close as possible to the opera stage to take pictures. Those who are interested in opera makeup may come at 6:30 P.M. to see the artists doing their own makeup at the opera stage and take pictures of them. And those who want to take pictures with the performers or talk to them are most welcome to do so after the performance at 8:30 P.M. Our performers are effectively bilingual: they speak good English and Mandarin and they have been with the Chinese Theatre Circle to almost half the world.
>
> Tonight, we will be performing the excerpt called "None Gives Way on the Wedding Night," an episode taken from the very famous Cantonese opera called *The Arrogant Princess.* It's a very hilarious piece of opera excerpt, telling the story of the arrogance of a princess, so much so that she refused to give way to the prince consort on her wedding night. Well, you'll see how things go. And with subtitles on both sides of the stage, English on your right and Chinese on your left, we believe you should be able to enjoy the show. And now, ladies and gentlemen, please put your hands together to welcome our two young artists this evening from the Chinese Theatre Circle, Joanna See Toh Hoi Siang and Garrett Khong Yew Cheong in this excerpt called "None Gives Way on the Wedding Night" from *The Arrogant Princess.*

While the audience applauded, the percussion ensemble played a rhythmic segment, later joined by the melodic group, followed by the entrance of the actor and actress. The play lasted for about forty minutes and ended at approximately 8:25 P.M. that evening. At the end of the performance, both the actor and actress, who had moved behind the white panels, acknowledged the audience's applause by returning to the center of the stage. Using hand gestures and pointing toward the orchestra on both sides of the stage, they displayed their appreciation to the musicians. Wong then returned to the stage to thank the audience and invite them to take photographs with the actor and actress, who were already below the stage preparing to pose for photographs (figure 33).

The performance outlined above constructs a specific notion about traditional Chinese street opera in Singapore. The speech given by Wong prior to the performance presents an interesting image of Chinese street opera in Singapore and deserves closer analysis. The main section of the speech is repeated prior to every performance; only the introduction and sometimes the conclusion vary.

The introduction begins by welcoming visitors to Clarke Quay. It then proceeds to validate the authenticity of the performance by emphasizing its continuity with traditional or customary practices. Compare the slightly different version below with the speech above:

Figure 33: Performers from the Chinese Theatre Circle posing for photographs with the audience (November 1997).

> Good evening ladies and gentlemen, welcome to Clarke Quay Festival Village. We apologize for the delay in opening the show; it's due to the rain. And because of the rain, we are putting our orchestra on the stage. In fact, this is the traditional way of the orchestra layout of a Chinese opera stage: the percussionists on your left and the wind and string instruments on your right. With the help of subtitles this evening, with English on your right and Chinese on your left, we hope you'll be able to follow the story. Whilst the projectionists are preparing for the projectors and the subtitles, let me say a few words this evening. (November 14, 1997)

While it was the usual practice of the Chinese Theatre Circle to position the orchestra in front and below the stage during their performances at Clarke Quay to enable the audience to have a closer view of the instruments, there were occasions when the orchestra was placed on the stage. For whatever reason this is done, the concept of tradition is emphasized in the two speech excerpts above, and, likewise, for the description of the musical prelude. On some occasions when the orchestra was placed below the stage, Wong introduced the musicians after his general introduction in a manner that called for applause from the audience: he indicated that both the *gaohu* and *zhonghu* players are from an operatic institution in the Canton province in China, and that the lead percussionist is the "most experienced Cantonese opera percussionist in Singapore" (November 27, 1997). Thus, in addition to emphasizing traditional aspects of the performance event, Wong attempted to establish authenticity by pointing out performers from mainland China and performance quality by listing credentials of the orchestra members.

The main section of Wong's speech begins by acknowledging the sponsors and performers of the Traditional Chinese Street Opera performance series, namely Clarke Quay Singapore and the Singapore Tourist Promotion Board (renamed Singapore Tourism Board in November 1997). Chinese street opera is proclaimed as a phenomenon that existed in the past: "The Chinese street opera *was* a very popular street entertainment" (my emphasis), which implies that street opera no longer exists or is not as popular in Singapore today. Furthermore, the sentence implies that the Chinese Theatre Circle series in Clarke Quay is the only extant form of Chinese street opera in Singapore. Chinese street opera is then localized within the history of Clarke Quay and contextualized as a form of entertainment during religious and festive seasons. No reference whatsoever is given to the ongoing street performances by professional opera troupes that are presented almost every night in multiple locations around Singapore.

The speech then introduces the Chinese Theatre Circle as "Singapore's premier Cantonese opera group" and "a professional arts company" that boasts numerous performances worldwide (with an alphabetical list), has won many awards, and organizes the annual Chinese Opera Festival to "preserve and promote" Chinese opera. Besides implying that the Chinese Theatre Circle is the only opera group that performs Chinese street opera in Singapore today, in this section of the speech, Chinese street opera is practiced by a "professional arts company" that specializes in Cantonese opera. In fact, the Chinese Theatre Circle started as an amateur opera group in 1981 and was designated a "nonprofit professional" company by the National Arts Council in 1995.

According to the speech, Chinese street opera is being revived and nurtured as an art form by a Cantonese opera group that has achieved honors and recognition both locally and in many foreign countries. The paragraph beginning with "in an effort to keep the age-old tradition alive" addresses the audience directly and positions the whole performance event as a tourist attraction or rather, as a conspicuous consumption of the exotic and traditional. The audience is invited to take photographs of the performance, observe opera makeup, and converse with the performers. The performers of the Traditional Chinese Street Opera are young and bilingual, proficient in both English and Mandarin, and, as if to validate their artistry, have performed worldwide with the company.

In sum, this speech suggests that traditional Chinese street opera in Singapore is a historical phenomenon that no longer exists in Singapore today. It is only through the efforts of the Chinese Theatre Circle, supported by Clarke Quay Singapore and the Singapore Tourism Board, and visitors to Clarke Quay who make up the audience, that Chinese street opera is being preserved, promoted, and secularized in the form of Cantonese opera. Any religious and ritual connotations that traditionally characterized Chinese street opera in Singapore are obliterated in this performance event. In the new form of presentation, traditional Chinese street opera in Singapore is performed by artists who are educated, who have performed in both local and foreign contexts, and who possess a level of artistry that is honored in Singapore.

THE CHINESE THEATRE CIRCLE

The Chinese Theatre Circle (CTC) was formed as an amateur Cantonese opera group in 1981 by Joanna Wong, Leslie Wong, and Lou Mee Wah. Joanna Wong joined the Kong Chow Wui Koon (Kong Chow Association) Music and Opera Troupe in 1967, and Lou became a member of that group in 1971 as Wong's student.[7] Wong and Lou have performed together frequently since 1978, with Wong taking the *dan* (female) roles and Lou the *sheng* (male) characters. In addition to performances, CTC organizes the annual Chinese Opera Festival in Singapore that began in 1992, in which overseas Cantonese opera groups participate in performances, master classes, and dialogue sessions. Since 1995, CTC has also conducted lecture-demonstrations in schools as part of the National Arts Council's Arts Education Programme.[8] CTC hosts small-scale performances in community clubs and presents an average of four large-scale performances annually. The group has also given numerous performances and workshops outside Singapore, and is said to have pioneered the simultaneous projection of opera script and its translation during performances.

CTC has received several awards as individuals and as a group. Joanna Wong was awarded the Cultural Medallion in 1981, the highest award for those who have contributed to the promotion of arts and culture in Singapore. Her student Lou Mee Wah achieved that honor in 1997. See Toh Hoi Siang, one of the performers mentioned above in CTC's Traditional Chinese Street Opera series, received the Outstanding Young Persons of Singapore Award in 2000. Perhaps the most significant award was the 1997 "Excellence for Singapore" award, given to institutions that have brought honor to Singapore by achieving high standards and wide recognition in their field, both locally and abroad.

In 1995, CTC was incorporated as a nonprofit professional Chinese opera company known as the Chinese Theatre Circle Limited, and is reputed to be the first of its kind in Singapore. The term "professional" as it is used to describe CTC implies that the group performs Chinese opera on a full-time basis, like professional opera troupes that perform street opera regularly. The main distinction between them is this: CTC remains a nonprofit organization and receives support from the National Arts Council, like other amateur opera groups, but professional opera troupes are profit-oriented companies that do not receive state funding.[9]

CTC is comprised of a chairman, opera instructors, artistic directors, and musicians. Leslie Wong serves as the chairman of the company, while Lou is an instructor and performer who only became a full-time member of CTC in 1993. Joanna Wong was the registrar of the National University of Singapore until her recent retirement and also serves as the artistic director for CTC. The majority of the performers of CTC have full-time occupations such as managers and executives of companies and, to quote one full-time staffer interviewed at Clarke Quay, "other high-post jobs" (personal communication, November 21, 1997). CTC's performances are funded partially by national institutions like the National Arts Council and, in the case of their performance series at Clarke Quay, by the Singapore Tourism Board. Aside from salaried, full-time members, other CTC members receive only a nominal fee whenever they perform, and profits from tickets sales are redirected into the company's fund for future group activities. At Clarke Quay, each participant is given about S$30 (US$19) per performance for transportation and food expenses.

CTC is the first nonprofit professional company to specialize in Chinese opera performance (www.ctcopera.com.sg). Even with the adjective "professional" in the title, its history, ideology, and performance practices are similar to amateur opera groups: only its organizational structure differs from amateur groups (as prescribed by policies of the National Arts Council). Given those differences, CTC is still distinct from professional opera troupes in Singapore whose subsistence depends entirely on profits from their performances. More importantly still, like amateur opera groups, CTC is not traditionally associated with the Chinese street opera performance style.

Representing Chinese Street Opera

As described in chapter 2, Chinese street opera is performed by professional opera troupes almost every day in Singapore today, and usually in religious contexts where it is known as *choushenxi,* a social phenomenon that has existed since the early days of the Chinese immigrants. Very often, several troupes perform in different venues at the same time. By excluding references to these professional troupes and their performances, the Traditional Chinese Street Opera series at Clarke Quay attempts to construct new notions of traditional Chinese street opera in contemporary Singapore.

The CTC's performance is shaped as an authentic representation of traditional Chinese street opera through references to traditional operatic practices. In this sense, it alludes to Edward Bruner's first meaning of authenticity with an emphasis on "mimetic credibility." By referencing historical aspects of attending Chinese opera performances and the traditional placement of the instrumental ensembles, the Traditional Chinese Street Opera event draws its authenticity from general practices of Chinese opera, thus making itself more "credible and convincing" (Bruner 1994, 399). Yet, while certain features are emphasized as customary, other inauthentic elements are conveniently obscured. One example is the absence of backdrops. Professional troupes always feature several changes of backdrops, which depict the settings of the play such as a court, garden, and temple, in a single performance. The performance by CTC at Clarke Quay, however, has a stationary backdrop that features a fairy and the Chinese name of CTC—Dunhuang Jufang—both images unrelated to any plays it performs. To be sure, there are certain constraints in such cultural performances for tourists, and it is not my intention to pinpoint which element is or is not authentic. Rather, it may be more useful to consider the processes through which "authenticity" is acquired, as I shall discuss below.

One of CTC's objectives is to familiarize its audience with Chinese opera through its didactic approaches, thus demystifying the genre. This is achieved in the following ways: (1) locating it in a middle- to upper-class modernized entertainment location; (2) merging the performance with the crowd by holding makeup demonstrations and photo sessions in the audience area; (3) verbally introducing the performance and projecting the script and its translation; and (4) constructing it as a purely secular event. Clearly, these elements contrast with the everyday Chinese street opera performances by professional troupes described in chapter 2. While conventional street opera is distanced from its audience, the Traditional Chinese Street Opera at Clarke Quay is consciously "bringing Chinese opera to the people" (to paraphrase one of CTC's community projects that began in 1984; see www.ctcopera.com.sg).

Providing projections of the script and its translation is one way to familiarize the audience with the performance. These efforts do not go unnoticed: after a performance on the evening of November 21, 1997, I overheard a Taiwanese couple commenting that it was useful to have the Chinese script projected as they would not have understood the performance otherwise. This raises an interesting issue on the ethnicity/genre of Chinese street opera in Singapore. As described in chapter 2, the two predominant types of Chinese street opera performed by professional troupes in Singapore today are Chaozhou and Fujian operas. Cantonese opera, on the other hand, is limited to occasional performances during the Hungry Ghost Festival (seventh month of the lunar calendar), organized by local agents who engage overseas performers for lead roles and local performers for minor roles (W. Lai 1986, 27).

I noted above that the announcement placed on the opera stage at Clarke Quay reads "Traditional Chinese Street Opera" in English and "street Cantonese opera" (*jietou yueju*) in Chinese characters. An immediate question arises: to what extent does Cantonese opera represent the Chinese street opera tradition in Singapore? Interestingly, when planning the Traditional Chinese Street Opera series at Clarke Quay, the Singapore Tourism Board invited several amateur Chinese opera troupes of different genres to perform for the event, but only CTC was able to undertake it.[10] In other words, it was not so much an issue of which genre appropriately represents the street opera tradition in Singapore, but simply to have a visual display of street opera appropriate for the tourist context. Projecting the Chinese script and its translation surely enhances the effectiveness of the event, but it also diminishes the significance of ethnicity in the Chinese street opera tradition in Singapore. With the Chinese script, anyone who reads Chinese can understand the performance regardless of the language used, while the English translations cater to most of the visitors to Clarke Quay. Through its performance in a tourist context, the Traditional Chinese Street Opera series transcends ethnic differentiations of Chinese opera to foreground "street opera" as a genre in itself.[11]

The event's credibility is further generated by framing itself as part of an evolutionary trajectory of Chinese street opera in Singapore. The performance suggests that while traditional street opera used to be a communal, festive event, especially during religious occasions, it is now preserved, promoted, and developed as a secular art form. The absence of references to the everyday street opera performances and other operatic genres renders an exclusive image for the event. Traditional Chinese street opera in Singapore has now become an object of artistic pursuit, exclusive to an elite community of educated and widely traveled practitioners.

The performers at Clarke Quay are young and bilingual, as emphasized in the introductory speeches. The event's emphasis on the young and bilingual attributes of the performers at Clarke Quay has two implications: (1) that it is unusual to be young and bilingual and to be involved in Chinese street opera performance, and (2) that Chinese street opera is no longer an outmoded tradition but has become an "in" tradition in which the educated, younger generation of Singaporeans actively participate. The kind of Chinese street opera promoted in Clarke Quay and by other amateur groups (as I shall elaborate in chapter 6) is different from that practiced by professional opera troupes in the past and today in Singapore. In this way, the tradition of Chinese street opera is appropriated by an elite community to create and establish its group identities to the public through performance. Through the production of an event promoted as "Traditional Chinese Street Opera," CTC and Clarke Quay not only construct a new image for Chinese street opera, but also present and affirm new status, knowledge, and power to appropriate and resignify a tradition that is generally recognized as the domain of another community.

As an upscale site for entertainment catering mainly to young Singaporeans and visitors to Singapore, Clarke Quay spatially enhances the Traditional Chinese Street Opera performance event as an exclusive circumstance. Chinese street opera is projected as an event purely for secular entertainment, not unlike the merry-go-round. The performance event locates street opera within the continuum of activities that is out of everyday life, creating a marked contrast to professional Chinese street opera, where the majority of its practitioners perform for a living. The embodiment of tradition in the performance event in the modern context of Clarke Quay enhances the experience of a phenomenon that is unusual and ephemeral, yet real and compelling.

On November 27, 1997, I was filming a performance by CTC at Clarke Quay when three women and five children stopped in front of the stage next to me (from their accents, I could tell they were Singaporeans). The adults commented that there was going to be a Chinese opera performance and suggested that they stay to watch. One of the kids groaned at the suggestion, to which a woman rebutted, "We are here at Clarke Quay to learn about the history of Singapore. You young people should learn more about the history of Singapore." I scribbled her comments in my notebook because I was struck by how the Chinese opera performance at Clarke Quay, and Clarke Quay itself, were perceived as "authentic" reflections of the history of Singapore.

Thus far, I have outlined two factors that contribute to creating authenticity at Clarke Quay. First, the introductory speech before the performance claims that what the audience is viewing preserves original aspects of the street opera tradition (Bruner's third meaning of authenticity; see Bruner 1994, 400). Second, the context of Clarke Quay, with its history, architecture, spatial organization, and activities, produces its own authenticity and further enhances that of the performance, just as the performance constitutes the emergent meaning of the locale. In this way, Clarke Quay is similar to the New Salem Historic Site discussed in Bruner's essay in its "verisimilitude" and "genuineness" (Bruner's first and second meanings of authenticity; 1994, 399).

The authenticity of the Traditional Chinese Street Opera series may also be attributed to marketing strategies in tourist brochures. *The Singapore Visitor*, a weekly guide for tourists in Singapore, introduces Clarke Quay and its street opera performance in the following manner: "It seems that Clarke Quay has always been 'the' place to be for fun . . . even 100 years ago when it was known as 'Festival Quay.' Religious and cultural festivals were celebrated here, complete with street performers. Clarke Quay is bringing back these days and recapturing the 'spirit' of traditional street entertainment with Chinese 'Wayang' (street opera) which you can enjoy every Wednesday, Thursday and Friday at 7:45 P.M." (Singapore Visitor 1997). The "Entertainment Delights" section in *New Asia Singapore: Mature Travellers* highlights the street opera performance as follows: "Of the cultural shows, one of the most memorable has to be the Chinese street opera or 'wayang.' An iridescent display of vibrance and movements, the performances take place in the evenings (Wednesdays, Thursdays and Fridays) at Clarke Quay throughout the year" (Singapore Tourism Board 1997, 21). In an article titled "Street Theatre," published in *Changi: The Magazine*, a publication distributed to passengers entering or leaving the Singapore Changi Airport, Clarke Quay's Traditional Chinese Street Opera is contextualized in a nostalgic rhetoric of a decline of tradition:

> It is sad that this ancient art is dying in Singapore but you can still happen upon a vibrant street performance in Chinatown during Chinese holidays or catch a scaled down show at tourist venues.
>
> Chinese Opera performances are staged every Thursday and Friday evening at the Gas Lamp Square in Clarke Quay by the Chinese Theatre Circle. This is a professional Cantonese Opera group established to preserve and promote Chinese opera, drama, dance and music. Translations can be provided for English speakers. (Singapore Changi Airport 1997, 21)

As with the introductory speech preceding performances, the above publications position the Traditional Chinese Street Opera series at Clarke Quay in terms of its originality ("bringing back these days . . .") and the survival of a declining tradition in contemporary Singapore. While the event is recognized as a cultural show performed at a tourist venue, the "authenticity" discourse is not diminished. On the contrary, the event's authenticity is enhanced despite, or perhaps because of, its focus on cultural tourism.

Unlike tourists attending concerts of traditional Naxi music in Lijiang County in northwest Yunnan province who may be able to juxtapose their experiences of modern traditions with the more conservative Naxi music to form their opinions on the latter's authenticity (Rees 1998), tourists at Clarke Quay are not likely to be exposed to conventional street opera performances by professional troupes. For them, then, Traditional Chinese Street Opera at Clarke Quay is their sole point of reference. Yet, if we assume that the experience of the three women and five children is applicable to others, how does this case of cultural tourism create and sustain its own authenticity?

I suggest that Clarke Quay's Traditional Chinese Street Opera series achieves its authenticity because its performance process reflects broader changes in the meanings and values of national culture in contemporary Singapore. In some ways, the event's authenticity depends on context as a "place"—Clarke Quay, near Chinatown, in a rapidly modernizing country. However, as Gary Tomlinson cogently states in his conception of authenticity in music, "The most profound and authentic meanings of music will be found not in musical works themselves but behind them, in the varieties of discourse that give rise to them" (Tomlinson 1988, 135–36). For this reason, the event's authenticity is also derived from the more subtle performative context—specific performance practices (such as the introductory speech), types of performing institutions and support, parity between tradition and modernity (such as the performers' ability to excel in Cantonese opera and be young, educated, and bilingual). Indeed, the evolutionary trajectory in which the event is marketed and performed affirms an authenticity defined in terms of its propensity to credibly adapt itself to new contexts.[12]

If the Clarke Quay Adventure attraction described above covers Singapore's history in a ride, we might also regard Clarke Quay as a microcosm of contemporary Singapore. The confluence of the modern and traditional, the Western and Asian at Clarke Quay reflect a prevailing trend in Singapore today described as "cultural cosmopolitanism" (T. Koh 1989, 723). Viewed in this way, Clarke Quay as a tourist locale is "a showcase of post-modernism: a concoction of something 'native' and something borrowed, something old and something new" (Leong 1997a, 530). Yet even in such a context, I suggest that cultural authenticity is further enhanced rather than "eclipsed by estrangement" (ibid.).

The authenticity of the Traditional Chinese Street Opera at Clarke Quay is sustained by feeding off a broader notion of culture in Singapore today, just as it simultaneously constitutes it. Its authenticity emerges from its viability in current cultural aesthetics and values in Singapore, and its relevance is derived from its novelty, not its traditionalism (see Taruskin 1988, 152). It highlights Singapore's perpetual concern for salvaging cultural heritage for the purposes of displaying its history to Singaporeans and tourists in Singapore.[13] To paraphrase Clifford Geertz, we might say that the Traditional Chinese Street Opera at Clarke Quay is "a story we tell us about ourselves" (Geertz 1973, 448): it provides a metacommentary upon the role of cultural traditions amid processes of modernization in Singapore, and the planning of culture and the arts around this concern. In this way, tourism and culture are constitutive of each other.[14]

6 *Chinese Opera and the Concept of Culture in Singapore*

The general perception of the state of Chinese opera in Singapore today is marked by the rhetoric of decline and revival: "while the professional groups were fading from the scene, many amateur groups sprang up to fill the vacuum," states Chua Soo Pong, director of the Chinese Opera Institute (S. Chua 1995, 96). Literature on Chinese opera in Singapore attributes the decline to four main reasons: (1) general disinterest in Chinese opera among the younger-generation Singaporeans, (2) decrease in the number of older-generation opera enthusiasts, (3) influx of modern technology and entertainment, and (4) fall in performance standards of professional troupes. At the same time, these publications praise amateur troupes for their success in developing and sustaining the Chinese opera tradition in Singapore: "Around 1969, amateur Chinese opera activities took a turn. Through the efforts of a group of enthusiasts whose objective was to raise the standard of amateur performance and to attain higher artistic achievement, amateur performances improved in quality. Other groups followed the examples set by them and with competition amongst these opera enthusiasts, amateur performances reached greater heights" (J. Wong 1995, 105; see also Chong 2003, 465–67).

Professional and amateur Chinese opera troupes are positioned as contrasting entities in these observations. Indeed, the decline of professionals is depicted as an inevitable corollary of the rise of the amateurs:

> Though most professional companies have vanished from the scene, some have managed to exist by remaining as street performances during religious festivals. Revival of local professional companies is a Herculean feat as there is no second generation to succeed the old performers and neither are there opera schools or teachers to provide the training.
>
> However, prospects appear much brighter in the amateur opera scene. While the local professional opera troupes wane, amateur groups have sprung up over the years. Many of the amateur groups are able to put up performances yearly, and in doing so, have gathered more young people into the groups to preserve this stylised and traditional art. (J. Wong 1985, 25; see also J. Wong 1976)

To be sure, there was a general decrease in the number of professional opera troupes in Singapore and a concomitant rise of amateur troupes since the 1960s. What is significant, however, is the interpretation of this scenario, which focuses on an absolute notion of artistic standards: amateurs are commonly described as having "a higher standard of performance which often transcended those by professionals" (Liu and Phillips 1988, 60; see also *Straits Times*, September 30, 1990).

Considering the immense popularity of professional opera troupes in the first half of the twentieth century, what happened in the 1960s that resulted in a decline of performance standards? Given that professional and amateur troupes were historically distinct from one another, what is the basis for comparing them under the same rubric after the 1960s? Focusing solely on some universal view of performance standards minimizes the critical role of context in the shaping of aesthetic distinctions between professional and amateur opera troupes in Singapore. One way to effectively understand the social positioning of professionals and amateurs is to explore the development of Chinese opera in Singapore after the 1960s and to situate it within the changing contexts of cultural production in contemporary Singapore.

Elevating Chinese Opera

In 1977, the Singapore Tourism Board and the Ministry of Culture organized the Hong Lim Park Chinese Opera Series. Hong Lim Park is a public space in the Central Business District near Chinatown, and what is significant about this series is that the opera groups that performed were predominantly amateurs. In 1983, the Hong Lim Park Chinese Opera Series staged twelve productions by six amateur Chinese opera groups, featuring Cantonese, Chaozhou, Hainan, Peking, and Fujian operas.

Writing about the 1983 performance in an article titled "Chinese Opera in the Park," Chua Soo Pong begins by reminiscing about his childhood experiences with Chinese street opera. He compares his observations of past performances with one he recently attended by a "Teochew opera group which was performing outside the roadside temple off Braddell Road" (S. Chua 1984, 9), and notes the sparse audience in contrast to the audience size in past performances. The performance Chua observed was presented by a professional group, as he later affirms.

He proceeds to point out that "this experience has confirmed the general observation about the decline of 'street opera' performed by the professional groups" (ibid.), and he attributes the paucity of audience to the usual reasons, such as declining performance standards of professional troupes and the influx of mass media entertainment in the 1950s and 1960s. Significantly, Chua challenges both reasons, stating that "[such] reasoning is disproved when the performances of the 'Chinese opera series' organized by the Tourist Promotion Board and the Ministry of Culture since 1977 at the Hong Lim Park have proved to be successful especially in terms of audience numbers" (ibid.).

Note that the Hong Lim Park Chinese Opera Series consisted primarily of amateur opera troupes performing in the street opera context. Using audience statistics for an amateur performance of Chinese street opera to affirm the continual popularity of professional Chinese street opera conflates the amateur and professional operatic traditions under a single rubric of "Chinese street opera." This foregrounds Chinese street opera as a genre in and of itself and diminishes any differences in the way it was historically performed, just as the "Traditional Chinese Street Opera" event at Clarke Quay effaces ethnicity to emphasize the street opera context. Here, two distinct social and musical organizations are compared on the same platform. More importantly, such comparisons presuppose that Chinese street opera performed by amateur opera troupes is an accepted norm, even though the street opera performance style has hitherto been the sole domain of professional opera troupes.

Chua's introductory remarks to the Hong Lim Park Chinese Opera Series reveal the expectations of this performance series and the assumptions about amateur and professional Chinese opera troupes in Singapore in the 1980s: "Hong Lim Park . . . has been selected . . . to stage annually a series of opera shows during the months of June and July presented by more experienced Chinese opera groups known to be able to maintain a high standard of performance. The objectives of these series are to raise the standard of local opera and thereby regain its audience and cultivate new talents and audience for this beautiful ancient art" (ibid.). Amateur opera troupes are thus perceived to embrace high standards and considered carriers of a traditional art form. Labeling this series a "most worthy cultural promotion scheme," Chua attributes its success to four factors: (1) easy accessibility to the performance venue, (2) competitive performance context, (3) proper performance management such as the projection of Chinese script and its English translation, and (4) availability of good publicity in the mass media.

The Hong Lim Park Chinese Opera Series not only assumes that the amateur and professional operatic traditions are similar, but it foregrounds the amateurs as cultural bearers of Chinese opera in Singapore. In other words, the process of elevating the amateurs is espoused from a "culture" standpoint, which produces a set of new meanings and values for Chinese street opera, as I shall elaborate below.[1]

The success of this performance series, and others similar to it, generated and affirmed a new performance practice for amateur opera troupes in the 1970s and 1980s and redefined the Chinese street opera tradition. While professional opera troupes used to perform Chinese street opera as secular entertainment, this function is now taken over by amateurs. Although professional opera troupes continue to perform Chinese street opera in Chinese customary and religious contexts today, their social significance as performers of the Chinese street opera tradition is effectively diminished in this comparison with amateur troupes as a result of the "culture" rhetoric. The conventional notion of Chinese street opera as a practice of everyday life associated with the professional troupes is gradually being appropriated by the amateurs as a contemplative pursuit of culture.

Conflating the professional and amateur operatic traditions under the name "Chinese street opera," as the Hong Lim Park Chinese Opera Series has done, negates the historical and social conditions of both groups as distinct organizations in Singapore. Chinese street opera is now secularized and recontextualized within a framework of "culture," appropriated from the functional domain of the professional opera troupes and upheld by the amateurs as a kind of aesthetic practice.

In her essay on culture and the arts in Singapore, Koh Tai Ann adopts a similar viewpoint on Chinese opera that collapses the professional operatic practice into the amateur framework: "In being forced off the streets and in losing its customary association with the rural, with temples, market-places and folk festivals, Chinese opera in Singapore, removed from its supporting socio-cultural context, has become secularised, its cultural messages now rooted in the new orthodoxy of contingent state-derived values" (Koh 1989, 721). The first half of the quotation refers to conventional street opera performances by professional troupes; the secularized performance context bound by state values points to street opera performances by the amateurs in Singapore after the 1960s. Rather than being "forced off the streets" and losing their customary associations, professional opera troupes in Singapore have continued to perform Chinese street opera under the patronage of Chinese religious institutions.

What has emerged is a new frame of reference within which new meanings and values of Chinese street opera were shaped. Chinese street opera was gradually becoming a sanitized art form, performed by amateur troupes and supported by the state. In this framework in a shifting cultural context, professional Chinese street opera performances were slowly obliterated.

The Hong Lim Park Chinese Opera Series continued for eight years before it was moved indoors. The expressed purpose for the new performance context was "to merge with the multicultural Traditional Theatre Festival held in 1986" in keeping with the ideology of multiculturalism that has hitherto been the basic pillar of nationalism in Singapore (T. Koh 1989, 721).[2] Quoting the title of a newspaper article written by Sng Poh Yoke of the Chinese Opera Society (Singapore), Koh remarks that this strategy marks "the end of *wayang,* the birth of an art" (ibid.). In her article, Sng commends the Hong Lim Park Chinese Opera Series for having "succeeded in giving the traditional art form a new lease of life" but is concerned that "open air performances have also perpetuated . . . the belief that opera is only street entertainment." By moving indoors, Sng claims that "this year's Festival *elevates* Chinese opera to the realm of art" (Sng 1986; my emphasis). Amateur opera troupes are not only guardians of the Chinese street opera tradition as a local heritage but practitioners of Chinese opera as an art form, recognized in the context of a national festival.

The distinction between street and indoor performances described above alludes to the early twentieth century when Chinese opera performance was popular both as street opera and in indoor theatres. By the mid-1980s, however, the contrast between street and indoor performances was imbued with specific values that derived from, as it further accentuated, differences between amateur and professional opera troupes. Insofar as professional troupes continue to perform Chinese street opera in temples and other outdoor sites for purely religious functions, they are deemed to be of a lower and nonartistic status. The amateurs, on the other hand, are privileged as representatives of Chinese opera in both its heritage (street opera performance) and artistic (indoor performance) manifestations.

From the 1960s to 1980s, then, the development of Chinese opera was projected in an evolutionary trajectory, from Chinese opera as customary and religious street performances to Chinese opera as an elevated art form performed indoors. From the 1980s on, the state's focus on Chinese opera was less about contrasting professionals and amateurs, street and indoor performances, or high and low artistic standards, but on salvaging the declining Chinese street opera tradition as a heritage in Singapore.

Chinese Street Opera as Heritage

One example that showcases the cultural significance of Chinese opera in contemporary Singapore was the inauguration and fund-raising dinner of the Chinese Opera Institute in May 1996. The Chinese Opera Institute is a nonprofit organization supported by the National Arts Council and functions as "a training and research centre responsible for the promotion of all facets of Chinese opera, both practical and theoretical." Recognizing that "Chinese opera is a cultural legacy of Singapore that should be preserved and promoted among our people, especially the younger generation," the Chinese Opera Institute aims to be "a creative platform for artistes and audience who are dedicated in making a renaissance of Chinese opera in Singapore" (Chinese Opera Institute 1996).

The fund-raising dinner on May 19, 1996, featured performances of Peking, Cantonese, Chaozhou, Fujian, and Kun operas. Except for the Peking opera excerpt, performers from China, Taiwan, and Hong Kong presented the other operatic genres.[3] The music ensembles accompanying each performance comprised musicians from various amateur opera troupes in Singapore. Professional opera troupes were conspicuous by their absence from this gala event conceived as a showcase of Chinese opera as a national heritage. Implicit in this event, then, is that local amateur opera troupes have the role of preserving and promoting Chinese opera as a cultural tradition in Singapore, a role affirmed by the overseas Chinese opera communities.

Professional troupes fared only marginally better in another event organized by the Chinese Opera Institute, called "Traditional Theatre in the Park" (June 5–8, 1997). Modeled on the Chinese street opera performance style, this event was not unlike the Hong Lim Park Chinese Opera Series and was held in an open area located in the heart of Orchard Road, Singapore's major shopping district. Among the numerous sponsors for this event were the National Arts Council and the Singapore Tourism Board. In many respects, the event was similar to the Traditional Chinese Street Opera series at Clarke Quay.

Traditional Theatre in the Park included performances of various Chinese opera genres and also featured the Malay *bangsawan* and the Indian *kathak* dance. Of the sixteen Chinese opera performances in this series, only one professional opera troupe—Lau Sai Thor Guan Teochew Wayang—was represented, while the remaining excerpts were performed by amateurs. Lau Sai Thor Guan performed on June 7, 1997, and was accompanied by a musical ensemble from the Thau Yong Amateur Musical Association. As with other amateur performances in the series, Chinese script and English synopsis of its performance were projected onto the two side panels of the stage, a practice not associated with Lau Sai Thor Guan's daily street opera performances (figure 34). Regardless of Lau Sai Thor Guan's presence as a professional opera troupe, Traditional Theatre in the Park was a reconstructed form of Chinese street opera consciously set apart from conventional performances by professional troupes. One might even say that through the Traditional Theatre in the Park event, a professional troupe has been subsumed under a reinvented street opera tradition defined by amateurs.

Perhaps a more important feature of Traditional Theatre in the Park lies in its emphasis on creativity and innovation, a central facet associated with amateur opera troupes. For example, *Zhao Nu Qing* (*The Lady Zhao*), a new Chaozhou opera written by Tan Ooh Chye, a member of the

Figure 34: Lau Sai Thor Guan Teochew Wayang performed at Traditional Theatre in the Park on June 7, 1997, with an instrumental ensemble from the Thau Yong Amateur Musical Association and projections of Chinese script and English synopsis (photo by Low Eng Teong).

Thau Yong Amateur Musical Association and head of the arts management department at the Nanyang Academy of Fine Arts, was premiered by the Thau Yong Amateur Musical Association during the series. The following evening, the Siong Leng Musical Association performed an excerpt from the Indian epic *Ramayana* in the style of Fujian *liyuanxi* adapted by Chua Soo Pong.[4]

Innovation was also the underlying concern for the 1998 Chinese Opera in the Park series (March 12–15, 1998), presented as part of the Eighth Chinese Cultural Festival (February 14–March 15, 1998). Organized by the Chinese Opera Institute, this series was titled "New Street Opera: Innovations and Discovery," and was performed in the same park along Orchard Road where Traditional Theatre in the Park had been held a year earlier.

A newspaper article exoticized this event by urging audiences to "See Chinese Opera under the Stars" with a subtitle "An Attempt to Introduce the Magic of the Art Form to English-educated and non-Chinese Singaporeans" (*Straits Times*, March 11, 1998). It featured four amateur opera troupes that performed Cantonese, Chaozhou, Fujian, and Hainan operas on a makeshift stage, once again evoking the traditional imagery of Chinese street opera. Each performance was preceded by an introduction on the basic elements of Chinese opera in both English and Mandarin and accompanied by slide projections of the Chinese script and its English translation.

By the 1990s, then, in addition to evoking the Chinese street opera style, there was a conscious effort to transcend ethnic boundaries through street opera performance by amateur troupes, with corresponding emphases on new compositions, adaptations, and the provision of English introduction and translation. Indeed, consistent efforts were made by Chinese opera groups to perform Chinese opera in non-Chinese languages. For example, the Chinese Theatre Circle performed excerpts of the classic story of Madam White Snake (*Baishezhuan*) with English recitatives and arias on October 15, 1999. On August 25, 2001, it performed excerpts from the same play with Malay and English subtitles in collaboration with the Malay dance and theatre group Sri Warisan Som Said Performing Arts Limited (www.ctcopera.com.sg; see also *Straits Times*, December 5, 2000). In its continuing effort to promote multiculturalism through Chinese opera, the Chinese Opera Institute coordinated a performance of the Hindu epic *Ramayana* in the style of Huangmei opera (*huangmeixi*), adapted by the institute's director, Chua Soo Pong, on Saturday, April 17, 2004, in which thirty-six students from the Bukit Panjang Government High School performed (*Xinmin Ribao*, April 14, 2004; *Berita Minggu*,

April 18, 2004; *Straits Times*, April 19, 2004).[5] On August 26, 2005, the Chinese Theatre Circle premiered *Intrigues in the Qing Imperial Court*, composed by its chairman, Leslie Wong, at the Festival of World Cultures in the Republic of Ireland and proclaimed it the "first Chinese opera sung in English in the world" (www.ctcopera.com.sg). Toward the end of the twentieth century and into the twenty-first, the public perception of Chinese opera in Singapore has come to be dominated by amateur opera troupes and other nonprofit cultural institutions that function like amateur organizations, as they now embrace both Chinese street opera performances and the artistic, contemplative, and innovative presentations of Chinese opera in indoor theatres.

The Chinese street opera tradition constructed in the events described above is characterized by a set of practices that distinguishes the amateurs from professional opera troupes. Professional Chinese street opera performances are functional, strictly bound by religious events, and follow a largely traditional mode of performance practice. Members of professional troupes are generally middle-aged and above, have very little formal education, and perform Chinese opera for a living. The majority of them do not speak English and many are also non-Mandarin speakers who have spent a large part of their lives performing Chinese opera.

In contrast, amateur Chinese street opera is performed in public spaces located in business, tourist, and shopping areas, and framed in both artistic and cultural terms. Often supported by a large cast of performers and musicians, amateur performances feature elaborate props, special effects, and extensive sound systems. They cater to a wide audience with their projection of Chinese script and English translation, their coverage of a wide range of Chinese opera genres, and a didactic approach toward Chinese opera. The amateur organizational framework comprised of mainly educated, middle-class personnel who advocate Chinese opera as an artistic pursuit further enhances such a form of performance practice.

Arts and Cultural Identity

Aesthetic distinctions between amateur and professional troupes manifested in the reshaping of Chinese street opera from the 1960s were not merely an espousal of artistic achievements but also an indication of the cultural anxiety that has confronted (and continues to challenge) Singapore since its independence in 1965. The development of Chinese opera more than reflects the concerns for nation-building in Singapore: the performance aesthetics emerging through the new kind of Chinese street opera performed by amateur troupes structures the meanings and values of a Singaporean form of cultural nationalism.

For much of the decade following Singapore's 1965 secession from Malaysia, the government focused on political consolidation and economic development as part of its nation-building strategy. In the decade following independence, Singapore might have been described as a "new social order characterised by instrumental rationality and a population with strong achievement motivation" (B. Chua 1995, 105): a disciplined and educated workforce were the primary ingredients of industrial success. Indeed, broad cultural development—"intellectual, spiritual and aesthetic development" (Kroeber and Kluckhohn 1952, 76; see also R. Williams 1976, 76, and T. Koh 1989, 710–11)—"had to abide by the dictates of the logic of the economy" (B. Chua 1995, 105): "The need to survive as an island nation without natural resources and with a declining trading economy had dictated that the rhetoric and the substantive task of nation-building be exclusively concerned with improving the material conditions of the population" (ibid., 119).

Constructing a culture based on industrial success and economic development thus transcended the symbolic aspects of cultural construction. To the extent that ethnic traditions were practiced as symbols of communal identities, they were "restricted to largely privatised celebration of festivals, dances and ornamental adornments" (ibid., 107).[6] Such pragmatic attitudes to culture elevated the importance of material achievement in Singapore: symbolic culture was limited to displays of various ethnic traditions, subsumed within the overarching privileged form of material culture. Preoccupation with economic development and an emphasis on science and technology in the 1960s and the early 1970s further created a rift between social practices that contributed directly to the material development of society, and others that merely constitute symbolic culture.

Socially, one of the government's main concerns was to unite the ethnically diverse population in Singapore, and the primary aim in the late 1970s and 1980s was the construction of an overarching national identity based on the ideology of multiculturalism.[7] The ideal of a national culture in Singapore was envisaged as one that transcended the respective ethnic cultures that constitute the population: "The government's policy was not to 'assimilate,' but to 'integrate' our different communities, in other words, to build up common attributes such as one common working language, same loyalties, similar values and attitudes, so as to make the different communities a more cohesive nation" (statement from the Prime Minister's Office quoted in T. Koh 1989, 711).

To this end, the government introduced new education and social policies. There were four distinct education systems during the colonial times and the early years after Singapore's independence, each using one of the official languages as the major medium of instruction (English, Mandarin, Malay, or Tamil). In 1987 English was instituted as the sole medium of instruction in schools to ensure national cohesiveness through the use of "one common working language" (Kuo 1985, 183). At the same time, a second language—the ethnic or "mother tongue"—was retained and made compulsory for students for the purpose of enhancing ethnic identity through language. By the 1980s, a gradual emphasis was placed on ethnic traditions in terms of language, religion, customs, and other expressive forms: "there is encouragement not only of traditional religion but also of the so-called traditional arts to remind the different communities of their cultural roots; to express individually the identity of each community and collectively to express Singapore's multicultural identity; and as a means to create culture in itself" (T. Koh 1989, 712).[8] During this period, the importance of continued industrial growth and success was manifested in the encouragement of social values such as competitiveness and meritocracy, characteristics essential for capitalist economic development (B. Chua 1995, 120). At the same time, however, it was deemed equally important to promote ethnic identity through the encouragement of tradition and a return to cultural roots.

Economic prosperity in the 1960s and 1970s brought about a growing cult of materialism, along with "the related phenomena of cupidity, philistinism, political apathy, alienation and, for many people, a sense of spiritual deprivation" (Ho 1989, 678). Concerns about the gradual demise of ethnic cultures in Singapore as a consequence of the influx of Western values grew in the late 1970s. Singapore's colonial legacy, its strategic location at the crossroads between the West and Southeast Asia, and the adoption of English as the first language meant that the population was constantly interacting with the "'yellow' inflow of immorality and of narcissistic individualism from the West" (T. Koh 1989, 719). "Yellow" colloquially means "decadent" and is generally used to refer to negative influences from Western (particularly American) cultures. To stem these perceived negative influences, symbolic aspects of culture were salvaged in the 1980s. In particular, the government decided to "create national solidarity by reinforcing 'traditional Asian values'" (ibid.). The inculcation of so-called Asian values and ethnic roots were regarded as essential defenses against the encroachment of Western social values (Clammer 1985, 22–30; Tamney 1996).

In this context, education policies were extensively reviewed, and one of the outcomes was the institutionalization of moral education and religious knowledge programs in schools in 1984 (Ling 1989; Tamney 1996, 25–55). Cultural festivals for each major ethnic group featuring traditional arts, rituals, costumes, and food were periodically organized and supported by the government (A. Lai 1995). In other words, traditional art forms, especially Asian art forms, constituted an important resource in the process of constructing national identity and culture in Singapore.

CONFUCIANISM AS A CULTURAL FRAMEWORK

In the process of cultural formation in Singapore, Confucianism figured prominently in the salvaging of Asian values and ethnic traditions in the 1980s. The Confucianist discourse is often rationalized as the cultural underpinning that perpetuated rapid economic development in East Asia during the postwar period, particularly in Japan. In Singapore, the 1980s marked a period of satisfactory economic achievement and material standards after two decades of industrial expansion since independence. To combat the perceived negative influences of materialism and individualism, Confucianism was adapted as what might be called a "state apparatus" (Althusser 1984). As Lee Kuan Yew candidly states, "Confucianism must adjust and change with changing structures of economy and society" (Lee 2000, 49). The Confucian pantheon of ideas were reduced to "universal" attributes that represented the centrality of education, filial piety, loyalty and reciprocity in hierarchical relationships, and harmonious collectivism, applicable to the multiethnic and multireligious context in Singapore. Though not strictly a religion, a course on Confucian ethics was inserted in 1982 into the moral education program in schools and taught alongside other religious studies (Ling 1989, 701).

Related to the institution of Confucianism was the reinstatement of "culture" in the 1980s, previously sidelined by the state's emphasis on economic, industrial, and political achievements. Significantly, the salvage of "culture" was, in part, a reaction by the state, when it recognized that its autocratic approach to governance was losing ground with the populace. While hard-line policies were accepted in the first two decades after independence, framed in terms of pragmatic and legal-rational ideals such as industrialization, economic reform, legal establishment, and the institutionalization of education, or what may be called "political nationalism" (Hutchinson 1987, 1–2), the increased affluence of Singaporeans in the late 1970s and 1980s and the perceived negative effects of Westernization necessitated the co-option of culture as an ideological apparatus ("cultural nationalism"), perpetuated particularly through the arts.[9]

The catchphrases in the 1980s were "toward a cultured society" and "excellence in everything" (T. Koh 1989, 716). In its election manifesto in 1984, the People's Action Party pledged to develop Singapore into a society that is "culturally vibrant" and to mold Singaporeans into "a cultured people finding fulfilment in non-material pursuits" (quoted in T. Koh 1989, 713). Likewise, according to a speech by then First Deputy Prime Minister and Minister for Defence Goh Chok Tong (who became prime minister from 1990 to 2004 and senior minister from 2004 to the present):

> As we advance to become a developed economy, our people will want similar progress in the social and cultural fields. They will want a more aesthetic and invigorating environment which will allow them to lead a fulfilling life. We must expect this as, once basic needs are secure, a society will want to pursue the higher goals and the individual's self-fulfilment. . . .
>
> Now what is a cultivated society? By a cultivated society I mean a society of well-read, well-informed citizens, a refined and gracious people, a thoughtful people, a society of sparkling ideas, a place where art, literature and music flourish. It is not a materialistic, consumeristic society where wealth is flaunted and money spent thoughtlessly, in short, a *parvenu* society. (quoted in T. Koh 1989, 713–14)

By the 1980s then, "culture" includes contemplative practices of art, literature, and music, foregrounded as antidotes to materialism and consumerism. This concept of culture is equated to the promotion of the high arts, and cultural activity is synonymous with artistic activities.[10]

In "Culture and the Arts," an essay published in the monumental collection on the *Management of Success: The Moulding of Modern Singapore* in 1989, Koh Tai Ann groups cultural activities in Singapore into three categories: "(1) that which is seen as 'a luxury we cannot afford,' the arty-crafty, a merely ornamental, gracious accoutrement incidental to the more serious business of making a living and suggesting high-brow culture for the select few; (2) culturally symbolic expressions of communal identity associated with the more popular practice of the traditional arts (for example, Chinese music or opera, Indian dance, Malay drama, and Western ballet); (3) the pop culture of Westernized, cosmopolitan youth, until recently officially disapproved of and considered 'yellow'" (T. Koh 1989, 716).

Koh notes that the second category is "collectively the approved expression of an instant Singapore multicultural identity," manifest in the performances of traditional and Western art forms, usually presented in national celebrations, school concerts, community clubs, hotels, and tourist events. The concept of culture encapsulated in this category was the basis on which Chinese opera in Singapore was reconfigured after the 1960s.

Confucianism extends itself in Singapore through this avenue of culture. Under the culture rhetoric, Confucianism is espoused more as a behavioral framework than a mere set of ideas (Tu et al. 1992, 40). Moral education extends beyond the formal school system to national campaigns (Courtesy Campaign, Senior Citizens' Week, Racial Tolerance Day, Speak Mandarin Campaign), strict legal jurisdiction on public behavior (such as heavy fines for littering and spitting chewing gum), and national events (National Day, Cultural Months), with the aim of controlling emotions and behavior shaped by the ideology of nation-building.

The concept of culture in Singapore thus shifted from industrial pragmatism and its concomitant "Western" approaches in the 1960s and 1970s to an emphasis on symbolic practices of the high arts and "anti-Western" local and Asian traditions from the 1980s on. In some ways, this trajectory parallels the development of Chinese opera in Singapore, through efforts to elevate Chinese opera from its functional origins to an art form through state-sponsored festivals of amateur performances between the 1960s and 1980s, to the reshaping of Chinese street opera as an icon of local/Asian traditions from the 1980s.

Amateur Chinese Opera and Culture

It is the amateur troupes rather than the professionals that have come to represent the Chinese opera tradition in postindependence Singapore because amateurs embody the ideals of the prevailing, mainstream concept of what culture should be in Singapore. They are educated, work in white-collar occupations, and advocate for the practice of traditional theatre. Their main aim is to promote Chinese opera as an art form and engage in intellectual discourses, such as the analysis of musical modes, vocal styles, and performance techniques. With abundant support from both the state and private sectors, amateur troupes are able to perform with large ensembles, unique lighting effects, good sound systems, elaborate stage props, and overhead projections of the Chinese script and English translation, thereby enhancing their performance standards and reaching a wider audience.

Chinese street opera performance by amateurs is exoticized as a rustic, traditional practice and simultaneously projected as an art form that appeals to the modern sensibilities of the English-educated and non-Chinese communities. Amateur practitioners' abilities as individuals and organizations to sustain the dialectics between tradition and modernity enable them to become bearers of the Chinese opera tradition in Singapore. In contrast, performances by professional troupes are generally considered an unchanging historical product that is functional, apathetic, and nonaesthetic, and their performers are perceived to be uninterested in artistic discourses, performing only to make a living.

Chinese street opera performance by professional troupes has been systematically circumscribed outside the agenda of Chinese opera development in Singapore since the 1960s through a discernible shift in cultural aesthetics that valorize the amateurs. While the performance standards of professional troupes may have indeed declined, this should not be understood solely in any absolute "artistic" terms. The changing sociopolitical context in postindependence Singapore has created a new system within which the meanings and values of cultural practices and artifacts are evaluated. More to the point, the emerging aesthetic framework structures, and is structured by, the changing roles of Chinese opera in contemporary Singapore. So what was for professional troupes a trade for everyday subsistence has become a cause for negative typification through the social patterning of a new cultural paradigm. What constitutes such an aesthetic/cultural paradigm and how does it function? I propose four interrelated perspectives to understand the formation of this new paradigm in the process of cultural nationalism in Singapore: (1) invention of tradition, (2) art-culture system, (3) cultural distancing, and (4) culture as capital.

INVENTING AMATEUR CHINESE STREET OPERA

As discussed in chapter 3, amateur opera troupes historically are not associated with the tradition of Chinese street opera performance in Singapore. Thus, their enactment of street opera in contemporary Singapore is an invented tradition. Eric Hobsbawm notes that the invention of traditions is "highly relevant to that comparatively recent historical innovation, the 'nation,' with its associated phenomena: nationalism, the nation-state, national symbols, histories and the rest" (Hobsbawm 1992, 13). Singapore is a case in point.

Hobsbawm asserts that the continuity between invented traditions and their references to a historic past is "largely factitious" (Hobsbawm 1992, 2). In other words, responding to new situations, these invented traditions make references to the past and/or construct their own histories. Indeed, exalting amateur troupes and showcasing them in cultural events while displacing the professionals fabricate a different history of Chinese opera in Singapore. This history is no less real or authentic: the cultural significance of amateur Chinese street opera in late twentieth-century Singapore lies in its ability to innovate and historicize itself to create its own tradition.[11]

Hobsbawm further notes, "Where the old ways are alive, traditions need be neither revived nor invented" but cautions that "where they are invented, it is often not because old ways are no longer available or viable, but because they are deliberately not used or adapted" (Hobsbawm 1992, 8). The prominence of amateur street opera over the professionals clearly illustrates this point, which reflects "the culture of the selective tradition," that is, a process where specific social practices are highlighted and preferred over others (Williams 1961, 49).[12] Why is there a preference for amateur over professional troupes? I suggest that this is because of the production of what James Clifford calls the "art-culture system" that structures new forms of cultural aesthetics and standards of evaluation imposed upon, and espoused through the performing arts (Clifford 1988, 215–30).

AMATEUR CHINESE STREET OPERA AND THE ART-CULTURE SYSTEM

The art-culture system that Clifford proposes defines a conceptual space within which different cultural commodities produce varying meanings and values of culture and the arts: "The system classifies objects and assigns them relative value. It establishes the 'contexts' in which they properly belong and between which they circulate" (Clifford 1988, 223).

The process of cultural nationalism in Singapore constructs a system of meanings and values in which art and cultural practices are situated. This system is firmly rooted in the state's ideology of a national culture, espoused through national campaigns and changes in the education system (T. Koh 1989, 725–42). Culture is framed in terms of a reverence for ethnic diversity, a concern for "Asian roots," and an engagement with "intellectual and artistic works and activity such as literature, music, painting, theatre, and so forth" (ibid., 710). The goal of this cultural ideology is to create and maintain a suitable moral and aesthetic social paradigm that parallels the successful environment brought about by Singapore's economic achievements and technological advancement. As Richard Fox asserts, "A national culture starts out as a nationalist ideology, that is, a consciousness or perception of what the nation is or should be, which then may gain public meaning and be put into action" (Fox 1990, 4). Central to the effectiveness of the state's cultural ideology is the management of culture by shaping aesthetics in the arts. Indeed, it is through the arts that the meanings and values of the state's cultural ideology are manifested and made public, Chinese street opera being a key example.[13]

Chinese street opera performed by amateur troupes embodies the positive aspects of culture delineated by the state. The amateur engages in intellectual discourses through its practices, and its performances transcend ethnic boundaries and cater to a broad audience. Its organizational rhetoric is firmly rooted in history, local tradition, and social altruism, and, at the same time, powerfully aligned to the contemporary pursuits of learning, creativity, and innovation. The aesthetic framework produced by amateur Chinese street opera performance achieves a positive value through its convergence with the framework of cultural nationalism in Singapore: culture defined in terms of artistic achievement, importance of education, affirming national identity through local traditions, constructing an Asian identity as a conduit for regional coalition, and achieving global status through innovation, modernization, and industrialization. Both frameworks construct and reproduce each other simultaneously to create a broader art-culture system.

As part of the societal fabric, the art-culture system reflects and simultaneously articulates prevailing social norms and values. With reference to Chinese opera, the art-culture system in Singapore generates a particular framework of performance aesthetics within which professional and amateur opera troupes are compared to each other. The system reflects a social preference for the amateurs not only because they fulfill the aesthetic criteria articulated by the system, but also because they constitute a symbol, and indeed, an organizational model that Singapore aspires to achieve. To paraphrase Daniel Neuman in his study of musical organizations in North India, the characteristics, practices, and ideologies of the amateur Chinese opera troupe in Singapore constitutes a microcosm of what the Singapore government wants the country to be—educated, historically informed, culturally vibrant, technologically advanced, and artistically well versed (Neuman 1990, 205).

Insofar as avocation—rather than vocation—is a trademark of the amateur identity, the conspicuous presence of amateur troupes at state-sponsored events and in writings about Chinese opera in Singapore further perpetuates the social norm that favors the acquisition of a transcendent or aesthetic sensibility toward the arts. In other words, the emphasis is on participation in the field of arts for leisure, knowledge, contemplation, self-development, and more importantly, for the enhancement of the arts and culture.

CULTURAL DISTANCING AND SOCIAL IDENTITY

The art-culture system generated in the process of cultural nationalism in Singapore privileges the possession of an aesthetic "distance" in artistic pursuit and simultaneously encourages its acquisition. Amateur opera troupes exemplify the concept of aesthetic distance in artistic practices, which presupposes and perpetuates the notion that art transcends everyday experiences. In other words, if the practice of art is mundane and involved with ordinary daily necessities, it is then devalued when scrutinized with a gaze predisposed toward the aesthetic. In cultural terms, "There is no 'distancing' . . . in the culture of everyday life" (Fiske 1992, 154).

Insofar as an aesthetic distance in the practice of art is socially preferred in Singapore, the concept of "cultural distance" is privileged as a social practice. The practice of cultural distancing favors the aesthetic appreciation of art and "encourages reverence or respect for . . . an art object endowed with authenticity and requiring preservation" (Fiske 1992, 154). Furthermore, Pierre Bourdieu notes that "the work of art is the objectification of a relationship of distinction and that it is thereby explicitly predisposed to bear such a relationship in the most varied contexts" (Bourdieu 1984, 227). Thus, achieving cultural distance through a transcendent practice of art presupposes a pursuit for social distinction, in terms of merit and in the form of a different identity.

The mission, organizational structure and practice, and the overall ethos of the amateur opera organizations work toward preserving and promoting Chinese opera as cultural heritage and a traditional art form. Amateur opera troupes are model organizations in a social context that privileges and exemplifies the practice of the "aesthetic," in other words, a distanced approach toward art and, by extension, culture. Conversely, despite the almost daily performances by professional opera groups in Singapore, they are not as highly esteemed as the amateurs because they are not seen as preservers of the Chinese opera tradition as a cultural form. To members of professional opera troupes, the practice of Chinese opera is constrained by the mundane and economic necessities of everyday life, not distanced from it.

The separation of the "aesthetic" from the "mundane" as a practice of cultural distancing becomes socially significant within the art-culture system in which professional and amateur Chinese opera troupes are relativized against each other. In the process of building a new cultural identity for Singapore, the art-culture system "construct[s] an aesthetic which not only refuses to assign any value at all to material conditions, but validates only those . . . which transcend them" (Fiske 1992, 154). In such a context, Chinese street opera performances by professional opera troupes are considered inconsequential and relegated outside modernity in Singapore, while amateur Chinese street opera continues to gain cultural currency. It is important to note that the critique of professional Chinese street opera performance as crude, noninnovative, nonartistic, and declining in standards—in contrast to that of the amateurs—is a recent phenomenon that emerged after the 1970s during the formative period of the art-culture system in Singapore.

ACQUIRING CULTURAL CAPITAL

The practice of cultural distancing, embodied and encouraged by amateur opera troupes, constitutes "a marker of distinction between those able to separate their culture from the social and economic conditions of the everyday and those who cannot" (Fiske 1992, 154). Chinese opera performance defines a boundary between the artistic and everyday social practices for amateur performers. The relish for distance in the practice of Chinese opera is a process of constructing a cultural identity and inhabiting a definable social space, generally characterized by high educational level, high income, and the practice of acquiring cultural capital without an emphasis on economic returns. The Confucian ideology that permeates the amateur opera organization further encourages the didactic and moralistic values of artistic achievement, and perpetuates the "distanced" approach toward art.

According to Pierre Bourdieu, cultural capital is the resource of knowledge, experience, and disposition toward cultural practices and cultural goods (Johnson 1993, 7). The acquisition of cultural capital is dependent upon an aesthetic disposition toward various forms of social practices, and this capital can only be acquired "by means of a sort of withdrawal from economic necessity," which largely depends on the possession of substantial economic capital to begin with (Bourdieu 1984, 54; see also Bourdieu 1993, 67–68).

Insofar as economic means are a prerequisite for accumulating cultural capital, it is the social elites, already in possession of sufficient economic power, who obtain or are capable of sustaining this capital. In other words, the concept of cultural capital defines, and is structured by, the elite community. More importantly, the form in which cultural capital is shaped is "based on a particular form of *belief* concerning what constitutes a cultural (e.g. literary, artistic) work and its aesthetic or social value," and such a belief, "in its most traditional and canonical form," prescribes transcendental qualities to the practice of art and assigns absolute value and autonomy to works of art (Johnson 1993, 9; emphasis in original).

The concept of culture in Singapore prescribed through the art-culture system is analogous to Bourdieu's concept of cultural capital. Amateur opera troupes form the middle-class, elite community who practices Chinese opera in a pursuit of the aesthetic. Their performance reveals an underlying belief system that privileges a specific set of aesthetic values in social practices and emphasizes the pursuit of cultural distancing. This belief system, in turn, parallels and supports the political ideology of cultural construction in contemporary Singapore. The practice of cultural distancing expresses the ethos of an elite community and affirms its social superiority in relation to the larger population.

The concern for cultural distance therefore creates a dichotomous identity between professional and amateur opera troupes by fabricating a social boundary between them and, by extension, between two different social classes. This boundary defines, as it is defined by, the performance practices of the professionals and amateurs. For the amateur, Chinese opera is a form of cultural capital. "Performing" this cultural capital within the art-culture system that sustains it legitimizes its practices as authentic by way of being authoritative (Bruner 1994, 400). Indeed, the fetish for authenticity differentiates one group from another and generates social distinction: "There is a particular set of issues concerning authenticity . . . which revolves around the issues of good taste, expert knowledge, 'originality,' and social distinction, [and] is especially visible in the domain of art and art objects" (Appadurai 1986, 45). The constant assertion of authenticity is in itself a strategy to ensure the amateurs' position as cultural advocates within the constructed cultural space that is constituted simultaneously by their social identities and operatic practices. I have not come across any professional performers who discuss the issue of authenticity, however it is defined.

According to Bourdieu's study of the field of cultural production, in the process of acquiring cultural capital, the elite community is also affirming its high social status by making its practices seem "naturally" superior to others. The broader social preference for a distant relationship in the practice of art as exemplified by the amateurs legitimizes them as superior to the professionals, especially since their group ideology is analogous to and also constitutes the state's cultural ideology manifested in the art-culture system.

In this way, musical practices are predisposed, unconsciously or deliberately, to fulfill a social function of defining group identities and legitimizing social differences (Bourdieu 1984, 1–7). Indeed, the fact that amateurs are wealthy enough to afford a leisurely pursuit of music without profit motivation reinforces class distinctions and the importance of socioeconomic power in legitimizing an art form. Through Chinese opera performance, amateurs affirm their alliance with the contemporary processes of cultural nationalism in Singapore. Likewise, they articulate their social differences from professional opera troupes through performance.[14]

Chinese street opera thus becomes a means for the state to imbue its cultural ideology by associating what it defines as "culture" with specific organizational and performance aesthetics of amateur troupes. While amateur Chinese street opera may not be historically and socially consistent insofar as street opera is the traditional domain of the professionals, it is appropriate to its exponents—the amateurs—in their role as part of a dominant, traditionalistic, and humanistic social class in postindependence Singapore (Levenson 1957, 332–33).

It is through the aesthetic rhetoric of art, in this case of Chinese opera, that the state's cultural ideology achieves its ethnic neutrality. The meanings and values of culture espoused through amateur Chinese street opera performance are neither limited to the Chinese community nor to Chinese opera. After all, virtues of heritage, multiculturalism, creativity, and knowledge, among other cultural modes of thought and practice, are broadly applicable. Furthermore, the cultural paradigm effaces the political ideology that sustains it. Indeed, the management of art and culture, by virtue of itself, is "sanitized [and] distanced from the structures of power and interest that, inescapably, are a condition and consequence of its emergence and development" (Alvesson and Willmott 1996, 12). To put it in another way, the discourse on art and culture depoliticizes the ideological apparatus that frames and constitutes it.

This discourse on art and cultural aesthetics is not ephemeral but firmly rooted in pragmatic terms: in Singapore's definition of nation-building, "cultural" achievement occupies a parallel position to "scientific" success in the industry and economy (see Ministry of Information and the Arts 2000). Broadly speaking, then, music performance imbues visibility to, and enhances the meanings and values of, floating cultural signifiers, such as the rhetoric of artistic standards, without foregrounding the political engine that produces them.

Conclusion

Thursday to Saturday, February 19–21, 1998. The Chinese Opera Society (Singapore), an amateur opera society that promotes Chinese opera in Singapore, organized an event called Street Wayang Revisited as part of the annual Chinese Cultural Festival. The event consisted of three nights of performance of the popular Chaozhou opera *Liu Ming Zhu* (*The Story of Liu Ming Zhu*) by the Sing Yong Hoe Heng Teochew Wayang, a professional Chaozhou opera troupe in Singapore.[1] The ticketed performance, presented in what was called the "street wayang-style" (*Straits Times*, February 4, 1998), took place in the Bras Basah Park in the shopping and business district in downtown Singapore.

Accompanying the performance was a month-long exhibition (February 13–March 15, 1998) at the Singapore History Museum displaying old costumes, props, scripts, and other Chinese opera paraphernalia, many of which belonged to Sing Yong Hoe Heng. Organized at a cost of approximately S$15,000 (US$9,375), the exhibit was widely publicized and well attended, and was partially sponsored by the Singapore Press Holdings and National Arts Council among other national institutions.

Aimed specifically at younger-generation Singaporeans, the English-speaking communities, expatriates, and tourists, Street Wayang Revisited used slide projections of the Chinese script and corresponding English translations during the performance. The stage was double the size of the usual makeshift stages used by professional opera troupes, the performance area was sheltered and well ventilated with mobile fan units, and hawkers were engaged to serve food at this three-day event. Approximately five hundred people watched the final performance on Saturday, February 21, 1998 (*Straits Times*, February 21, 1998).

The following Monday, on February 23, 1998, Sing Yong Hoe Heng resumed its daily practice and staged performances for a ritual celebration in an open space next to Newton Circus, a popular area with tourists, expatriates, and younger Singaporeans. This time, however, a photograph published in the Chinese newspaper shows only a scattering of twelve people or so in the audience. The same newspaper article aptly questions this phenomenon with a metaphorical title: "Shuguang Zhaxian Haishi Xiyang Yuhui?" ("Emerging Sunshine or Lingering Sunset?" *Lianhe Zaobao*, March 7, 1998b; see also *Lianhe Zaobao*, March 7, 1998a). The same opera troupe performed in two different contexts with contrasting outcomes.

The concept of the Street Wayang Revisited event raises an interesting question, similar to the one that has guided this study: why "revisit" Chinese street opera (*wayang*) when a dozen professional troupes perform it almost every day around Singapore? One response is that the two events described above represent different cultural meanings and values even though both were Chinese street opera performed by the same troupe.

Street Wayang Revisited is cultural in the sense that it featured a traditional Chinese street opera performance in the artistic setting of a festival staged by art and cultural organizations to celebrate Chinese culture. The latter event is cultural in that Chinese street opera performed as a ritual, that is, *choushenxi*, is a deep-rooted tradition for the Chinese community. If success is measured by the size of the audience watching the performances, then the success of Street Wayang Revisited affirms a preference toward a type of Chinese street opera performance framed by a specific notion of culture.

Street Wayang Revisited was more than a mere revival of tradition. It was one in a series of amateur Chinese street opera events described in chapter 6, a new mode of performance practice for amateur opera troupes that began in the 1970s, partially or wholly sponsored by the state. The event, and indeed the entire concept of amateur Chinese street opera, has redefined the meanings and values of Chinese street opera in contemporary Singapore, hitherto the domain of professional opera troupes. This process of constructing a new performance tradition for a specific social organization, based on an existing tradition that continues to be practiced by another, offers insights into the intersection of music performance, ideology, class distinction, and heritage in the process of shaping a national culture in a rapidly modernizing country.

For the 1998 Chinese Cultural Festival, the two main Chinese opera events—Street Wayang Revisited and New Street Opera: Innovations and Discovery—were performed and staged by amateur opera troupes and national cultural organizations. In this performance context, revisiting Chinese street opera is more than a mere celebration of heritage. It is also an assessment of Singapore's current state of nationhood that frames it in relation to a manufactured past (Bruner 1994, 398). The past is manufactured not in terms of falsifying history but in creating new histories according to changing cultural ideologies.

Amateurizing the Chinese street opera tradition is as much (if not more so) an assertion of social distinction as it is a revival of tradition. Street Wayang Revisited featured a professional opera troupe, recasting what it did for a living in an event coordinated by an amateur opera society that pursues Chinese opera as an art form, within the context of a national cultural festival. In the same way that Lau Sai Thor Guan Teochew Wayang, the only professional opera troupe that appeared at the 1997 Traditional Theatre in the Park, performed in the amateur Chinese street opera tradition—well-equipped performance space, large accompanying ensemble, projections of Chinese script and English synopsis, preperformance introductions in English and Mandarin, to name a few characteristics—Sing Yong Hoe Heng Teochew Wayang's performance at Street Wayang Revisited is framed within the amateur Chinese street opera tradition. The effectiveness of this particular cultural performance lies in its use of a professional troupe to revisit and reflect on professional Chinese street opera in Singapore—in the amateur context.

In this way, the event's achievements are indicative of the successful appropriation of the Chinese street opera tradition by amateur opera troupes and cultural organizations in Singapore, and more importantly, a recognition of the cultural paradigm that frames and is simultaneously structured by their performance practices. A newspaper report on this event is titled "Wayang Back with a Spunky Maiden," the phrase "spunky maiden" referring to a character in the play *Liu Ming Zhu*. A photograph caption reads, "The sights and sounds of Singapore past: Street *wayang* in full swing with a Teochew-opera presentation, staged by the Chinese Opera Society" (*Straits Times*, February 21, 1998). While the term "wayang" used to refer mainly to street opera performances by professional opera troupes, it now refers to the amateur Chinese street opera tradition, thus affirming a shift in musical and cultural meanings and values in Singapore since the 1970s. The media's focus on the stark contrast between Sing Yong Hoe Heng's performances at the Street Wayang

Revisited event and at its routine daily performance barely a week later further exemplifies this changing cultural paradigm in Singapore in the late twentieth century.

The nation-building process in Singapore after 1965 was as much motivated by global movements of capitalism and consumerism as it was by an emphasis on local cultures. Central to the effectiveness of the state's ideology is the management of culture through aesthetics of the arts, and mediating such universal and local modes of social changes are cultural organizations such as the amateur Chinese opera troupe. No longer bounded by ethnicity, its organizational culture—with emphasis on education, social altruism, respect for heritage, and a passion for culture—is touted as a universal model applicable to all segments of Singapore society, a cultural microcosm capable of reproducing new political and ideological structures and imperatives.

As part of the middle class in Singapore, members of amateur Chinese opera troupes play a role in shaping a Singaporean culture through their history, structure, and performance of Chinese street opera. They have become, in effect, cultural entrepreneurs at a particular point in Singapore's history, and they have continued in this role because their organizational structures and practices interconnect with the state's concept of a Singaporean national culture.[2]

The rhetoric of culture is framed as a necessary pantheon of values concomitant to the process of economic and industrial advancement. The physical structure of the amateur Chinese opera organization that constitutes the interface in the production of culture is rendered invisible. What remains is a myth—no less real than the physical organization—structured and rationalized by values and morals. In the same way, Confucianism, as a major perpetrator of these values and morals, sheds its Chineseness and is molded as a set of overarching values for being Singaporean. In this way then, amateur Chinese opera troupes become "dramatic enactments of the rationalized myths pervading modern societies" (Meyer and Rowan 1977, 348).

Amateurs function as mediators of cultural knowledge, shaping and producing specific cultural understanding, and transmitting such forms of knowledge to the general populace through lecture-demonstrations in schools and public performances. In this process, knowledge also becomes a form of cultural capital, which further enhances the role of amateurs in shaping culture in Singapore. In this sense, knowledge management serves a broader political, social, and cultural purpose (McAdam and McCreedy 1999, 93–94).

The concept of national culture in Singapore is "dictated by those who do participate successfully," not unlike the "Big Men" theory in organizational studies (Hendry 1999, 567). Indeed, the art-culture system in Singapore defines the middle- and upper-class habitus exemplified in the amateur opera organization, whose members, through their practice of "positive" social ideals, continue to perpetuate the system. In this way, culture becomes a form of proprietary knowledge, externalized through socialization among a select group.[3] Amateur Chinese opera troupes are able to align their ideology, structure, and practices to that of the state's framework for cultural nationalism, thus constructing a "trope of amateurism" that defines an aesthetic vocabulary. In contrast, professional opera troupes do not practice such cultural tropes nor do they perform according to the aesthetics of the amateurs in their everyday practices. They are thus relegated to the outside of the conceptual boundaries of the art-culture system. Viewed in this way, the management of culture is predisposed to accentuate issues of social status and power (Fournier and Grey 2000, 9).

In this study, I have illustrated that the aesthetic distinctions between the professional and amateur performance traditions have been conditioned by shifting sociopolitical contexts in Singapore since its independence in 1965. The development of Chinese street opera in Singapore enables us to assess the changing social dynamics in a modernizing society, where cultural values and preferences are constantly negotiated through various expressive forms. Performing Chinese street opera is a means through which the identity politics of nation, organizations, and individuals are constantly constructed, affirmed, or even transcended.

NOTES

Introduction

1. Statistics Singapore (http://www.singstat.gov.sg/).

2. Singapore's management of ethnicity, multiculturalism, and national identity has been widely studied. See, for example, Benjamin (1976), S. Chew (1987), B. Chua (1998), Kong and Yeoh (2003), A. Lai (1995), Siddique (1989), and Vasil (1995). For an overview on the study of ethnicity, see R. Cohen (1978) and Vincent (1974); on ethnicity and nationalism, see Eriksen (1993) and B. Williams (1989).

3. The national anthem is sung in Malay, and even though proficiency in the Malay language is not compulsory for non-Malays, Malay is the national language in Singapore (see PuruShotam 1998).

4. The earliest record of Chinese inhabitants on the island of Singapore is generally attributed to Wang Dayuan's *Daoyi Zhilue* (*Description of the Islands*) published in 1349 (Cui 1994, 2).

5. Yen (1986, 1–10) describes the processes of Chinese immigration. For information on population growth in Singapore, see Saw (1991). Song (1967), Wang (1989), and Yen (1986) situate the dramatic migratory patterns within the establishment of the British Straits Settlement and its socioeconomic expansion. See also Purcell (1948, 1965) and Tan (1989) on Chinese in Malaya and Southeast Asia.

6. Peranakans, otherwise known as *baba* (male) or *nonya* (female), are Chinese who speak Malay and adopt certain aspects of the Malay culture, but practice Chinese religions and festivals; see Clammer (1979) and Rudolph (1998). In this study, names of people in Chinese are written with surname first, and Chinese terms are romanized according to Mandarin pronunciation in *hanyu pinyin*. References to certain places (for example, Canton), ethnic communities (for example, Cantonese), and genre (for example, Cantonese opera) are listed according to established conventions. "Fujian" and "Chaozhou" are used in place of "Hokkien" and "Teochew" respectively throughout this book, except in official names (for example, Sin Sai Hong Hokkien Wayang).

7. See Pan (1999, 200–217) for an overview of Chinese in Singapore.

8. Although the Speak Mandarin campaign was instituted only in 1979, campaigns to promote the study of Mandarin began in the late nineteenth century (PuruShotam 1989, 506–7).

9. On role types in Peking opera, see Scott (1957, 58–91) and Wichmann (1991, 7–12). See also Riley (1997, 12–53) on performance training in Peking opera.

10. See Yung (1989) on Cantonese opera music, Pian (1971, 1975), Scott (1957, 41–57), and Wichmann (1991, 53–175) on music of Peking opera, and Liang (1985, 230–67) for an overview of music in traditional Chinese opera.

11. The terms *xi* and *ju* refer to a play or drama, and may be used interchangeably. *Yue* refers to the Canton province (and also the neighboring Guangxi province): *yueju* (Cantonese opera) is the Chinese term for opera from this region. For introductions to Chinese opera in Singapore, see S. Chua (1996), Kamisango (1984), and Perris (1978).

12. *Gezaixi* is also known as *xiangju,* an operatic genre that developed in the *xiangjiang* (Xiang River) area in south Fujian province after *gezaixi* was introduced from Taiwan in the 1920s (Liu and Wang 1986, 393–431).

13. By the Song dynasty (960–1279 AD), *sanyue* was also known as *baixi* (Yang 1981, 333).

14. On the history and development of Chinese opera, see Yung (1989, 1–10) and Zhou (1960, 1979). On Song *zaju* and *nanxi,* see Dolby (1976, 14–39; 1983a), Yang (1981, 332–66), and Zhang and Guo (1992, 42–75, 106–23, 233–301, 403–50); on Yuan *zaju,* see Crump (1990), Dolby (1976, 40–59; 1983b), Johnson (1980), Shih (1976), Sieber (2003), and Yang (1981, 459–630); on *chuanqi,* see Birch (1995, 1–19), Dolby (1976, 71–101), Hu (1983), and Wong et al. (1972); on the social contexts of Chinese drama in the Ming and Qing dynasties, see Tanaka (1985). See Lopez (1991) and Wong (1994) for annotated bibliographies of Chinese drama.

15. Of particular cultural importance was the region south of the Yangzi River known as Jiangnan (literally "river south"), which includes the provinces of Jiangsi, Zhejiang, Jiangsu, and Anhui. For a brief overview of musical traditions in the Jiangnan region as they relate to *jiangnan sizhu* (Jiangnan "silk and bamboo") music, see Witzleben (1995, 5–22).

16. On Kun opera, see Dolby (1976, 71–113) and Tsiang (1932). For an overview of Peking opera and its social history, see Dolby (1976, 157–83), Guy (2005), and Mackerras (1972). On the general development of *qiang* and regional operas, see Dolby (1976, 114–56), Mackerras (1972, 4–15; 1983a, 98–106), Yang (1981, 858–64, 980–86), Zeng (1976), and Zhang and Guo (1992, 453–872; 875–1149). For a brief survey of regional operas, see Dolby (1976, 219–30) and Minsu Quyi (1983).

17. Consumption patterns, taste, lifestyle, and attitudes of the newly rich middle class provide a measure by which Singapore is perceived as a "middle-class society" (Chua and Tan 1999). On middle-class identities and the arts, see, for example, DiMaggio (1982) and Paritta (2002).

18. For an overview on music and identity, see Frith (1996).

Chapter 1: Chinese Opera in Singapore

1. For a study of interactions between China and Southeast Asia, and the early formation of Chinese communities in Southeast Asia, see Wu (1993, 1–45).

2. For a study of Chinese opera, religious procession, and the framing of ethnic space in modern Singapore, see Yung (1997, 193–222).

3. See color plate 14 in Jayapal (1992; after p. 38) for an illustration of Tian Fu Gong (romanized as Thian Hock Keng Temple) in early twentieth-century Singapore.

4. Reprinted as "In High Spirits" in Wise (1996, 165–69).

5. See Trocki (1990) for a study of the opium trade and the Chinese community in colonial Singapore. My maternal grandfather, Ng Jin Sim (1902–2001), migrated to Singapore in the early 1920s and was an ardent fan of Chaozhou opera. In the

1930s and 1940s, he set up gambling stalls in the vicinity of Chinese street opera performances and also in the amusement parks. During my visits to street opera troupes at their performance sites, there were times when I saw groups of people playing cards or mahjong (a form of Chinese gambling) backstage while others were performing. If the stage was a permanent one, which usually had a semi-covered basement, they would congregate in the basement for their games while the performance continued above them.

6. These rituals form part of Chinese opera performance, particularly during *choushenxi,* for purposes of spirit-cleansing and blessings. For a study of these two operatic rituals in Singapore, see Yung (1997, 133–66) on *Liuguo Fengxiang* and Yung (1997, 167–91) on *Liyu Tiaolongmen.*

7. Reprinted as "Chinese Theatre" in Bastin (1994, 174–81), 176.

8. Reprinted as "A Favourite Place for Europeans" in Wise (1996, 161–64), 163.

9. Cui (1994, 11–14). For a succinct study of these events, see Fairbank and Goldman (1998, 206–34). On the impact of Chinese exclusion acts in the United States, see Pan (1999, 262–65); on reasons for population increase of Chinese in Southeast Asia, see Wu (1993, 227–80, 588–98); on patterns of Chinese migration, see Pan (1999, 46–71) and Wang (1989).

10. A population census of Singapore taken in 1849 categorized professions into merchants and clerks, mechanics, agriculturists, laborers, servants, and miscellaneous, and did not have a category for performing artists (Jackson 1850). This suggests that the profession of performing artists rose to prominence in the latter half of the nineteenth century, alongside the increase in Chinese immigrants to Singapore. The other occupation classes listed in the 1881 census are domestic, commercial, agricultural, industrial, and unclassified.

11. On economic growth and Chinese entrepreneurship in Singapore or Southeast Asia in general, see Cui (1994, 125–49), Heng and Sieh (2000), Mackie (2003), Wu (1993, 370–423), and Yong (1987, 41–82).

12. On "Greater Town" and "Lesser Town" in Singapore, see Wang (1997, 1–10). For an approximate comparison, an average laborer in the 1850s earned between $3 and $3.50 per month, or approximately one cent per day (Blythe 1951, 34). See Cui (1994, 94) or Pitt (1988, 60) for the Chinese text. From *Xinjiapo Fengtuji (A Description of Singapore)* by Li Chung Chu, or Li Zhongjue in pinyin (Singapore: Nanyang Shuju Youxian Gongshi [Nanyang Bookstore Private Limited], 1947), 13.

13. See Liu and Phillips (1988) and Tang (1976) on architectural and ownership records of Chinese theatres, and Wang (1997, 47–52, 53–58, 70–77) for further descriptions of theatres. "Wayang Street" was probably named after the two Chinese theatres along the street, and was later changed to "Eu Tong Sen Street" between 1915 and 1918, named after its owner, Eu Tong Sen (Pitt 1988, 62–63; see also Liu and Phillips 1988, 29–30, and Wang 1997, 53–58). Hainan opera is also known as *qiongju,* Qiong being the alternative name for the Hainan region.

14. For a map showing the divisions of different ethnic communities in Raffles's town planning of Singapore, see Jayapal (1992, 9): Chinatown is located to the west of the river shown on the top left corner of the map.

15. See "Greater Town" in Wise (1996, 134). See also Archives and Oral History Department (1983, 20–21) and Cui (1994, 40–41). Kreta Ayer is located within the broader confines of Chinatown, and is generally regarded as Chinatown proper.

16. In Cantonese, Li Chun Yuan is romanized as Lai Chun Yeun; Qing Wei Xin and Qing Sheng Ping are romanized as Heng Wai Sun and Heng Seng Peng, respectively. In Chaozhou, Yi Yuan and Zhe Yuan are referred to as Ee Hng and Tiat Hng, respectively. For a succinct description of Chinese opera theatres in Singapore, see Liu and Phillips (1988, 28–35).

17. Today, although Chinatown has become an emblem of a pan-Chinese community in Singapore, it is still known for its Cantonese character in terms of its inhabitants, historical buildings, and food.

18. Map adapted from Tang (1976, 141), who suggests a correlation between identities of opera theatres and the Chinese communities residing around them.

19. *Bahe* refers to the eight divisions in the traditional categorization of Chinese opera according to role types and duties of personnel: Zhao He Tang for *sheng* (male), Fu He Tang for *dan* (female), Qing He Tang for *jing* (painted face), Xin He Tang for *chou* (clown), Yong He Tang for *wu* (military), De He Tang for *dawu* (martial arts), Shun He Tang for those in charge of sourcing for performances, and Pu He Tang for musicians and those responsible for stage settings (Pitt 1988, 59). In this way, Bahe Huiguan functions like a clan association. For an overview of overseas Chinese associations, see Pan (1999, 74–95).

20. A copy of the bylaws is reproduced in Liu and Phillips (1988, 27).

21. See Pitt (1988, 61–62) for more information on Li Chun Yuan. Wang (1997, 47–52) notes that Li Chun Yuan existed in 1887, Cui (1994, 94) points out that the theatre is on an 1893 map of Singapore (see map in Pitt 1988, 62), and other sources affirm that the theatre was designed circa 1897 (Liu and Phillips 1988, 29).

22. In the 1920s, men and women watching Chinese street opera were also segregated by a rope strung loosely on poles laid perpendicular to the stage to protect any harassment of women in the crowd (personal communication, Ng Jin Sim, August 21, 1997). During this period, the Qing Sheng Ping theatre along Eu Tong Sen Street (Wayang Street), known for its Peking opera performances, also had separate areas for men and women and charged cheaper ticket prices for women (Wang 2000, 104–7).

23. In 1996 and 1997, I observed this phenomenon of reserving seats using tissue papers instead of handkerchiefs at the annual opera gala hosted by the Lorong Koo Chye Sheng Hong Temple (see chapter 4).

24. Reprinted as "The Daily Double" in Wise (1996, 232–35), 232–33.

25. This phenomenon is hardly seen in Singapore today. In 1995, the Chinese Theatre Circle began a performance series known as "Cantonese Opera Lunchtime Melodies" at the Dragon Phoenix Restaurant in Singapore, "thereby reviving a form of ethnic culture which had disappeared from the local scene in the early 1960s" (Chinese Theatre Circle 1995). A three-hour performance was held the first Sunday of the month and showcased vocal students of the Chinese Theatre Circle (personal communication, Joanna Wong, August 1, 1997).

26. These figures are supported by the 1938 report on the Federated Malay States (comprising Pahang, Perak, Selangor, and Negeri Sembilan), which notes that the trends for wages and living costs in Singapore and the Federated Malay States follow each other closely. The report states that estimated earnings for Chinese laborers were between sixty and sixty-five cents a day (Colonial Reports 1939, 51–52).

27. Author's translation from Chinese. The first announcement of the troupe was published in *Lat Pau* on December 22, 1893, and news of their performance in

Singapore remained in print for eighteen consecutive days. The last publication on January 8, 1894, was a short review of their final performance on January 6, 1894. Wang Fang provides a succinct overview of the troupe's activities in Singapore, including a copy of the first advertisement, the final review, and a brief survey of the troupe's history (Wang 2004, 20–30). The subject of the performance is real historical events: the Great Taiping Rebellion (1851–1864) began in Guangxi, west of Guangzhou (Canton) in south China, and was a confrontation between militant Chinese evangelists and the Manchu court (Fairbank and Goldman 1998, 206–12). Jiujiang is located in the northern part of the Jiangxi province.

28. On August 20, 1887, the *Illustrated London News* published an illustration titled "Celebration at Singapore: Jubilee Performance at a Wayang, or Chinese Theatre" (see Jayapal 1992, 52), showing that Chinese opera was used to commemorate the fiftieth anniversary of the reign of Queen Victoria (1819–1901; reigned 1837–1901). For a brief description of the activities of Chinese in Queen Victoria's Jubilee celebrations in Singapore, see Song (1967, 227–28).

29. Emperor Guangxu (Song romanizes the name as Kwang-su) was the penultimate emperor of China who reigned from 1875 to 1908. Guangxu became emperor in 1875 when he was only four years old, with Empress Dowager Cixi in power, and formally ascended the throne when he was married in 1889.

30. Seah Liang Seah (1850–1925) is the son of Seah Eu Chin (1805–1883), a prominent Chinese businessman in Singapore who is credited as the first local Chinese to write about the Chinese community in Singapore (Song 1967, 73–75).

31. *Lat Pau*, September 4, 1905, 4. See Pitt (1988, 58) for a transcription of this announcement.

32. On the complexities of the term *huaqiao*, see Wang (1989).

33. For an analysis of the republican revolution, see Fairbank and Goldman (1998, 235–53); on its influence on Chinese in Singapore, see Cui (1994, 182–85); on responses of Southeast Asian Chinese, see Wu (1993, 493–538, 625–30).

34. The Manchus from Manchuria (northeast China) established the Qing dynasty in 1644. The Han Chinese trace their ancestry to the Han dynasty (206 BC–220 AD). Of the fifty-six ethnic groups in China, the Han Chinese constitute a majority of more than 92 percent.

35. On Chiang Kai-shek's northern expedition, see Fairbank and Goldman (1998, 283–89); on Chinese resistance against Japan between 1937 and 1945, see Fairbank and Goldman (1998, 321–30); on anti-Japanese resistance from Chinese in Southeast Asia, see Cui (1994, 189–201) and Wu (1993, 687–751).

36. On the Shandong Relief Fund, see Yong (1987, 179–88); on the Jinan incident, see Wu (1993, 635–39).

37. The Chew Wah Lim Club (romanized in the Chaozhou vernacular as Chui Huay Lim Club) was the first Chinese social club in Singapore established in 1849 by the Chaozhou community in Singapore. It is not clear who or which group presented the Chinese vernacular dramas, but the Hoi Thin variety shows were performed by the Hoi Thin Amateur Dramatic Association; for a picture of the association, see Liu and Phillips (1988, 38).

38. Wong and Tan (2004, 280) briefly describe amusement parks in Singapore and Shanghai in their detailed study of the New World amusement park.

39. Malay theatrical performances consisted mainly of *bangsawan* (see Tan 1993), and Malay theatre groups also performed English plays such as those by

Shakespeare. The use of *huaju* as a symbol of modernization in early twentieth-century China is attributed to its origins in the translations of Western dramas and novels, emphasis on social commentary, and its connection to intellectuals (Mackerras 1975, 120; 1983a, 107); on the development of *huaju* in Shanghai, see Gunn (1984); on examples of *huaju* plays, see Mackerras (1987); on contemporary *huaju*, see Conceison (2004). On the first *gewutuan* from China to perform in Singapore, see Wang (1988, 111–16).

40. A lesser known amusement park, Lao Shijie (Old World), also known as Huanle Yuan (Joyous Garden), was built in the late 1920s, located at the junction of Tanjong Pagar Road and Cantonment Road. Described as "The Most Colourful Town in the World" (Bastin 1994, 231), New World was situated at the junction of Serangoon Road and Rangoon Road (see also Wang 1988, 32–38). Great World was at the junction of Kim Seng Road and Jalan Bukit Ho Swee (see Wang 1988, 47–52), and Happy World, also known as Fanhua Shijie (Flourishing World), was located along Geyland Road (Pitt 1988, 65; see also Wang 1988, 39–46).

41. See Rudolph (1996) on activities in the amusement parks and Wong and Tan (2004, 291–94) on *bangsawan* in the New World amusement park. *Wayang Peranakan* is a genre of drama performed in the Peranakan vernacular with dialogue, comic skits, singing, dancing, and musical accompaniment (Rudolph 1998, 327–31, 358–65, 446–50).

42. Writing in the 1950s, William Newell noted that the four main groups of Chinese opera performers in Malaya were the Cantonese, Chaozhou, Fujian, and Hainan (Newell 1961, 67). On Chinese opera and performing arts in contemporary Malaysia, see Tan (1980; 2000a; 2000b).

43. For a study of the New World amusement park in Singapore and the role of its spatial design and entertainment programming in shaping cosmopolitan mass culture in early twentieth-century Singapore, see Wong and Tan (2004).

44. For a discussion of the May Fourth Movement, see Fairbank and Goldman (1998, 267–69); on education of Chinese in Singapore, see Cui (1994, 150–68).

45. See Levine (1988, 184–219) on the structuring of public space to shape social behavior and meanings of culture; see B. Chua (1991) on transformation of public spaces and social life in Singapore.

46. The term "women squadron" is a translation borrowed from an interview transcript of Tong Pak Meng (b. circa 1905), a Cantonese opera actor who performed actively at the New World amusement park (Liu and Phillips 1988, 52–53; see also National Archives Microfiche A000921/16).

47. Liew Seng Wah (b. 1914) was a Cantonese opera actor who specialized in the role of *wusheng* (male warrior); see Liu and Phillips (1988, 50–51) for an interview transcript.

48. On the role of the Qing court in the development of Peking opera, see Mackerras (1972, 116–53).

49. For example, ticket prices at Qing Sheng Ping in 1928 ranged between twenty cents and $1.10 for day shows, and between twenty cents and $1.30 in the evenings. For comparison, a good quality pair of rubber-sole, white canvas shoes cost twenty-three cents (Wang 2000, 104–7).

50. Historically, the term *xizi* carries derogative connotations of being unrefined, uneducated, and low class (Wang 1990, 76–77). It is interesting that *xizi* in Singapore were respected for their upright nature and allowed to perform publicly during the Japanese occupation. This corroborates Pitt Kuan Wah's observation

that the listing of actors, artists, and musicians in the class of "Professionals" in the 1881 population census was a noteworthy indication of differences in attitudes toward *xizi* in China and Singapore (Pitt 1988, 58).

51. For an overview of the Japanese occupation in Singapore, see Cui (1994, 212–24), Thio (1991), and Turnbull (1989, 187–215).

52. In 1955, the employment of children under twelve was forbidden in Malaya. Stricter restrictions on immigration from China at this time reduced the inflow of Chinese opera actors in Malaya, and regulations on child employment further reduced young recruits for Chaozhou opera troupes (Newell 1961, 68).

53. *Bayi* refers to the eight main areas of the Chaozhou region in the Canton province (Cui 1994, 57). See Liu and Phillips (1988, 54–55) for pictures of child actors. On child actors in Chinese opera in eighteenth- and nineteenth-century China, see Mackerras (1972, 41–42).

54. See Cai (2003, 71–74) for a brief analysis of *Su Liu Niang*.

Chapter 2: Chinese Street Opera and Professional Opera Troupes

1. *Fuzhouxi* is sometimes known simply as *minju* and developed in the north Fujian province centered on Fuzhou city (Dolby 1976, 224–25). *Puxianxi* developed in Putian county that comprises Putian and Xianyou cities in north Fujian province (Liu and Wang 1986, 432–62). On the history of Fujian opera, see Lin et al. (1983); for a brief overview of operas in the Fujian province, see Mackerras (1975, 125–45); on Fujian opera and its music, see Liu and Wang (1986, 331–67).

2. *Gaojiaxi* is an operatic genre that developed in south Fujian province and was popular in Taiwan and Southeast Asia in the early twentieth century. Characterized by its robust aura and military actions, *gaojiaxi* in Southeast Asia was gradually replaced by *gezaixi* from the 1930s onwards. The music of *gaojiaxi* is based primarily on *nanqu* (also known as *nanyin* or *nanguan*) and also incorporates folk tunes and influences from Peking opera and *liyuanxi* (Liu and Wang 1986, 496–520). Traditionally, the term *liyuan* is a reference for a theatre, or more broadly, the practice of Chinese opera. *Liyuanxi* (Pear Garden Theatre) is an operatic genre from south Fujian province and its music is also based on *nanqu* (Liu and Wang 1986, 462–96). For writings on *liyuanxi*, see Mackerras (1975, 125–27) and Wang (1992a); on *nanqu*, see Liu and Wang (1986, 234–56).

3. Between 1945 and 1949, the Nationalist party (Guomindang) that established the Republic of China in 1912 fought a losing battle with the Chinese Communist Party and systematically retreated to Taiwan. Taiwan was a Japanese colony from 1895 when it was ceded after the first Sino-Japanese war and returned to Chinese rule in October 1945. The central government of the Republic of China relocated to Taiwan after the Chinese Communist Party formally established the People's Republic of China in October 1949 (see Fairbank and Goldman 1998, 331–41). Han Chinese from the coastal provinces of Fujian and Guangdong, particularly the south Fujian and Kejia (Hakka) ethnic groups, have migrated to Taiwan since the sixteenth century and constitute approximately 85 percent of Taiwan's population today.

4. The performance style of Fujian puppet theatres is similar to *gezaixi* and retains traditional aspects of the *gezaixi* tradition. In his observations of Chinese drama in Malaya, Ly Sinko claims that the "most conservative Chinese theatre

which can be seen in Malaya is perhaps represented by the puppet plays" (Ly 1965, 171). For an introduction to puppet theatre in Singapore, see Wang (2000, 139–44, 145–46); on hand puppet theatre in Malaysia, see Tan (1981). For a brief overview of Fujian *gezaixi* in Singapore, see Wang (2000, 68–73).

5. On the development of *yiyangqiang,* see Wu and Liu (1993, 287–92), Yang (1981, 859–62, 980–81), and Zhang and Guo (1992, 478–88, 817–72); on *kunshanqiang,* see Wu and Liu (1993, 275–86), Yang (1981, 862–66), and Zhang and Guo (1992, 461–78, 743–817); on *bangziqiang* and *erhuangqiang* (related to *pihuangqiang*), see Wu and Liu (1993, 292–96), Yang (1981, 981–83), and Zhang and Guo (1992, 892–902).

6. On Chaozhou musical systems, see also Chen (1991), Dujunco (2002), and Zhang (1980).

7. On Chaozhou opera in Singapore, see Chiam (1979), Li (1971), Ong (1958), and Phang (1998); on Chaozhou opera, see Chaojuzhi Pianji Weiyanhui (1995).

8. On Cantonese opera and its music, see Chan (1986) and Yung (1989). See Chan and Yung (2000), Leung (1977), and Riddle (1978; 1983) for studies on Cantonese opera in North America, and Leung (1979) on Cantonese opera in Canton city, China.

9. When theatres and amusement parks closed and state regulations limited the number of spaces for street performances in the 1970s, Chinese opera troupes disbanded, focused on performances in Malaysia and Thailand, or reorganized the troupe: Tin Ying and Kong Fai managed to maintain their operations by reducing costs and reorganizing their personnel structure (Pitt 1988, 69).

10. In the 1950s, the average size of Chaozhou opera troupes was usually larger than Cantonese opera troupes, each troupe supporting between twenty and a hundred employees (Newell 1961, 68).

11. For pictures of Lau Chit Kee Hiang (or Lao Yizhixiang in pinyin), see Vente and Lim (1984).

12. Cai (2003, 26–32) describes a similar situation with Sing Yong Hoe Heng Teochew Wayang.

13. For brief biographies of Chaozhou opera performers who have gone through the traditional Chinese opera training system in Singapore, see Cai (2003, 26–32, 40–46). See also the interview transcripts of Chinese opera performers listed under National Archives Microfiche in the bibliography.

14. Examples of these are the Chek Hoon (Zhiyun [Knitted Clouds]) Teochew Wayang and Hokkien Lam Geh (Southern Arts Troupe). For a brief introduction to Chek Hoon Teochew Wayang, see Cai (2003, 33–36).

15. Lau Sai Thor Guan Teochew Wayang, for example, is one of the most popular troupes in Singapore today, but before the 1970s, it was known for performing more frequently in Peninsular Malaysia and also in Sabah and Sarawak in East Malaysia. New professional opera troupes continue to form sporadically as offshoots of older troupes, often with the prefix "New" in their names: for example, Xin Lao Sai Tao Yuan (New Lau Sai Thor Guan) Teochew Wayang and Xin Xin Rong He Xing (New Sing Yong Hoe Heng) Teochew Wayang were formed after 2000.

16. See *Straits Times* (1974a-d) on restrictions imposed on Chinese street opera performance in Singapore.

17. In Newell's observations of Chinese opera in Malaya in 1955, he notes that the Chaozhou opera company he worked with paid about US$165 in wages for sixty-three people, or an average of US$2.60 per person (Newell 1961, 68).

18. Chaozhou opera was known as *chaoyin* (Chaozhou tune) during the Qing dynasty (1644–1911) and as *chaoqiang* (Chaozhou tune-system) or *chaodiao* (Chaozhou mode) in the Ming dynasty (1368–1644). *Chaoju* (Chaozhou opera) is a modern name coined after the establishment of the People's Republic of China in 1949.

19. The *qizaiban* of *gaojiaxi* and *qiyiban* of *gezaixi* have roots in *liyuanxi*. *Liyuanxi* is colloquially known as *qiziban* (seven-person troupe), based on its seven role types (Liu and Wang 1986, 462). Traditionally, *liyuanxi* comprised two groups: *xiaoliyuan* (little *liyuan*) with child performers and *daliyuan* (big *liyuan*) with adults. *Daliyuan,* also known as *laoxi* (old show), is further categorized into *shanglu laoxi* ("upper-road" show) and *xianan laoxi* ("down-south" show), where *shanglu* refers to regions north of Quanzhou city (in Fujian Minnan area) including Jiangxi and Zhejiang provinces, and *xianan* refers to the Quanzhou area. *Gaojiaxi* is also known as *jiujiaoxi* (nine role-type play) with two more roles in addition to the seven in *liyuanxi* (Liu and Wang 1986, 497).

20. This festival is believed to be based on the ritual play *Mulian Jiumu* (*Mulian Rescues His Mother*; see Johnson 1989; Wang 1992b). On the Yulan festival, see Kani (1984); on Chinese opera and rituals of the Cantonese and Fujian communities, see Tanaka (1984); on *diaoxianxi* in the *Beidouxi* (Big Dipper) propitiation ritual, see Yung (1997, 59–97); on the myth of *Beidouxi,* see Yung (1997, 99–131). In Malaysia, the Yulan festival is also known as the Phor Tor festival, named after the deity Phor Tor Kong, or God of Hell (Tan 1988).

21. On Chinese deities and temples in Singapore, see Cui (1994, 60–65) and Sakai (1981).

22. Pitt notes that a permanent opera stage was built in front of Tian Fu Gong around the 1880s (before 1893), which was later demolished (Pitt 1988, 64–65). Vaughan also describes an opera stage in front of Tian Fu Gong, which dates the stage to before 1880, since his description was first published in 1879 (Vaughan 1971, 53–59). On *nanyin* in Singapore, see Lay (1998).

23. On *getai* in Malaysia, see Tan (1984).

24. On *qiongju* in Singapore, see Wan (1996) and Wang (2000, 116–22, 123–29, 130–33, 135–38).

25. On ritual plays in Fujian opera, see Cheung (1993, 92–116).

26. On *Liuguo Fengxiang,* see Yung (1997, 133–66); on *Liyu Tiaolongmen,* see Yung (1997, 167–91). *Pantao Dahui* is specifically associated with the Sing Yong Hoe Heng Teochew Wayang.

27. I observed this ritual return of the deity on December 18, 1996, at an evening performance by Sin Sai Hong Hokkien Wayang. It is important to select the "properly attired" person to receive the deity: according to Chinese beliefs, red is an auspicious color, while white symbolizes death—the latter is thus not suitable to bring back the troupe's deity. On Chinese opera and rituals in Singapore, see Tanaka (1984) and Yung (1997).

28. For more information on Lau Sai Thor Guan Teochew Wayang, see Cai (2003, 22–25) and Wang (2000, 20–22). On Sin Sai Hong Hokkien Wayang, see Perris (1978) and Wang (2000, 63–67).

29. In the late 1990s, evening performances began at 8 P.M. and ended at 11 P.M. Today, performances begin at 7:30 P.M. and end by 10:30 P.M.

30. Older temples in Singapore today maintain a permanent stage situated in front of the temple and facing its main entrance, though these are few and far

between. These stages are more spacious and comfortable than the makeshift ones.

31. Fujian opera troupes performing *xiangju, gaojiaxi,* and *puxianxi* also pay respects to Tiandu Yuanshuai. Troupes performing Fujian *liyuanxi,* however, recognize Langjun Xianshi as their patron deity. Tiandu Yuanshuai is venerated as the patron saint of the performing arts and invoked in spirit exorcisms in Quanzhou, Fujian province. Xuantian Shangdi sits among the pantheon of Taoist gods and is revered as the divine protector during the Ming dynasty (1368–1644) and for his powers of exorcism.

32. For similar observations in Chaozhou instrumental music, see Dujunco (2002, 212) and Lau (2001, 54).

33. The tuning of both *erxian* and *yehu* is usually based on pitch F: *erxian* is tuned to pitches 5 (inner string) and 1 (outer string) and *yehu* is tuned to pitches 1 and 5 or 6 and 3.

34. Understandably, then, when the troupe performs during the month of the hungry ghost for the purpose of entertaining spirits, the *haotou* cannot be played and must be stored.

35. Other instruments that may be used in a Chaozhou opera ensemble include *pipa* (four-stringed plucked lute), *erhu* (two-stringed bowed fiddle), *banhu* (two-stringed bowed fiddle), violoncello, *dizi* (transverse bamboo flute), and *dongxiao* (vertical bamboo flute) in the *wenchang,* and different varieties of woodblock, cymbals, and gongs in the *wuchang.*

36. A genre of traditional opera of the Sibe community in Xinjiang, northwest China, also uses a *kudiao* (Harris 2004, 73).

37. Other instruments in Fujian *gezaixi* include the *sanxian* (three-stringed plucked lute), *dongxiao* (vertical bamboo flute), *taiwandi* ("Taiwan" vertical flute, also known as *bangzixiao* [wooden flute]), and *yamudi* ("mother duck" flute, also known as *shuguan* [vertical flute]) in the *wenchang.* Early *gezaixi* emphasized the *wenchang* with basic rhythmic accompaniment; *wuchang* later developed through influences from Peking opera.

38. A *xiaoxian* play such as *Xianji Songzi* (*Fairy Delivering the Deity*) requires only two main performers, but eleven to thirteen performers are needed to enact *Liuguo Fengxiang* (*Minister of the Six States*) in the *daxian* category.

39. See Vente and Lim (1984, 29, 33) for pictures of meal times on stage.

40. See Cheung (1993) for a detailed discussion of performance strategies in Fujian opera troupes.

41. However, animosity may emerge between the audience and banquet guests over the use of the chairs. On Thursday, August 28, 1997, at a Hungry Ghost Festival celebration at Block 339, Ang Mo Kio Avenue 1, Sin Sai Hong's performance coincided with the evening's banquet cum auction of *fuwu* (prosperous goods). I observed an argument between the host and the audience because too many chairs were taken by the audience for the performance, leaving insufficient seats for banquet guests. When the host offered to let the audience have the chairs after the banquet, the audience argued that the performance would be over by then. This incident suggests that the audience at *choushenxi* is not all from the same group of guests of the event's host, and that certain Chinese opera troupes in Singapore continue to attract ardent fans.

42. This amount is comparable to the five dollars per song request at teahouses that presented Chinese opera described in chapter 1 (see also Pang 1997, 35). In

1938, Chinese laborers in the Straits Settlements earned between fifty and seventy cents daily (Colonial Reports 1940, 42). Therefore, as with teahouses during the same period, even though Chinese street opera performance would have attracted more working-class people, song requests were probably limited to the wealthier group.

43. *Chuanqing* is also known as *luoke* (placing a gesture), where *ke* traditionally refers to specific movements in Chinese opera.

44. While working backstage with Goh Gek Lam of Lau Sai Thor Guan on the evening of August 21, 1997, I met a middle-aged lady who was a fan of the troupe. She fondly recalled watching the troupe when she was younger and remembered Goh as a young girl performing on stage.

45. Auntie Ng is the spouse of Johnnie Ng of Lau Sai Thor Guan. Sometime in 1997, I had a conversation with a fan of Sing Yong Hoe Heng Teochew Wayang, whom I shall not name. She was then a leading member of a performing arts institution and criticized the poor performance standard of Lau Sai Thor Guan. She even expressed doubts on Johnnie Ng's capability as manager and teacher of the troupe because of his "western" name.

46. Sing Yong Hoe Heng last performed on January 14, 2001, before it officially disbanded after a history of 174 years; see Cai (2003, 26–32) and Wang (2000, 54–57).

47. This information is based on interviews with Tan Teck (b. 1929), who is active in organizing Hungry Ghost Festival celebrations and end-of-year thanksgiving rituals on behalf of the community at the Toa Payoh Lorong 4 market, and has served as *luzhu* on many occasions.

48. Johnnie Ng notes that before the 1960s, Lau Sai Thor Guan was known for its use of *huojing* (live props). For water scenes, they would use a huge tank filled with water, and stagehands would create waves by rotating a mechanism. In addition, actual boats would be used in the tank and fighting scenes were performed in the water. Today, a piece of blue cloth held by stagehands is used to portray a water scene (Cai 2003, 23). Similarly, a lead *huadan* (young female) performer in Sin Sai Hong Hokkien Wayang notes with nostalgia that the troupe had at least four musicians in both the *wuchang* and *wenchang* in the 1960s and 1970s, with each musician playing one instrument. That produced a much fuller sound than the present custom, where there is usually only one percussionist.

49. Victoria Theatre is part of a larger complex of buildings in Singapore's civic and financial district that dates back to 1862, now used primarily for the performing arts.

50. *Hanju* developed in and around the Hubei province and is based on the *xipi* and *erhuang* tune systems. *Hanju* was popular in Singapore in the 1920s, and at least five amateur opera troupes were known for their *hanju* performances (Wang 2000, 38–40).

Chapter 3: Amateur Chinese Opera and Confucianism

1. When professional opera troupes perform in the *qingchang* style, the vocalists conventionally sit in a circle and face the musicians (see figure 4).

2. Buckley (1984, 585–92), Lee (1978, 64–87), Song (1967, 402–4), and Vaughan (1971, 95–104) describe violent confrontations that occurred between different

Chinese communities (generally known as *bang*; see Mak 1982 and Cheng 1985) in 1851, 1854, 1871, 1876, and 1906, when economic and political changes instituted by the British administrators were deemed to threaten their interests.

3. See Cui (1994, 76) for a list of voluntary Chinese associations and the schools they built in pre–World War II Singapore.

4. On Ping Sheh, see also Pang (1997) and Wang (2004, 56–60, 89–96).

5. On overseas Chinese nationalism, see, for example, Yen (1976).

6. For an introduction to the Er Woo Amateur Musical and Dramatic Association, see Lau (2005, 34–36), Tan (1996), and Wang (2000, 27–37).

7. *Konghuay* is the dialect romanization of the Chinese term *gonghui*, which refers to an association. *Khek* refers to *Hakka* in dialect romanization or *Kejia* in *pinyin*.

8. For an introduction to the Hymn Rhyme Sing Opera Club, see Wang (2000, 130–33); on Siong Leng Musical Association, see Lay (1998); on Thau Yong Amateur Musical Association, see Lau (2005, 36–38).

9. The Registry of Societies is a unit within the Ministry of Home Affairs in Singapore. Under the Societies Act, groups of ten or more people formed with specific organizational objectives and not already registered under any law are required to register for a fee.

10. The name of the group, Puning Huiguan Xichangban, is quite unusual. *Xichangban* may be translated as "practice-singing class," which perhaps reflects their relatively recent formation, and that the group sings more than acts out Chinese opera excerpts.

11. The session I observed on May 17, 2004, had a substitute instructor (Ms. Lin) who also taught at the Kit Yang Hway Kuan (Kit Yang Association). She did not use musical instruments but played minus-one recordings to accompany the singing. The regular instructor (Mr. Hwang) and a former instructor (Mr. Wu) use *erhu* and *yangqin* respectively as a way of teaching intonation (personal communication, Tan Yang Ngor, May 20, 2003).

12. In more practical terms, it is also economically more viable for amateur performers, with their higher levels of education, to seek employment outside Chinese opera performance.

13. In a study of amateur performers in Japanese Noh theatre, Johnson suggests that their participation is more "for reasons of self-discipline than self-gratification in either aesthetics or recreation" (Johnson 1982, 116).

14. For a brief discussion of the social status of Peking opera performers, see Mackerras (1972, 218–22); see also Birch (1995, 1–19) for a succinct description of Chinese drama and its social context in the Ming dynasty (1368–1644). On amateur and professional theatrical groups in post-1949 China, see Mackerras (1983b, 160–66).

Chapter 4: Reinstating Patronage and Tradition

1. The temple is generally known as Cheng Huang Miao (or Sheng Hong Temple in the local Fujian vernacular), a generic reference for a temple dedicated to the patron deity (or deities) of a particular area. Thus, Cheng Huang Miao is often translated as City-God Temple and its deity is known simply as City-God. Lorong Koo Chye refers to the name of the area in which the temple is located, histori-

cally known for the farming of chives: "Lorong" is the Malay term for "Way" and "Koo Chye" is the Fujian term for chives. Thus, Lorong Koo Chye Sheng Hong Temple may be translated as "Chives Way Temple."

2. Announcements were published in Chinese only during my field research from 1996 to 1998, and for the first time in both Chinese and English in 2005.

3. In 1998, the temple sponsored two performances, one on the actual birthday on the twenty-eighth day of the fifth month (June 22), and the other on the same day in the leap fifth month (July 21).

4. Tan Chiew Hai assists in the daily operations of the Lorong Koo Chye Sheng Hong Temple and also serves as a member of the organizing committee for its temple festival.

5. Thus, in 1997, Chinese opera performances at the Lorong Koo Chye Sheng Hong Temple ended on the twenty-eighth day of the sixth month (August 1, 1997), two days before the first day of the seventh month, and in 1998, on the twenty-ninth day of the sixth month (August 20, 1998), two days before the seventh month.

6. Between 1996 and 2005, more than ten troupes from Singapore and Malaysia, and sometimes troupes from mainland China and Taiwan, perform annually at the temple: in 1996, ten troupes performed, thirteen in 1997, fifteen in 1998, fourteen in 1999, thirteen in 2000, fourteen in 2004, thirteen in 2005. Troupes perform for at least two days, and in a single year, the more popular troupes may be invited for performances at different periods of time during the celebration, sometimes performing for up to twenty days in total.

7. From 1996 to 2000 and also in 2004 and 2005 (information unavailable for 2001 through 2003), Kim Eng (Golden Eagle) Teochew Opera was engaged to perform on the birthday itself, an arrangement that is both pragmatic and convenient. Since the troupe is normally available on and around the deity's birthday every year and is one of the more popular Chaozhou opera troupes with a huge following, the festival committee decided to confirm this arrangement on a long-term basis. Kim Eng Teochew Opera was formed in 1980 and disbanded in 2007; for a brief introduction, see Cai (2003, 37–39).

8. The system is somewhat arbitrary and is only used to determine the amount of payment to opera troupes (personal communication, Tan Chiew Hai, August 6, 1997).

9. The two highest paid Fujian opera troupes, Hokkien Sio Kee Lin Troupe and Hokkien Lam Geh (Southern Arts) Troupe, consistently performed for the most number of days at the temple from 1996 to 2000 and also in 2004 and 2005. Hokkien Sio Kee Lin Troupe is the first local *gezaixi* troupe formed circa 1920s when *gezaixi* became popular in Southeast Asia (Wong et al. 1972, 5): "Kee Lin" is the Fujian pronunciation of *qilin,* a mythical animal that resembles an antelope.

10. This play was first performed by the troupe on January 6, 1997, near Block 230, Tampines Street 21 (east Singapore), and later became one of the most well-loved plays in the troupe's repertoire. Auntie Ng receives calls every afternoon from fans asking what play is being performed that evening. She states that whenever the troupe performs *Yijin Ronggui,* callers invariably confirm that they will attend the performance. On June 28, 1997, at the Lorong Koo Chye Sheng Hong Temple, Auntie contends, the majority of the audience was there to watch this play, and therefore, the troupe had to perform it so as not to disappoint them.

11. The Lorong Koo Chye Sheng Hong Temple has organized performances by the following overseas troupes: Xiamen Tongan Huaxing Xiangjutuan from China (1993), Tainan Yingyi Gezaixituan from Taiwan (1994), Chen Meiyun Gejutuan from Taiwan (2000), and Xiamen Gezaixi Jutuan from China (1999, 2001, and 2004).

12. Other donors may give only to specific performers, a practice that Johnnie Ng discourages in order to avoid rivalry within the troupe.

13. Ward (1979) notes the dual roles that Chinese opera performers embody in ritual events: as an actor or actress as well as a priest. See also Yung (1997, 216–18) for a discussion of this issue.

14. In these cases, I was told that the money collected would go to the individual performers. I wonder if this was why barricades were put up in front of the stage in the 1997 and 1998 opera gala, that is, to prohibit both performers and audience from such practices, which are ultimately for personal gain (I do not recall seeing barricades when I first attended the opera gala in 1996).

15. On the efficacy of performance in shaping culture and identities, see Fine and Speer (1992).

16. On ritual and theatre, see Chan (2006), Turner (1982a, 1982b), and Ward (1979).

Chapter 5: Tourism and Cultural Authenticity in Chinese Opera

1. Probably the only place in Singapore today where one can view Cantonese opera over a meal, the Chinese Opera Teahouse is located on Smith Street in Chinatown. A similar setting, the Oriental Opera Teahouse on Bukit Pasoh Road, allows visitors to observe Cantonese opera performances by members of the Tung On Wui Kun (Tung On Association) Cantonese Opera Troupe over drinks (http://frannxis.tripod.com/frontpage/id37.html).

2. For studies on tourism and local cultures, see Deitch (1989), Duggan (1997), and Dunbar-Hall (2001).

3. The first series ended on December 31, 1996, and because it proved to be a popular attraction, it was instituted again in 1997, this time increasing to three performances a week. In 1998, performances were reduced to twice a week, and the series ended shortly afterwards. Nonetheless, issues that have emerged through the "Traditional Chinese Street Opera" series at Clarke Quay continue to be applicable to the understanding of Clarke Quay in particular and of cultural construction in Singapore in general.

4. See color plate 2 in Jayapal (1992; after p. 38) for an illustration of a sugar godown in mid-nineteenth-century Singapore. For an introduction to coolies, see Wang (1988, 161–69).

5. A story on Clarke Quay and Boat Quay titled "Quayside Story: The River Shows Us Where We're Going . . . and Where We've Been" (Koh 1997) reveals their symbolism of traditional and modern Singapore.

6. For a succinct description of musical instruments used in Cantonese opera, see Yung (1989, 23–31).

7. The Kong Chow Wui Koon was established in 1843 and its opera group was formed in 1947. See Lai (1986, 37–42) for a brief description of the Chinese The-

atre Circle; see Cheong (1996) and Lai (1987) for an overview of Cantonese opera in Singapore.

8. Under this program, CTC performed in twenty-four schools in 1995, twenty-one in 1996, and thirty-three in 1997 (Chinese Theatre Circle 1997). For more information on the National Arts Council Arts Education Programme, see http://www.nac.gov.sg/aep.

9. The National Arts Council (NAC) is a government body that oversees the organization of various national arts festivals, provides performance grants, and initiates arts education programs in schools. An arts group can register itself under three categories: (1) as a society; (2) as a company limited by guarantee; (3) as a nonprofit professional company, limited by guarantee. CTC is registered as a nonprofit professional company, which means it has a board of directors that advises and oversees the operation of the group. NAC encourages arts groups to become full-time, nonprofit professional companies through several means. First, it provides an initial grant to assist the setting up of the company. Second, if the company employs more than five full-time staff in the areas of administration and artistic direction, NAC subsidizes the salaries of up to two artistic directors.

10. This information is based on comments by Joanna Wong after my presentation of an earlier version of this chapter at the Centre for Advanced Studies, National University of Singapore, March 24, 2000.

11. See Leong (1997b) on tourism and its implications on ethnicity in Singapore.

12. See Duggan (1997). This approach to authenticity alludes to Paul Gilroy's conception of "music as a *changing* rather than an unchanging same" (Gilroy 1993, 101; emphasis in original).

13. For an overview of heritage marketing, see Dominguez (1986).

14. See Picard (1997) for an analysis of how Balinese cultural identities have developed through tourism.

Chapter 6: Chinese Opera and the Concept of Culture in Singapore

1. On the politics of the concept of culture, see Dominguez (1992).

2. See Benjamin (1976) and B. Chua (1998) on multiracialism and cultural construction in Singapore, and Barth (1969) on issues of ethnicity, cultural boundary, and difference.

3. Phan Wait Hong, a veteran Peking opera performer in Singapore and a cultural medallion recipient, performed the Peking opera excerpt that evening. For an introduction to Phan, see Liu and Phillips (1988, 49) and Wang (2000, 100–103); see also National Archives Micicrofiche (A000368/11) for a transcript of interviews with Phan.

4. The Siong Leng Musical Association later represented Singapore at the Eleventh World Festival of Amateur Theatre at Le Mondial du Theatre in Monaco (August 21–30, 1997) with a performance of *Ramayana*.

5. The multiethnic cast included eight Malay students, one Indian, and one Filipino, who learned the Chinese script using the *hanyu pinyin* system. *Huangmeixi* is a form of regional opera that developed in Anhui, Jiangxi, and Hubei provinces in East China.

6. An effect of, or perhaps a reason for, this compartmentalized form of cultural expression is the diffusion of political potential of different ethnic constituencies (B. Chua 1995, 120).

7. For further discussion on national identity and multiculturalism in Singapore, see, for example, Chew (1991), Chiew (1983), Chua and Kuo (1991), Lai (1995, 178–87), and Siddique (1989).

8. See Tong et al. (1992) for an overview of traditional Chinese customs in contemporary Singapore.

9. See Wee (2002a, 130–33) for a discussion on what he calls "national culturalism," based on Arjun Appadurai's notion of "culturalism" defined as "identity politics mobilized at the level of the nation-state" (Appadurai 1996, 15). See also Handler (1985) for a case study on nationalism and culture in Quebec.

10. See Speeches (1996a, 1996b) for an understanding of the government's position on arts and culture in Singapore in the 1990s; see Koh (1980) for a study of culture and globalization in Singapore; see Peterson (2001) and Wee (2002b) for studies on English theatre and cultural identities in Singapore.

11. In his study of Cuban musical sources in Puerto Rico, Peter Manuel argues that the processes of appropriating and resignifying Cuban music as symbols of Puerto Rican cultural identity involve "distortions of historical fact" (Manuel 1994, 250). For further studies on invention of traditions, see Handler and Linnekin (1984), and Hanson (1989).

12. Raymond Williams outlines three levels of culture: (1) lived culture of a particular time and place, (2) recorded culture, and (3) the culture of the selective tradition (Williams 1961, 49).

13. Issues on art and cultural aesthetics are applicable to other performance genres and ethnic communities. For example, the setting up of the Singapore Indian Orchestra in 1985 and the Singapore Malay Orchestra in 1991 are bound within broader discourses on foregrounding ethnic traditions in Singapore, as well as the negotiations between traditional art forms and modernizing tendencies.

14. See Chua and Tan (1999) for an analysis of how the middle class shapes cultural standards in Singapore, and Paritta (2002) for a discussion of middle-class culture and Thai identity in the practice of Thai traditional dance. See also Broyles (1992), Kidd and Roberts (1985), Kift (1996), Levine (1988), and Rubin (1992) for discussions on class and cultural production. On elite culture identity and power, see Cohen (1981) on Africa and Pinches (1999) on Asia. The relationship between cultural capital and social superiority may be understood in conjunction with a similar notion in tourism studies concerning authenticity and social distinction: middle-class tourists' "thirst for cultural authenticity seems at once a recognition of the supposed cultural impoverishment that has accompanied economic success and world domination and a reinforcement of the sense of social superiority" (Greenwood 1989, 184).

Conclusion

1. The Chinese Opera Society (Singapore) was established in August 1992 with the aims of promoting Chinese opera through English publications and performance subtitles, presenting performances of different operatic genres, and conducting lecture-demonstrations in schools and for the public.

2. See Chua and Tan (1999) for a study of how culture in Singapore is influenced by the middle class. This argument alludes to the concept of institutional isomorphism (DiMaggio and Powell 1983). For an introduction to the concept of cultural entrepreneurship, see DiMaggio (1982).

3. See McAdam and McCreedy (1999, 96–97) for a discussion of knowledge categories and processes of transferring knowledge.

GLOSSARY

General Terms

Anhui	安徽	province in eastern China
Anxi	安溪	county in southern Fujian province
Bai Lao Hui	百老彙	"Community Assembly" theatre in the New World amusement park
Baishezhuan	白蛇傳	play based on legend of Madam White Snake
baixi	百戲	variety show developed in the Han dynasty
Bajiao Ting	八角亭	"Octagon Pavilion" theatre in the New World amusement park
ban	板	wooden clappers; also refers to tempo
bang	邦	generic term for Chinese ethnic groups
bangsheng	幫聲	vocal feature of *yiyangqiang* and Chaozhou opera (see *zhansheng*)
bangzi	梆了	woodblock
bangziqiang	梆子腔	tune system developed in Shanxi and Shaanxi provinces
bangzixiao	梆子簫	vertical flute in Fujian *gezaixi* (also known as *taiwandi*)
banhu	板胡	two-stringed bowed fiddle
banqiangti	板腔體	tempo-variant form
banxianxi	扮仙戲	"plays mimicking deities": generic term for ritual plays
Baxian	八仙	Eight Immortals
Baxian Heshou	八仙賀壽	ritual play: "Birthday Greetings from the Eight Immortals"
Beidouxi	北斗戲	ritual play: "Big Dipper"
bo	鈸	cymbals
budaixi	布袋戲	cloth- (hand-) puppet theatre
Chai Chuan Tou	柴船頭	Clarke Quay
chaoju (*chaoyin, chaoqiang, chaodiao*)	潮劇(潮音, 潮腔，潮調)	Chaozhou opera
chaqian	茶錢	tea money

chaoyin	潮音	singing of Chaozhou opera without acting; Chaozhou opera was also known as *chaoyin* from the Qing dynasty to circa 1949
chaoyou (*chaodu*)	超度(超幽)	spirit ascension
Chaozhou	潮州	city in northern Guangdong province
chazuoshi	茶座式	teahouse seating style
chemafei	車馬費	travel expenses
Cheng Huang Miao	城隍廟	"City-God Temple": generic name for local city temples (see Lorong Koo Chye Sheng Hong Temple)
Chensan Wuniang	陳三五娘	play based on a love story between two characters in feudal China
Chew Wah Lim Club	醉花林俱樂部	first Chinese social club in Singapore established in 1849 by the Chaozhou community
chou	醜	role type: clown
choushenxi	酬神戲	thanksgiving performance
chuanqi	傳奇	drama in the *nanxi* tradition popular in Ming and Qing dynasties
chuanqing	傳情	sending affections (see *luoke*)
Chunxiangzhuan	春香傳	play based on character of Chunxiang
dabo	大鈸	large cymbals
Dabogong	大伯公	deity: "God of the Earth"
dadianhua	打電話	"to make a telephone call": process of assisting performers with phrase prompts
dagu	大鼓	large drum
daguangxian	大廣弦	large bowed fiddle in Fujian *gezaixi*
da liyuan	大梨園	"big" *liyuan*: *liyuanxi* with adult performers
damu	大幕	large screen
dan	旦	role type: female
Dan Gui Yuan	丹桂園	"Sweet-scented Osmanthum Garden" in nineteenth century Chinatown, Singapore
Danrong Bage Dabogong	丹戎巴葛大伯公	Tanjong Pagar "God of the Earth" temple
Daoyi Zhilue	島夷志略	*Description of the Islands* by Wang Dayuan, published in 1349
dapigu	打屁股	"to beat the bottom": strict training process of professional opera troupes

Dapo	大坡	"Greater Town" in old downtown Singapore
Da Shijie	大世界	Great World amusement park
dawu	打武	martial arts
Da Wutai	大舞台	"Great Stage" in the New World amusement park
daxi	大戲	grand opera
daxian	大仙	ritual play: "Big Deity"
De He Tang	德和堂	traditional division in Chinese opera for military roles
diao	調	modal system
diaoxianxi	吊綫戲	string-puppet theatre
difangxi	地方戲	regional opera
dingchounian	丁醜年	Year of the Ox (1997)
dizi	笛子	transverse bamboo flute
dongxiao	洞簫	vertical bamboo flute
dongzhi	冬至	winter solstice
ergutuan	二姑團	women squadron
erhu	二胡	two-stringed bowed fiddle
erhuang (*erhuangqiang*)	二黃	tune system developed in Yihuang county, Jiangxi province (see *xipi*)
erxian	二弦	two-stringed bowed fiddle
Fanhua Shijie	繁華世界	alternate name for Happy World amusement park
fanxian	反線	Chaozhou "inverted" mode
Fengli Shan	鳳梨山	"Pineapple Hill" in present-day Hougang, Singapore
fengluo	奉鑼	small gong in Fujian *gezaixi*
fengtiao yushun	風調雨順	calm and tranquil environment
Fu	福	deity: "Good Fortune"
Fu He Tang	福和堂	traditional division in Chinese opera for the female role types
Fujian	福建	province in southeastern China
fujianxi	福建戲	Fujian opera
fushui	符水	blessed water
fuwu	福物	prosperous goods
fuxian	副弦	"assisting" fiddle (also known as *yehu*)
Fuzhou	福州	city in northern Fujian province
fuzhouxi	福州戲	regional opera developed in north Fujian province (also known as *minju*)
gaohu	高胡	treble two-stringed bowed fiddle
gaojiaxi	高甲戲	Fujian opera from Minnan and Taiwan

gaojia xiban	高甲戲班	a category of Fujian *gaojiaxi* performance style
geji	歌姬	women entertainers
getai	歌台	"song-stage": modern theatre
gewutuan	歌舞團	song-dance troupe
gezaixi	歌仔戲	Fujian operatic genre developed in Taiwan (see *xiangju*)
gonghui	公會	Chinese association
guan	管	vertical, double-reed instrument
Guangdong	廣東	province in southern China
Guangdong Xiyuan	廣東戲院	"Cantonese Theatre" in the Great World amusement park
Guangxi	廣西	province in southern China
Guangxu	光绪	Chinese emperor who reigned from 1875–1908
Guangzhou	廣州	Canton
Guanyin	觀音	deity: "Goddess of Mercy"
guanyin	官音	"official tune": Peking opera
Guomindang	國民黨	Taiwanese government
guotai pingan	国泰平安	peace to the country
Haichun Fudeci	海唇福德祠	"Coastal Luck and Virtue Temple": Cantonese temple along Telok Ayer Street
Hainan	海南	island off China's southern coast
haiyanqiang	海鹽腔	tune system developed in Zhejiang and Jiangxi provinces
hanju	漢劇	Hakka opera developed in the Hubei province in central China
haotou	號頭	natural horn used in Chaozhou opera
hejing gaosheng	合境高升	prosperity to the community
hejing pingan	合境平安	peace to the community
Hougang	後港	town in northeastern Singapore
huaju	話劇	spoken drama
huadan	花旦	role type: young female
huangmeixi	黃梅戲	regional opera developed in Anhui, Jiangxi, and Hubei provinces
Huanle Yuan	歡樂園	alternative name for Old World amusement park
huapai	花牌	flower basket
huaqiao	華僑	overseas Chinese
Hubei	湖北	province in eastern China
huojing	活景	live props
huosanwu	活三五	Chaozhou "lively third and fifth" mode
Jiangnan	江南	region on eastern coast of China around the Yangzi river

jiangnan sizhu	江南絲竹	"silk and bamboo" instrumental ensemble from the Jiangnan region
Jiangsu	江蘇	province on the eastern coast of China
Jiangxi	江西	province in southeastern China
jiaose	角色	role types
jietou yueju	街頭粵劇	Cantonese street opera
jiexi	街戲	street show
Jinan	濟南	capital of Shandong province in eastern China
jing	净	role type: painted face
Jingchenghui	京城會	ritual play: "Meeting in the Capital"
Jing Chun Yuan	景春園	"Spring View Theatre" in late nineteenth-century Chinatown, Singapore
jingju	京劇	Peking opera
jingluo	京鑼	small gong used in Peking opera and Fujian *gezaixi*
Jiujiang	九江	city in Jiangxi province
jiujiaoxi	九角戲	"nine-role play": alternative name for *gaojiaxi*
ju	劇	drama/play
jushe	劇社	clubhouse for amateur opera troupes
Kejia	客家	Hakka
kezixian	殼子弦	"shell" two-stringed bowed fiddle
Kuaile Shijie	快樂世界	Happy World amusement park
kudiao	哭調	"crying tune" in Fujian *gezaixi*
Kunshan	崑山	city in Jiangsu province
kunshanqiang	崑山腔	tune system developed in Kunshan, Jiangsu province
kunqu (*kunju*)	昆曲(昆劇)	opera developed from *kunshanqiang*
Langjun Xianshi	朗君先師	"Master Teacher": patron deity for Fujian *liyuanxi* troupes
laosheng	老生	role type: old male
Lao Shijie	老世界	Old World amusement park
Lat Pau	叻報	Singapore's first Chinese newspaper, circulated between 1887–1904
Liangshanbo yu Zuyingtai	梁山伯與祝英台	The Butterfly Lovers
lianquti	連曲體	string-of-tune "medley" form
Li Chun Yuan	梨春園	"Spring Pear Theatre" in nineteenth-century Chinatown, Singapore
Li Shimin Jingpeng	李世民淨棚	ritual play: "Li Shimin Blesses the Stage"

Liuguo Fengxiang	六國封相	ritual play: "Minister of the Six States"
Liu Ming Zhu	劉明珠	play in the Chaozhou opera repertoire based on the character Liu Ming Zhu
liyuanxi	梨園戲	"Pear Garden Opera": Fujian opera in Minnan and Taiwan
Liyu Tiaolongmen	鯉魚跳龍門	ritual play: "Carp Jumps over the Dragon Gate"
Li Zhongjue	李鍾玨	Li Chung Chu, author of *Xinjiapo Fengtuji* [*A Description of Singapore*] published in 1897
Lorong Koo Chye Sheng Hong Temple	韭菜巴城隍廟	"Chives Way City-God Temple"
Lu	祿	deity: "Prosperity"
luo	鑼	gong
luoke	落科	sending affections (see *chuanqing*)
luzhu	爐主	"Urn Owner": head of the committee that organizes ritual event
Ma Che Jie	馬車街	street in nineteenth-century Singapore
Ma Jiao Jie	馬交街	street in nineteenth-century Singapore
Mazu	馬祖	"Mother Goddess" deity: primary deity for coastal and fishing communities with origins in northern Fujian province
Meixian	梅縣	area in northeastern Guangdong province
miaohui	廟會	temple festival
Min	閩	Fujian region
minju	閩劇	regional opera developed in northern Fujian province (also known as *fuzhouxi*)
Minnan	閩南	southern region of the Fujian province
Mulian Jiumu	目蓮救母	Buddhist play about Mulian saving his mother from hell
nanqu (*nanyin, nanguan*)	南曲 (南音, 南管)	vocal and instrumental genre from Fujian Minnan and Taiwan
Nantian Dajiudian	南天大酒店	Great Southern Hotel
nanxi	南戲	dramatic form developed in the Southern Song dynasty
Pantao Dahui	蟠桃大會	ritual play: "Meeting of the Heavenly Peaches" (also known as *Potao*)

piaofang	票房	amateur Peking opera groups
pihuangqiang	皮黄腔	tune system with both *xipi* and *erhuang*; musical basis of Peking opera
pipa	琵琶	pear-shaped four-stringed plucked lute
Potao	破桃	"Breaking the Peach": colloquial name for the *Pantao Dahui* ritual play
Pu He Tang	普和堂	traditional division in Chinese opera for musicians and stagehands
Puning	普寧	city in Chaozhou region
Putian	莆田	county in Fujian province
puxianxi	蒲仙戲	Fujian opera from Putian county (also known as *xinghuaxi*)
qiang	腔	tune system
qingchang	清唱	"pure singing": singing without actions
Qing He Tang	慶和堂	traditional division in Chinese opera for the role of painted face
qingsanliu	輕三六	Chaozhou "light third and sixth" mode
Qing Sheng Ping	慶升平	"Celebrating Prosperity and Peace" theatre built in late nineteenth-century Singapore
Qing Wei Xin	慶維新	"Celebrating Continuous Innovation" theatre built in late nineteenth-century Singapore
Qingxi Xianyou Bozhu	清溪顯佑伯主	"Virtuous and Blessed" deity of Lorong Koo Chye Sheng Hong Temple, originally from Anxi
qinzi	欽子	small knobbed gong in Chaozhou opera
qiongju	瓊劇	Hainan opera
Qiongzhou Huiguan	瓊州會館	Hainan Association
qipao	旗袍	traditional Chinese dress for women, also known as *cheongsam*
qiyiban	七藝班	"seven-artist troupe" for Fujian *gezaixi*
qizaiban	七仔班	"seven-person troupe" for Fujian *gaojiaxi*
qizidiao	七字調	"seven-syllable tune" in Fujian *gezaixi*
Quanzhou	泉州	city in Fujian Minnan region
quluo	曲鑼	"tune" gong in Chaozhou opera
qupai	曲牌	labeled tunes

Riguang Tai	日光台	"Sunshine Stage" in the New World amusement park
ru	儒	practices relating to Confucius
rujia	儒家	term referring to Confucius, people versed in Confucian practices, and amateur Chinese opera performers
rujia yueshe	儒家樂社	amateur Chinese music association
rujushe	儒劇社	amateur opera association
ruya de yeyu juyue zuzhi	儒雅的業餘劇樂組織	amateur Chinese opera and music organization
ruyue	儒樂	Confucian music; music practiced by amateurs
ruyueshe	儒樂社	amateur music association
sanxian	三弦	long-necked three-stringed plucked lute
sanxian	三仙	ritual play: "Three Deities"
sanyue	散樂	"variety music" dating back to Zhou dynasty
Shaanxi	陝西	province in northern China
Shandong	山東	province in northern China
shanglu laoxi	上路老戲	*liyuanxi* in regions north of Quanzhou
shanglu laoxiban	上路老戲班	a category of Fujian *gaojiaxi* performance style
Shantou	汕頭	city in Chaozhou region
Shanxi	山西	province in northern china
Shan Zai Ding	山仔頂	location in nineteenth-century Singapore
shayu	鯊魚	"sharks": fans of professional Chaozhou opera troupes
shayu guohai	鯊魚過海	"sharks crossing oceans," referring to distances traveled by Chaozhou opera fans to attend performances
shenbo	深波	"deep wave": large gong in Chaozhou opera
sheng	生	role type: male
Shijie	世界	"World": amusement park
Shou	壽	deity: "Longevity"
shuai po	摔破	"break up": action of intercepting *chuanqing* (or *luoke*)
shuguan	豎管	vertical flute in Fujian *gezaixi* (also known as *yamudi*)
Shun He Tang	順和堂	traditional division in Chinese opera for people in charge of sourcing for performances
Su Liu Niang	蘇六娘	play in the Chaozhou opera reper-

		toire based on the character Su Liu Niang
suona	嗩吶	double-reed, woodwind instrument
suqing	肅清	"purge and exterminate" campaigns during the Japanese occupation of Singapore
taiwandi	台灣笛	vertical flute in Fujian *gezaixi* (also known as *bangzixiao*)
Taizi Ye	太子爺	"Crown Prince": patron deity for Chaozhou opera troupes
Tiandu Yuanshuai	田都元帥	"Field Marshall": patron deity for Fujian *gezaixi* troupes
Tian Fu Gong	天福宮	"Heavenly Blessings Palace": Fujian temple along Telok Ayer Street
Tian Hou Gong	天後宮	"Heavenly Empress Palace": Hainan temple along Beach Road
Tianhou Shengmu	天後聖母	deity: "Heavenly and Holy Empress" (also known as Mazu)
Tianyan Dawutai	天演大舞台	Majestic Theatre
Tiaojiaguan	跳加官	ritual play: "Elevating Status"
tigang	題綱	outline of play used by Fujian opera troupes
tixian muouxi	提線木偶戲	string-puppet theatre
Tong Jing Tang	同敬堂	"Hall of Communal Respect": brothel in nineteenth-century Singapore
Tong Le Yuan	同樂園	"Mutual Happiness Theatre" in early twentieth-century Singapore
toushou	頭手	lead fiddle player
touxian	頭弦	lead fiddle (*erxian*)
Wang Dayuan	汪大淵	author of *Daoyi Zhilue*
wenchang	文場	"civil section": string division of Chinese opera ensemble
wu	武	role type: military
wuchang	武場	"military section": percussion division of Chinese opera ensemble
Wuchang	武昌	capital of Hubei province
Wufulian	五福連	set of ritual plays in Chaozhou opera
Wuhemiao	五合廟	"Five-consolidated Temple" in Singapore
wusheng	武生	role type: male warrior
Wuyinnian	戊寅年	Year of the Tiger (1998)
xi	戲	drama/play
Xiamen	廈門	Amoy: island city off the coast of Fujian province
xianan laoxi	下南老戲	*liyuanxi* in Quanzhou

xiangju	薌劇	counterpart of Taiwanese *gezaixi* in Fujian Minnan region
Xiangjiang	薌江	Xiang River; area in Fujian Minnan where *xiangju* developed
Xianji Songzi	仙姬送子	ritual play: "Fairy Delivering the Deity"
Xianyou	仙遊	city in Putian
Xiao Guang Han	小廣寒	"Little Winter Space" theatre in Great World amusement park
xiao liyuan	小梨園	"little" *liyuan*: *liyuanxi* with child performers
xiaobo	小鈸	small cymbals
xiaodiao	小調	"little tune": traditional folk tunes
xiaogu	小鼓	small drum
xiaoluo	小鑼	small gong
Xiaopo	小坡	"Lesser Town" in old downtown Singapore
xiaosheng	小生	young male role
xiaoxian	小仙	ritual play: "Small Deity"
xifan	戲飯	rice cooked onstage by professional opera troupes
xiguan	戲館	administrative and/or living quarters for professional opera troupes
Xin He Tang	新和堂	traditional division in Chinese opera for clown roles
Xin Shijie	新世界	New World amusement park
xinghuaxi	興化戲	Fujian operatic genre from Putian county (also known as *puxianxi*)
Xinjiapo Fengtuji	新加坡風土記	*A Description of Singapore* by Li Chung Chu, published in 1897
xipi	西皮	tune system developed in Hubei province (see *erhuang*)
Xiyuanjie	戲院街	"Theatre Street" (Smith Street)
Xiyuan Hengjie	戲院橫街	"Theatre Side Street" (Trengganu Street)
Xiyuan Houjie	戲院後街	"Theatre Back Street" (Temple Street)
xizi	戲子	term referring to professional opera performers
xizi juewucuo	戲子絕無錯	phrase referring to the uprightness of *xizi*
Xuantian Shangdi	玄天上帝	"Supreme Divine Emperor of the Dark Heavens": patron deity for Chaozhou opera troupes
yamudi	鴨母笛	"mother duck" end-blown flute

		in Fujian *gezaixi* (also known as *shuguan*)
Yang Chun Yuan	陽春園	"Spring Theatre" in late nineteenth-century Chinatown, Singapore
yangqin	揚琴	dulcimer played with thin bamboo beaters
yehu	椰胡	"coconut" two-stringed bowed fiddle
yeyu	業餘	amateur
Yihuang	宜黃	county in Jiangxi province where the *erhuang* tune system was developed
Yijin Ronggui	衣錦榮歸	"Glorious Homecoming": play in the Chaozhou opera repertoire
yiyangqiang	弋陽腔	tune system developed in the Yiyang county of Jiangxi province
Yong He Tang	永和堂	traditional division in Chinese opera for military roles
Yi Yuan	怡園	"Joyous" theatre in late nineteenth-century Chinatown, Singapore
Yong Le Yuan	永樂園	"Everlasting Happiness" theatre in early twentieth-century Singapore
Yue	粵	Canton region
Yuehai Qingmiao	粵海清廟	"Temple of the Canton Sea": Chaozhou temple along Phillip Street
yueju	粵劇	Cantonese opera
yueju	越劇	regional opera developed in Shanghai
yueqin	月琴	short-necked plucked lute
Yulan	盂蘭	"Hungry Ghost Festival" during the lunar seventh month
yuyaoqiang	餘姚腔	tune system developed in Jiangsu and Anhui provinces
zaju	雜劇	dramatic form developed during the Song and Yuan dynasties
zhangu	戰鼓	barrel drum used in Cantonese opera and Fujian *gezaixi*
Zhangzhou	漳州	city in the Fujian Minnan region
zhansheng	展聲	"extended voice": technique of emphasizing phrase endings by singing in unison (see *bangsheng*)
Zhao He Tang	兆和堂	traditional division in Chinese opera for male roles
Zhao Nu Qing	趙女情	*The Lady Zhao*, Chaozhou opera play composed by Tan Ooh Chye

Zhejiang	浙江	province in southeast China, Singapore
zhengyin	正音	"proper tune": Peking opera
Zhe Yuan	哲園	"Philosophical" theatre in late nineteenth-century Chinatown, Singapore
zhezixi	折子戲	excerpt plays
zhiye	職業	professional
zhonghu	中胡	"mid-range" two-stringed bowed fiddle
zhongsanliu	重三六	Chaozhou "heavy third and sixth" mode
zouchang	走唱	"walk singing": itinerant style of performance for professional Chaozhou opera troupe

Names of Troupes and Associations

Bahe Huiguan (also known as Li Yuan Tang)	八和會館
Cai Qing Yuan Muou Xiban	蔡慶元木偶戲班
Chaozhou Bayi Huiguan	潮州八邑會館
Chek Hoon Teochew Wayang	織雲潮劇團
Chen Meiyun Gejutuan	陳美雲歌劇團
Chinese Theatre Circle	敦煌劇坊
Er Woo Amateur Musical and Dramatic Association	餘娛儒樂社
Fenghuang Ban	鳳凰班
Fu Xiang Sheng Ban	福祥升班
Gek Choo Hong Troupe	玉珠鳳劇團
Hoi Thin Amateur Dramatic Association	海天游艺会
Hokkien Lam Geh Troupe	南藝閩劇團
Hokkien Sio Kee Lin Troupe	福建筱麒麟劇團
Hyme Rhyme Sing Opera Club	瓊聯聲劇社
Kheng Lian Yew Dramatic Society	瓊聯友劇社
Kim Eng Teochew Opera	金鷹潮劇團
Kit Yang Hway Kuan Chaozhou Opera Troupe	揭陽會館潮劇團
Kong Chow Wui Koon Music and Opera Troupe	岡州會館樂劇部
Kong Fai Cantonese Opera Troupe	光輝粵劇團
Kreta Ayer Cantonese Song and Opera Troupe	牛車水粵曲歌劇團
Lak Aik Amateur Musical and Drama Association	六一儒樂社
Lao Quanan Zhangzhongban	老泉安掌中班
Lao Sanduo Ban	老三多班
Lau Chit Kee Hiang	老一枝香潮劇團
Lau Sai Thor Guan Teochew Wayang	老賽桃源劇團
Lao Sanzhengshun Teochew Wayang	老三正順潮劇團

Leling Beijing Opera Troupe	樂齡京劇團
Li Yuan Tang	梨園堂
Nan Hwa Amateur Musical and Dramatic Association	南華儒劇社
Nanyang Diyiban	南洋第一班
Nanyang Khek Community Guild Opera Group	南洋客屬總會漢劇部
Nanyang Pho Leng Hui Kuan	南洋普寧會館
Ping Sheh (Singapore Amateur Beijing Opera Society)	平社
Puning Huiguan Chaoqu Xichangban	普寧會館潮曲習唱班
Pu Qun Ying Ban	普群英班
Qing Bai Nian Ban	慶百年班
Qing Feng Nian Ban	慶豐年班
See Quee Choon Opera	四季春閩劇團
Shuangmingfeng Minjutuan	雙明鳳閩劇團
Singapore Bukit Panjang Hokkien Konghuay Recreation Club	武吉班讓福建公會康樂股
Singapore Hainan Society Opera Group	新加坡海南協會戲劇組
Sin Guat Hong Wayang	新樂凰歌仔戲
Sing Yong Hoe Heng Teochew Wayang	新榮和興潮劇團
Sin Poh Hong Troupe	新寶鳳歌仔戲
Sin Sai Hong Hokkien Wayang	新賽鳳福建劇團
Sin Yen Ling Hokkien Wayang	新燕玲歌劇團
Siong Leng Musical Association	湘林音樂社
Tainan Yingyi Gezaixituan	台南鶯藝歌仔戲團
Thau Yong Amateur Musical Association	陶融儒樂社
Tian Yun Peking Opera Society	天韻京劇團
Tien Heng Kang Heng Nam Dramatic Association	新興瓊南劇社
Tin Ying Cantonese Opera Troupe	天鷹粵劇團
Tung On Wui Kun Cantonese Opera Troupe	東安會館粵劇團
Xiamen Gezaixi Jutuan	廈門歌仔戲劇團
Xiamen Huaxing Xiangjutuan	廈門華興薌劇團
Xin Tiancai Ban	新天彩班
Xin Yilixing Ban	新怡梨興班
Yushan Fengnu Ban	玉山鳳女班
Zhen Fu Sheng Ban	振福升班

BIBLIOGRAPHY

Althusser, Louis. 1984. "Ideology and Ideological State Apparatuses (Notes Towards an Investigation)." In *Essays on Ideology,* 1–60. London: Verso. Originally published in *La Pensée,* 1970.

Alvesson, Mats, and Hugh Willmott. 1996. *Making Sense of Management: A Critical Introduction.* London: Sage Publications.

Ang, Ien, and Jon Stratton. 1995. "The Singapore Way of Multiculturalism: Western Concepts/Asian Cultures." *SOJOURN: Journal of Social Issues in Southeast Asia* 10, no. 1: 65–89.

Appadurai, Arjun. 1986. "Introduction: Commodities and the Politics of Value." In *The Social Life of Things: Commodities in Cultural Perspective,* ed. Arjun Appadurai, 3–63. Cambridge: Cambridge University Press.

———. 1996. *Modernity at Large: Cutural Dimensions of Globalization.* Public Worlds 1. Minneapolis: University of Minnesota Press.

Archives and Oral History Department. 1983. *Chinatown: An Album of a Singapore Community.* Singapore: Archives and Oral History Department and Times Books International.

Baily, John. 1979. "Professional and Amateur Musicians in Afghanistan." *World of Music* 21, no. 2: 46–60.

Barth, Fredrik. 1969. "Introduction." *Ethnic Groups and Boundaries: The Social Organization of Culture Difference,* ed. Fredrik Barth, 9–38. Oslo: Universitetsforlaget for Scandinavian University Books.

Bastin, John, comp. 1994. *Travellers' Singapore: An Anthology.* Kuala Lumpur, Malaysia: Oxford University Press.

Benjamin, Geoffrey. 1976. "The Cultural Logic of Singapore's Multiracialism." In *Singapore Society in Transition,* ed. Riaz Hassan, 115–33. Kuala Lumpur: Oxford University Press.

Berita Minggu. 2004. "Gadis Melayu Berlakon Epik Hindu Dalam Opera Cina" [Malay Girl Performs Hindu Epic in Chinese Opera Style]. April 18.

Birch, Cyril. 1995. *Scenes for Mandarins: The Elite Theater of the Ming.* New York: Columbia University Press.

Blythe, W. L. 1951. *Colony of Singapore Annual Report, 1950.* Singapore: Government Printing Office.

Bourdieu, Pierre. 1984. *Distinction: A Social Critique of the Judgement of Taste.* Translated by Richard Nice. Cambridge, MA: Harvard University Press.

———. 1993. "The Field of Cultural Production, or, The Economic World Reversed." In *The Field of Cultural Production: Essays on Art and Literature,* edited and introduced by Randal Johnson, 29–73. New York: Columbia University Press.

Broyles, Michael. 1992. *"Music of the Highest Class": Elitism and Populism in Antebellum Boston.* New Haven: Yale University Press.

Bruner, Edward M. 1994. "Abraham Lincoln as Authentic Reproduction: A Critique of Postmodernism." *American Anthropologist* 92, no. 2: 397–415.

Buckley, Charles Burton. 1984. *An Anecdotal History of Old Times in Singapore.* Singapore: Oxford University Press. Originally published by Fraser and Neave Limited, Singapore, 1902.

Cahill, James F. 1975. "Confucian Elements in the Theory of Painting." In *Confucianism and Chinese Civilization,* ed. Arthur F. Wright, 77–102. Stanford, CA: Stanford University Press. Originally published in 1964 by Atheneum Publishers.

Cai, Bixia. 2003. *Shicheng Chaojuqing* [Chaozhou Opera in the Lion City]. Singapore: Chinese Opera Institute.

Chan, Margaret. 2006. *Ritual Is Theatre, Theatre Is Ritual; Tang-Ki: Chinese Spirit Medium Worship.* Singapore: Singapore Management University.

Chan, Sau Yan. 1991. *Improvisation in a Ritual Context: The Music of Cantonese Opera.* Shatin, New Territories, Hong Kong: Chinese University Press.

Chan, Sau Yan, and Yung Sai-Shing. 2000. "Cantonese Operatic Clubs in New York Chinatown: A Fieldwork Report." In *Red Boat on the Canal: Cantonese Opera in New York Chinatown,* ed. Isabelle Duchesne, 70–99. New York: Museum of Chinese in the Americas.

Chaojuzhi Pianji Weiyanhui [Editorial Committee for Chaojuzhi]. 1995. *Chaojuzhi* [Journal of Chaozhou Opera]. Shantou, China: Shantou Dashue Chubanshe.

Chen, Wei. 1991. "Lun Chaozhou Yinyue De Gongdiao Xi" [Discussion on the Gong Modal System in Chaozhou Music]. *Zhongguo Yinyuexue* [Musicology in China] 3: 44–54.

Cheng, Lim-Keak. 1985. *Social Change and the Chinese in Singapore: A Socio-Economic Geography with Special Reference to Bang Structure.* Singapore: Singapore University Press.

Cheong, Yan Peng. 1996. "Yueju zai Xinjiapo: Koushu Lishi Gean Diaocha" [Cantonese Opera in Singapore: Case Studies through Oral History]. Honors thesis, Department of Chinese Studies, National University of Singapore.

Cheung, Hock Cheun. 1993. "Xinjiapo Jiexi Yanjiu" [A Study of Singapore Chinese Street Wayang]. Academic Exercise, Department of Chinese Studies, National University of Singapore.

Chew, Ernest C. T. 1991. "The Singapore National Identity: Its Historical Evolution and Emergence." In *A History of Singapore,* ed. Ernest C. T. Chew and Edwin Lee, 357–68. Singapore: Oxford University Press.

Chew, Sock Foon. 1987. *Ethnicity and Nationality in Singapore.* Monographs in International Studies Southeast Asia 78. Athens: Ohio University Center for International Studies.

Chiam, Siew Yim. 1979. "Xinjiapo de Chaoju" [Teochew Opera in Singapore]. Graduation essay (B.A. Hons.), Department of Chinese Language and Literature, Nanyang University.

Chiew, Seen-Kong. 1983. "Ethnicity and National Integration: The Evolution of a Multi-ethnic Society." In *Singapore: Development Policies and Trends,* ed. Peter S. J. Chen, 29–64. Singapore: Oxford University Press.

Chinese Opera Institute. 1996. *Chinese Opera Institute Inauguration and Fund-Raising Dinner Souvenir Programme.* May 19.

Chinese Theatre Circle. 1995. Program notes to *The First Emperor.* June 20.

———. 1997. Program notes to *Women Warriors of Yang Family.* October 25.

Chong, Terence. 2003. "Chinese Opera in Singapore: Negotiating Globalisation, Consumerism and National Culture." *Journal of Southeast Asian Studies* 34, no. 3: 449–71.

Chua, Beng Huat. 1991. "Modernism and the Vernacular: Transformation of Public Spaces and Social Life in Singapore." *Journal of Architectural and Planning Research* 8, no. 3: 203–21.

———. 1995. *Communitarian Ideology and Democracy in Singapore.* London: Routledge.

———. 1998. "Culture, Multiracialism and National Identity in Singapore." In *Trajectories: Inter-Asia Cultural Studies,* ed. Chen Kuan-Hsing, 186–205. New York: Routledge.

Chua, Beng Huat, and Eddie C. Y. Kuo. 1991. *The Making of a New Nation: Cultural Construction and National Identity in Singapore.* National University of Singapore, Department of Sociology Working Papers 104. Singapore: National University of Singapore. Also published in Chua 1995: 101–23.

Chua, Beng Huat, and Tan Joo Ean. 1999. "Singapore: Where the New Middle Class Sets the Standard." In *Culture and Privilege in Capitalist Asia,* ed. Michael Pinches, 137–58. London: Routledge.

Chua, Soo Pong. 1984. "Chinese Opera in the Park." *Performing Arts* 1, no. 1: 9–12.

———. 1992. "Teochew Culture on Stage: Er Woo Celebrates 80th Anniversary," *Er Woo Amateur Musical and Dramatic Association 80th Anniversary Souvenir Magazine.*

———. 1995. "Reaching Out for Cultural Roots: A Singapore Example in Reviving Traditional Theatre." In *Traditional Theatre in Southeast Asia,* ed. Chua Soo Pong, 91–102. Singapore: UniPress.

———. 1996. "Chinese Opera in Singapore." *The Arts* 3: 14–17. Singapore: Centre for the Arts, National University of Singapore.

Clammer, John R. 1979. *The Ambiguity of Identity: Ethnicity Maintenance and Change Among the Straits Chinese Community of Malaysia and Singapore.* Institute of Southeast Asian Studies, Occasional Paper 54. Singapore: Institute of Southeast Asian Studies.

———. 1985. *Singapore: Ideology, Society, Culture.* Singapore: Chopmen Publishers.

Clifford, James. 1988. "On Collecting Art and Culture." In *The Predicament of Culture: Twentieth-Century Ethnography, Literature, and Art,* 215–52. Cambridge, MA: Harvard University Press.

Cohen, Abner. 1981. *The Politics of Elite Culture: Explorations in the Dramaturgy of Power in a Modern African Society.* Berkeley: University of California Press.

Cohen, Ronald. 1978. "Ethnicity: Problem and Focus in Anthropology." *Annual Review in Anthropology* 7: 379–403.

Colonial Reports. 1939. *Annual Report on the Social and Economic Progress of the People of the Federated Malay States, 1938.* London: His Majesty's Stationary Office.

———. 1940. *Annual Report on the Social and Economic Progress of the People of the Straits Settlements, 1938.* London: His Majesty's Stationary Office.

Conceison, Claire. 2004. *Significant Other: Staging the American in China.* Honolulu: University of Hawaii Press.

Crump, J. I. 1990. *Chinese Theater in the Days of Kublai Khan.* Michigan Monographs in Chinese Studies 62. Ann Arbor, Michigan: Center for Chinese Studies, University of Michigan. Originally published in 1980, Tucson, Arizona: University of Arizona Press.

Cui, Guiqiang. 1994. *Xinjiapo Huaren: Chong Kaibu dao Jianguo* [The Chinese in Singapore: Past and Present]. Singapore: EPB Publishers Private Limited.

Deitch, Lewis I. 1989. "The Impact of Tourism on the Arts and Crafts of the Indians of the Southwestern United States." In *Hosts and Guests: The Anthropology of Tourism.* 2nd ed., ed. Valene L. Smith, 223–35. Philadelphia: University of Pennsylvania Press.

DiMaggio, Paul. 1982. "Cultural Entrepreneurship in Nineteenth-Century Boston: The Creation of an Organizational Base for High Culture in America." *Media, Culture, and Society* 4, no. 1: 33–50.

DiMaggio, Paul, and Walter W. Powell. 1983. "The Iron Cage Revisited: Institutional Isomorphism and Collective Rationality in Organizational Fields." *American Sociological Review* 48, no. 2: 147–60.

Directory of Associations in Singapore. 1983. *Xinjiapo Quanguo Shetuan Daguan* [Directory of Associations in Singapore, 1982–83]. Singapore: Historical Culture Publishers.

Dolby, William. 1976. *A History of Chinese Drama.* New York: Harper and Row Publishers.

———. 1983a. "Early Chinese Plays and Theater." In *Chinese Theater: From Its Origins to the Present Day,* ed. Colin Mackerras, 7–31. Honolulu: University of Hawaii Press.

———. 1983b. "Yuan Drama." In *Chinese Theater: From Its Origins to the Present Day,* ed. Colin Mackerras, 32–59. Honolulu: University of Hawaii Press.

Dominguez, Virginia R. 1986. "The Marketing of Heritage." *American Ethnologist* 3, no. 3: 546–55.

———. 1992. "Invoking Culture: The Messy Side of 'Cultural Politics.'" *South Atlantic Quarterly* 91, no. 1: 19–42.

Duggan, Betty J. 1997. "Tourism, Cultural Authenticity, and the Native Crafts Cooperative: The Eastern Cherokee Experience." In *Tourism and Culture: An Applied Perspective,* ed. Erve Chambers, 31–57. New York: State University of New York Press.

Dujunco, Mercedes M. 2002. "Ensembles: Xianshiyue." In *Garland Encyclopedia of World Music.* Vol. 7, *East Asia: China, Japan, and Korea,* ed. Robert C. Provine, Yosihiko Tokumaru, and J. Lawrence Witzleben, 211–16. New York: Routledge.

Dunbar-Hall, Peter. 2001. "Culture, Tourism, and Cultural Tourism: Boundaries and Frontiers in Performances of Balinese Music and Dance." *Journal of Intercultural Studies* 22, no. 2: 173–87.

Eriksen, Thomas Hylland. 1993. *Ethnicity and Nationalism: Anthropological Perspectives.* East Haven, CT: Pluto Press.

Fairbank, John King, and Merle Goldman. 1998. *China: A New History.* Enlarged ed. Cambridge, MA: Belknap Press of Harvard University Press.

Fine, Elizabeth C., and Jean Haskell Speer, eds. 1992. *Performance, Culture, and Identity.* Westport, CT: Praeger.

Fiske, John. 1992. "Cultural Studies and the Culture of Everyday Life." In *Cultural Studies,* ed. Lawrence Grossberg, Cary Nelson, Paula A. Treichler, 154–73. New York: Routledge.

Fournier, Valérie, and Chris Grey. 2000. "At the Critical Moment: Conditions and Prospects for Critical Management Studies." *Human Relations* 53, no. 1: 7–32.

Fox, Richard G. 1990. Introduction to *Nationalist Ideologies and the Production of National Cultures,* ed. Richard G. Fox, 1–14. American Ethnological Society Monograph series 2, ed. James L. Watson. Washington, DC: American Anthropological Association.

Frith, Simon. 1996. "Music and Identity." In *Questions of Cultural Identity,* ed. Stuart Hall and Paul du Gay, 108–27. London: Sage Publications.

Geertz, Clifford. 1973. "Deep Play: Notes on the Balinese Cockfight." In *The Interpretation of Cultures,* 412–53. New York: Basic Books.

Gilroy, Paul. 1993. *The Black Atlantic: Modernity and Double Consciousness.* Cambridge, MA: Harvard University Press.

Goffman, Erving. 1961. *Encounters: Two Studies in the Sociology of Interaction.* Indianapolis: Bobbs-Merrill.

Greenwood, Davydd J. 1989. "Culture by the Pound: An Anthropological Perspective on Tourism as Cultural Commoditization." In *Hosts and Guests: The Anthropology of Tourism.* 2nd ed., ed. Valene L. Smith, 171–85. Philadelphia: University of Pennsylvania Press.

Gunn, Edward. 1984. "Shanghai's 'Orphan Island' and the Development of Modern Drama." In *Popular Chinese Literature and Performing Arts in the People's Republic of China 1949–1979,* ed. Bonnie S. McDougall, 36–53. Berkeley: University of California Press.

Guy, Nancy A. 2005. *Peking Opera and Politics in Taiwan.* Urbana: University of Illinois Press.

Handler, Richard. 1985. "On Having a Culture: Nationalism and the Preservation of Quebec's Patrimoine." In *History of Anthropology.* Vol. 3, *Objects and Others,* ed. George Stocking, 192–217. Madison: University of Wisconsin Press.

Handler, Richard, and Jocelyn Linnekin. 1984. "Tradition, Genuine or Spurious." *Journal of American Folklore* 97: 273–90.

Hanson, Allan. 1989. "The Making of the Maori: Culture Invention and Its Logic." *American Anthropologist* 91, no. 4: 890–902.

Harris, Rachel. 2004. *Singing the Village: Music, Memory, and Ritual among the Sibe of Xinjiang.* British Academy Postdoctoral Fellowship Monograph. Oxford: Oxford University Press.

Hendry, John. 1999. "Cultural Theory and Contemporary Management Organization." *Human Relations* 52, no. 5: 557–77.

Heng, Pek Koon, and Sieh Lee Mei Ling. 2000. "The Chinese Business Community in Peninsular Malaysia, 1957–1999." In *The Chinese in Malaysia,* ed. Lee Kam Hing and Tan Chee-Beng, 123–68. Selangor Darul Ehsan, Malaysia: Oxford University Press.

Ho, Wing Meng. 1989. "Value Premises Underlying the Transformation of Singapore." In *Management of Success: The Moulding of Modern Singapore,* ed. Kernial Singh Sandhu and Paul Wheatley, 671–91. Singapore: Institute of Southeast Asian Studies.

Hobsbawm, Eric. 1992. "Introduction: Inventing Traditions." In *The Invention of Tradition,* ed. Eric Hobsbawm and Terence Ranger, 1–14. Canto edition. Cambridge: Cambridge University Press.

Hu, John. 1983. "Ming Dynasty Drama." In *Chinese Theater: From Its Origins to the Present Day,* ed. Colin Mackerras, 60–91. Honolulu: University of Hawaii Press.

Hutchinson, John. 1987. *The Dynamics of Cultural Nationalism: The Gaelic Revival and the Creation of the Irish Nation State.* London: Allen and Unwin.

Jackson, Louis S. 1850. "Census of Singapore and Its Dependencies Taken under Orders of Government in the Months of November and December, 1849." *Journal of the Indian Archipelago and Eastern Asia* 4: 107–8.

Jayapal, Maya. 1992. *Old Singapore.* Images of Asia series. Singapore: Oxford University Press.

Johnson, Dale R. 1980. *Yuarn Music Dramas: Studies in Prosody and Stucture and a Complete Catalogue of Northern Arias in the Dramatic Style.* Michigan Papers in Chinese Studies 40. Ann Arbor: Center for Chinese Studies, University of Michigan.

Johnson, David, ed. 1989. *Ritual Opera, Operatic Ritual: "Mu-lien Rescues His Mother in Chinese Popular Culture."* Chinese Popular Culture Project 1. Berkeley: University of California Press.

Johnson, Irmgard. 1982. "The Role of Amateur Participants in the Arts of No in Contemporary Japan." *Asian Music* 13, no. 2: 115–33.

Johnson, Randal. 1993. "Introduction: Pierre Bourdieu on Art, Literature, and Culture." In *The Field of Cultural Production: Essays on Art and Literature,* ed. Randal Johnson, 1–25. New York: Columbia University Press.

Juntaronanont, Pornpan, and Mak Lau Fong. 1994. *Mangu yi Xinjiapo Huaren Miaoyu ji Zongjiao Xishu de Diaocha* [A Survey on Temples and Religious Practices of Ethnic Chinese in Bangkok and Singapore]. Occasional series no. 9. Taipei, Taiwan: Institute of Ethnology, Academia Sinica.

Kamisango, Hiroyasu. 1984. "Xinjiapo de Huaren Difangxi Yinyue" [The Music of Chinese Opera in Singapore]. In *Guanyu Dongnanya Huaren Chuantong Xiju, Quyi Zonghe Diaocha Yanjiu* [Research on Southeast Asian Traditional Chinese Theatre]. Vol. 2, *Singapore and Malaysia,* ed. Onoe Kanehide, 17–92. Tokyo: Institute of Oriental Culture, University of Tokyo.

Kani, Hiroaki. 1984. "Guanyu Xinjiapo De Zhongyuanhui" [Regarding the Hungry Ghost Festival in Singapore]. In *Guanyu Dongnanya Huaren Chuantong Xiju, Quyi Zonghe Diaocha Yanjiu* [Research on Southeast Asian Traditional Chinese Theatre]. Vol. 2, *Singapore and Malaysia,* ed. Onoe Kanehide, 93–122. Tokyo: Institute of Oriental Culture, University of Tokyo.

Kidd, Alan J., and K. W. Roberts, eds. 1985. *City, Class,and Culture: Studies of Social Policy and Cultural Production in Victorian Manchester.* Manchester: Manchester University Press.

Kift, Dagmar. 1996. *The Victorian Music Hall: Culture, Class,and Conflict.* Translated by Roy Kift. Cambridge: Cambridge University Press. Originally published as *Arbeiterjultur im gesellschaftlichen Konflikt: Die Englische Music Hall im 19.* Jahrhundert. Klartext Verlag, Essen, 1991.

Koh, Joan. 1997. "Quayside Story: The River Shows Us Where We're Going . . . and Where We've Been." *I-S Magazine* 3, no. 8. Singapore: Asia City Publishing Group.

Koh, Tai Ann. 1980. "The Singapore Experience: Cultural Development in the Global Village." In *Southeast Asian Affairs 1980*, 292–307. Singapore: Institute of Southeast Asian Studies.

———. 1989. "Culture and the Arts." In *Management of Success: The Moulding of Modern Singapore*, ed. Kernial Singh Sandhu and Paul Wheatley, 710–48. Singapore: Institute of Southeast Asian Studies.

Kong, Lily, and Brenda Yeoh. 2003. "Nation, Ethnicity, and Identity: Singapore and the Dynamics and Discourses of Chinese Migration." In *The Chinese Diaspora: Space, Place, Mobility, and Identity*, ed. Laurence J. C. Ma and Carolyn Cartier, 193–219. Lanham, MD: Rowman and Littlefield.

Kroeber, A. L., and Clyde Kluckhohn. 1952. *Culture: A Critical Review of Concepts and Definitions*. New York: Vintage.

Kuo, Eddie C. Y. 1985. "Language and Identity: The Case of Chinese in Singapore." In *Chinese Culture and Mental Health*, ed. Wen-Shing Tseng and David Y. H. Wu, 181–92. New York: Academic Press.

———. 1996. "Confucianism as Political Discourse in Singapore: The Case of an Incomplete Revitalization Movement." In *Confucian Traditions in East Asian Modernity: Moral Education and Economic Culture in Japan and the Four Mini-Dragons*, ed. Tu Wei-Ming, 294–309. Cambridge, MA: Harvard University Press.

Lai, Ah Eng. 1995. *Meanings of Multiethnicity: A Case-Study of Ethnicity and Ethnic Relations in Singapore*. Kuala Lumpur, Malaysia: Oxford University Press.

Lai, Wai Yin. 1986. *Modernization of a Cultural Tradition: A Case Study of Cantonese Opera in Singapore*. Academic exercise, Department of Sociology, National University of Singapore.

———. 1987. "Ups and Downs of Cantonese Opera in Singapore." *Performing Arts* 4: 4–9.

Lat Pau. 1888a. "Danguiyuan Guan Yanhuo Ji" [An Account of a Fireworks Display in Danguiyuan]. March 9: 2.

———. 1888b. "Qietu Jiuhuo" [A Successful Theft]. April 16: 5.

———. 1889. "Guchui Huangren" [Honoring the Emperor]. March 8: 2.

———. 1890. "Qiongshe Jingyan" [An Extravagant Display]. September 11: 2.

———. 1891. "Mingyou Daole" [Famous Artists Perform in Singapore]. October 5: 6.

———. 1893. "Liyuan Zhengnao" [Squabble at the Opera]. January 2: 2.

———. 1893. "Jingban Daole" [Peking Opera Troupe Performs in Singapore]. December 25: 6.

———. 1905. "Jiangshang Mingling" [List of Awardees]. September 4: 4.

Lau, Frederick. 2001. "Performing Identity: Musical Expression of Thai-Chinese in Contemporary Bangkok." *SOJOURN: Journal of Social Issues in Southeast Asia* 16, no. 1: 37–69.

———. 2005. "Morphing Chineseness: The Changing Image of Chinese Music Clubs in Singapore." In *Diasporas and Interculturalism in Asian Performing Arts: Translating Traditions*, ed. Hae-Kyung Um, 43–60. London: RoutledgeCurzon.

Lay, Woon Wee. 1998. "Xinjiapo de Fujian Nanyin" [Fujian Nanyin in Singapore]. Honors thesis, Department of Chinese Studies, National University of Singapore.

Lee, Eu Fah Edmund. 2001. "Profile of the Singapore Chinese Dialect Groups." *Statistics Singapore Newsletter*. Singapore: Department of Statistics.

Lee, Kuan Yew. 2000. "Is Confucianism Dead?" *Newsweek* special issue, July–September: 49–50.

Lee, Ping. 1982. "Nanxi yu Chaoju" [Southern Opera and Chaozhou Opera]. *Xiju Yishu Zhiliao* [Information on Theatre Studies] 7: 1–20.

Lee, Poh Ping. 1978. *Chinese Society in Nineteenth Century Singapore.* Kuala Lumpur, Malaysia: Oxford University Press.

Leong, Wai Teng. 1997a. "Culture and the State: Manufacturing Traditions for Tourism." In *Understanding Singapore Society,* ed. Ong Jin Hui, Tong Chee Kiong, and Tan Ern Ser, 513–34. Singapore: Times Academic Press. Originally published in *Critical Studies in Mass Communication* 6, no. 4 (1989): 355–75.

———. 1997b. "Commodifying Ethnicity: State and Ethnic Tourism in Singapore." In *Tourism, Ethnicity, and the State in Asian and Pacific Societies,* ed. Michel Picard and Robert E. Wood, 71–98. Honolulu: University of Hawaii Press.

Leung, Chun-Kin. 1977. "Notes on Cantonese Opera in North America." *Chinoperl Papers* 7: 9.

———. 1979. "The Cantonese Opera in Guangzhou in 1979." *Chinoperl Papers* 9: 92.

Levenson, Joseph R. 1957. "The Amateur Ideal in Ming and Early Ch'ing Society: Evidence from Painting." In *Chinese Thought and Institutions,* ed. John K. Fairbank, 320–41. Chicago: University of Chicago Press.

Levine, Lawrence W. 1988. *Highbrow/Lowbrow: The Emergence of Cultural Hierarchy in America.* Cambridge, MA: Harvard University Press.

Li, Hui Zhen. 1971. "Chaoju zai Xinjiapo de Fazhan" [The Development of Teochew Opera in Singapore]. Graduation essay (B.A. Hons.), Department of Chinese Language and Literature, Nanyang University.

Liang, Mingyue. 1985. *Music of the Billion: An Introduction to Chinese Musical Culture.* New York: Heinrichshofen Edition.

Lianhe Zaobao. 1997. "Jiucaiba Chenghuangmiao Shilue" [A Historical Account of Lorong Koo Chye Sheng Hong Temple]. November 30.

———. 1998a. "Jiexi Shiyizhong Jiti Huiyi" [Street Opera as Collective Memory]. March 7.

———. 1998b. "Shuguang Zhaxian Haishi Xiyang Yuhui?" [Emerging Sunshine or Lingering Sunset?]. March 7.

———. 2004a. "Bendi Miaoyu Choushenxi Yueyan Yuewang" [Local Thanksgiving Performance Prospering]. May 15.

———. 2004b. "Chongjian Miaohui Renao Fengguang" [Busy Atmosphere of Temple Festivals Sees Resurgence]. May 16.

———. 2004c. "Kan Choushen Gezaixi" [Watching Thanksgiving Gezaixi]. May 25.

Lim, Joo Hock. 1967. "Chinese Female Immigration into the Straits Settlements, 1860–1901." *Journal of the South Seas Society* 22: 58–110.

Lin, Qingxi, Zheng Qingshui, and Liu Xiangru, eds. 1983. *Fujianxi Shilu* [Historical Records of Fujian Opera]. Fujian: Fujian Sheng Xiqu Yanjiushuo.

Lin, Yutang, ed. and trans. 1966. *The Wisdom of Confucius.* New York: Modern Library, Random House. Originally published in 1938.

Ling, Trevor. 1989. "Religion." In *Management of Success: The Moulding of*

Modern Singapore, ed. Kernial Singh Sandhu and Paul Wheatley, 692–709. Singapore: Institute of Southeast Asian Studies.

Liu, Chunshu, and Wang Yaohua. 1986. *Fujian Minjian Yinyue Jianlun* [A Brief Study of Fujian Folk Music]. Shanghai: Shanghai Wenyi Chubanshe.

Liu, Gretchen, and Angelina Phillips, eds. 1988. *Wayang: A History of Chinese Opera in Singapore.* Singapore: National Archives.

Lopez, Manuel D. 1991. *Chinese Drama: An Annotated Bibliography of Commentary, Criticism, and Plays in English Translation.* London: Scarecrow Press.

Lorong Koo Chye Sheng Hong Temple. 1999. *Zhongguo Xiamen Gezaixi Jutuan Lixin Yanchu Tekan* [Special Edition of the Performance of China's Xiamen Gezaixi Troupe in Singapore]. Singapore: Lorong Koo Chye Sheng Hong Temple.

———. 2000. *Taiwan Chen Meiyun Gejutuan Lixin Yanchu Tekan* [Special Edition of the Performance of Taiwan's Chen Meiyun Opera Troupe in Singapore]. Singapore: Lorong Koo Chye Sheng Hong Temple.

Ly, Sinko. 1965. "Chinese Drama in Malaya." *France-Asie* (Winter): 157–71.

Mackerras, Colin. 1972. *The Rise of the Peking Opera 1770–1870.* New York: Oxford University Press.

———. 1975. *The Chinese Theatre in Modern Times: From 1840 to the Present Day.* London: Thames and Hudson.

———. 1983a. "The Drama of the Qing Dynasty." In *Chinese Theater: From Its Origins to the Present Day,* ed. Colin Mackerras, 92–117. Honolulu: University of Hawaii Press.

———. 1983b. "Theater and the Masses." In *Chinese Theater: From Its Origins to the Present Day,* ed. Colin Mackerras, 145–83. Honolulu: University of Hawaii Press.

———. 1987. "Modernization and Contemporary Chinese Theater: Commercialization and Professionalization." In *Drama in the People's Republic of China,* ed. Constantine Tung and Colin Mackerras, 181–212. New York: State University of New York Press.

Mackie, Jamie. 2003. "Five Southeast Asian Chinese Empire-Builders: Commonalities and Differences." In *Chinese Migrants Abroad: Cultural, Educational, and Social Dimensions of the Chinese Diaspora,* ed. Michael W. Charney, Brenda S. A. Yeoh, and Tong Chee Kiong, 3–22. Singapore: Singapore University Press and World Scientific Publishing Co.

Mak, Lau Fong. 1982. *Chinese Secret Societies in Singapore and Peninsular Malaysia.* Singapore: Oxford University Press.

Makepeace, Walter, Gilbert E. Brooke, and Roland St. J. Braddell, eds. 1921. *One Hundred Years of Singapore: Being Some Account of the Capital of the Straits Settlements from Its Foundation by Sir Stamford Raffles on the 6th February 1819 to the 6th February 1919.* 2 vols. London: John Murray.

Manuel, Peter. 1994. "Puerto Rican Music and Cultural Identity: Creative Appropriation of Cuban Sources from Danza to Salsa." *Ethnomusicology* 38, no. 2: 249–80.

Mark, Lindy Li. 1990. "The Role of Avocational Performers in the Preservation of Kunqu." *Chinoperl Papers* 15: 95–114.

McAdam, Rodney, and Sandra McCreedy. 1999. "A Critical Review of Knowledge Management Models." *Learning Organization* 6, no. 3: 91–100.

Meyer, John W., and Brian Rowan. 1977. "Institutionalized Organizations: Formal Structure as Myth and Ceremony." *American Journal of Sociology* 83, no. 2: 340–63.

Ministry of Information and the Arts. 2000. "Renaissance City Report: Culture and the Arts in Renaissance Singapore." http: //www.mita.gov.sg/renaissance .htm.

Minsu Quyi. 1983. "Dalu Difangxi Jianjie" [Brief Discussion on the Regional Operatic Tradition in Mainland China]. *Minsu Quyi* [Chinese Folklore: Reports and Studies] 26: 77–86.

Moey, Kok Keong. 1995. "Shui Lai Kan Xi? Xinjiapo Huazu Difangxi de Guanzhong Goucheng" [Audience Composition of Chinese Regional Opera in Singapore]. Honors thesis, Department of Chinese Studies, National University of Singapore.

Nathan, J. E. 1921. *The Census of British Malaya (The Straits Settlements, Federated Malay States and Protected States of Johore, Kedah, Perlis, Kelantan, Trengganu and Brunei).* British Malaya: Malayan Civil Service.

National Archives Microfiche. Cheah Gek Song (A000932/06).

———. Chng Gek Huay (A000860/18).

———. Chung Hon Kee (A000919/17).

———. Kew Bee Kee (A000903/05).

———. Liew Seng Hwa (A000926/19).

———. Mak Siew Wai (A000946/14).

———. Ng Ah Keong aka Ng Ghuat Teng (A000884/07).

———. Pak Choy Yoke (A000952/05).

———. Phan Wait Hong (A000368/11).

———. Phua Tong Gek (A000816/05).

———. Soon Siew Eng (A000853/11).

———. Tan Yeo Toe (A000939/06).

———. Tong Pak Ming (A000921/16).

National Arts Council. 1996. *The Arts in Singapore: Directory and Guide 1996.* Singapore: Accent Communications and National Arts Council.

Neuman, Daniel M. 1990. *The Life of Music in North India: The Organization of an Artistic Tradition.* Chicago: University of Chicago Press.

Newell, William H. 1961. "The Chinese Theatre in Malaya." *Orient/West* 6, no. 9: 67–71.

Ong, Cheng Lian. 1958. *The Teochew Opera Troupes: A Study of the Business and Social Organisation of Opera Players.* Academic exercise, Department of Social Studies, University of Malaya.

Oral History Department. 1990. *Recollections: People and Places.* Singapore: Singapore University Oral History Department.

Pan, Lynn, ed. 1999. *The Encyclopedia of the Chinese Overseas.* Cambridge, MA: Harvard University Press.

Pang, Chai Ping. 1997. "Jingju zai Xinjiapo: Koushu Lishi Gean Yanjiu" [Peking Opera in Singapore: Case Studies through Oral History]. Honors thesis, Department of Chinese Studies, National University of Singapore.

Paritta, Chalermpow Koanantakool. 2002. "Thai Middle-Class Practice and Consumption of Traditional Dance: 'Thai-ness' and High Art." In *Local Cultures and the "New Asia": The State, Culture, and Capitalism in Southeast Asia,* ed. C. J.-L. Wee, 217–41. Singapore: Institute of Southeast Asian Studies.

Perris, Arnold. 1978. "Chinese Wayang: The Survival of Chinese Opera in the Streets of Singapore." *Ethnomusicology* 22, no. 2: 297–306.

Peterson, William. 2001. *Theater and the Politics of Culture in Contemporary Singapore.* Middletown, CT: Wesleyan University Press.

Phang, Shiak Chien. 1998. "Chaoju zai Xinjiapo: Koushu Lishi Gean Yanjiu" [Teochew Opera in Singapore: Case Studies through Oral History]. Honors thesis, Department of Chinese Studies, National University of Singapore.

Pian, Rulan Chao. 1971. "The Function of Rhythm in Peking Opera." In *Music of Asia,* ed. Maceda José, 114–31. Manila: National Music Council of the Philippines in cooperation with the UNESCO National Commission of the Philippines.

———. 1975. "Aria Structural Patterns in the Peking Opera." In *Chinese and Japanese Music-Drama,* ed. J. I. Crump and William P. Malm, 65–89. Michigan Papers in Chinese Studies 19. Ann Arbor: University of Michigan Press.

Picard, Michel. 1996. *Bali: Cultural Tourism and Touristic Culture.* Translated by Diana Darling. Singapore: Archipelago Press, Editions Didier Millet. Originally published in French as *Bali: Tourisme Culturel et culture touristique.* Paris: Editions L'Harmattan, 1992.

———. 1997. "Cultural Tourism, Nation-Building, and Regional Culture: The Making of a Balinese Identity." In *Tourism, Ethnicity, and the State in Asian and Pacific Societies,* ed. Michel Picard and Robert E. Wood, 181–214. Honolulu: University of Hawaii Press

Pinches, Michael, ed. 1999. *Culture and Privilege in Capitalist Asia.* The New Rich in Asia series, ed. Richard Robison. London: Routledge.

Pitt, Kuan Wah. 1988. "Xinjiapo Difang Xiqu Fazhan Shilue" [The Development of Chinese Wayang in Singapore]. *Asian Culture* 11: 56–75.

Purcell, Victor. 1948. *The Chinese in Malaya.* London: Oxford University Press.

———. 1965. *The Chinese in Southeast Asia.* 2nd ed. London: Oxford University Press.

PuruShotam, Nirmala Srirekam. 1989. "Language and Linguistic Policies." In *Management of Success: The Moulding of Modern Singapore,* ed. Kernial Singh Sandhu and Paul Wheatley, 503–22. Singapore: Institute of Southeast Asian Studies.

———. 1998. *Negotiating Language, Constructing Race: Disciplining Difference in Singapore.* New York: Mouton de Gruyter.

Rees, Helen. 1998. "'Authenticity' and the Foreign Audience for Traditional Music in Southwest China." *Journal of Musicological Research* 17, no. 2: 135–61.

Riddle, Ronald. 1978. "Music Clubs and Ensembles in San Francisco's Chinese Community." In *Eight Urban Musical Cultures: Tradition and Change,* ed. Bruno Nettl, 223–59. Urbana: University of Illinois Press.

———. 1983. *Flying Dragons, Flowing Streams: Music in the Life of San Francisco's Chinese.* Contributions in Intercultural and Comparative Studies 7. Westport, CT: Greenwood Press.

Riley, Jo. 1997. *Chinese Theatre and the Actor in Performance.* Cambridge Studies in Modern Theatre. Cambridge: Cambridge University Press.

Rubin, Joan Shelley. 1992. *The Making of Middlebrow Culture.* Chapel Hill: University of North Carolina Press.

Rudolph, Jürgen. 1996. "Amusements in the Three 'Worlds.'" In *Looking at Cul-*

ture, ed. Sanjay Krishnan, Sharaad Kuttan, Lee Weng Choy, Leon Perera, and Jimmy Yap, 21–33. Singapore: Artres Design and Communications.

———. 1998. *Reconstructing Identities: A Social History of the Babas in Singapore.* Aldershot, UK: Ashgate Publishing.

Sakai, Tadao. 1981. "Some Aspects of Chinese Religious Practices and Customs in Singapore and Malaysia." *Journal of Southeast Asian Studies* 12, no. 1: 133–41.

Saw, Swee-Hock. 1991. "Population Growth and Control." In *A History of Singapore,* ed. Ernest C. T. Chew and Edwin Lee, 219–41. Singapore: Oxford University Press.

Schein, Edgar H. 1985. *Organisational Culture and Leadership.* San Francisco: Jossey-Bass.

Scott, A. C. 1957. *The Classical Theatre of China.* London: George Allen and Unwin.

Seah, Eu Chin (Siah U Chin). 1848. "General Sketch of the Numbers, Tribes, and Avocations of the Chinese in Singapore." *Journal of the Indian Archipelago* 2: 283–90.

Shih, Chung-Wen. 1976. *The Golden Age of Chinese Drama: Yüan Tsa-chü.* Princeton, NJ: Princeton University Press.

Siddique, Sharon. 1989. "Singaporean Identity." In *Management of Success: The Moulding of Modern Singapore,* ed. Kernial Singh Sandhu and Paul Wheatley, 563–77. Singapore: Institute of Southeast Asian Studies.

Sieber, Patricia. 2003. *Theaters of Desire: Authors, Readers, and the Reproduction of Early Chinese Song-Drama, 1300–2000.* New York: Palgrave Macmillan.

Singapore Changi Airport. 1997. *Changi: The Magazine* (The Bi-Monthly Companion Magazine for Singapore Changi Airport). Issue 9 (February/March). London: Highbury House Communications.

Singapore Tourism Board. 1997. *New Asia Singapore: Mature Travellers.* Singapore: Singapore Tourism Board.

Singapore Visitor. 1997. *The Singapore Visitor: The Weekly Guide to Help You Enjoy Your Stay,* no. 1100/97 (June 7–13). Singapore: Creations and Communications.

Sng, Poh Yoke. 1986. "The End of Wayang, the Birth of an Art." *Sunday Times,* August 17.

Song, Ong Siang. 1967. *One Hundred Years: History of the Chinese in Singapore.* Singapore: University of Malaya Press. Originally published in 1923, London: John Murray.

Speeches. 1996a. "Building a Gracious Society." In *Speeches: A Bimonthly Selection of Ministerial Speeches,* 4–6. Singapore: Ministry of Information and the Arts.

———. 1996b. "Singapore's Deeper Commitment to the Arts." In *Speeches: A Bimonthly Selection of Ministerial Speeches,* 1–3. Singapore: Ministry of Information and the Arts.

Statistics Singapore. 2000. "Key Indicators of the Resident Population." http://www.singstat.gov.sg/keystats/c2000/indicators.pdf.

———. 2005. "General Household Survey 2005: Table 1 Resident Population by Age Group, Ethnic Group, and Sex." http://www.singstat.gov.sg/keystats/annual/ghs/r1/t1.pdf.

Stokes, Martin, ed. 1994. "Introduction: Ethnicity, Identity, and Music." In *Ethnicity, Identity, and Music: The Musical Construction of Place,* ed. Martin Stokes, 1–27. Providence, RI: Berg Publishers.

Straits Times. 1974a. "Clamp on Noise from Wayangs." July 20.

———. 1974b. "Noise Control: Wayangs Seek Deposit Cut." July 25.

———. 1974c. "Of Funeral Rites and Noisy Wayangs." July 26.

———. 1974d. "Plea for Cut in Wayang Fees." August 6.

———. 1990. "Amateurs Better Off Than Professionals." September 30.

———. 1996. "Complete Opera Lessons at CC [Community Centre]." July 30.

———. 1998a. "See Chinese Opera under the Stars." March 11.

———. 1998b. "Streets, Parks Used to Draw Wider Crowd." February 4.

———. 1998c. "Wayang Back with a Spunky Maiden." February 21.

———. 2000. "Wow, Wayang Sung in English!" December 5.

———. 2004. "The Ramayana as Chinese Opera." April 19.

Talbot, A. P. 1881. *Report on the Census of Singapore, 1881.* Straits Settlements: Colonial Secretariat.

Tamney, Joseph B. 1996. *The Struggle over Singapore's Soul: Western Modernization and Asian Culture.* De Gruyter Studies in Organization 70. Berlin: Walter de Gruyter.

Tan, Chee-Beng. 1989. "The Ethnic Chinese in Malaysia and Singapore." In *The Ethnic Chinese in the ASEAN States: Bibliographical Essays,* ed. Leo Suryadinata, 119–65. Singapore: Institute of Southeast Asian Studies.

Tan, Sock Lay. 1996. "Xinjiapo de Yeyu Chaoju Tuanti" [A Study of Amateur Teochew Opera Groups in Singapore]. Honors thesis, Department of Chinese Studies, National University of Singapore.

Tan, Sooi Beng. 1980. "Chinese Opera in Malaysia: Changes and Survival." *Review of South East Asian Studies* 10: 29–45.

———. 1981. "The Glove Puppet Theater (Po Te Hi) in Malaysia." *Asian Music* 13, no. 1: 53–72.

———. 1984. "Ko-Tai: Theatre in the Streets." *Aliran Monthly* 4, no. 2 (February): 19–21.

———. 1988. *The Phor Tor Festival in Penang: Deities, Ghosts, and Chinese Ethnicity.* Monash University Centre of Southeast Asian Studies Working Paper 51. Clayton, Victoria, Australia: Monash University.

———. 1993. *Bangsawan: A Social and Stylistic History of the Malay Opera.* Singapore: Oxford University Press.

———. 2000a. "The Chinese Performing Arts and Cultural Activities in Malaysia." In *The Chinese in Malaysia,* ed. Lee Kam Hing and Tan Chee-Beng, 316–41. South-East Asian Social Science Monographs. Selangor, Malaysia: Oxford University Press.

———. 2000b. "The Huayue Tuan (Chinese Orchestra) in Malaysia: Adapting to Survive." *Asian Music* 31, no. 2: 107–28.

Tanaka, Issei. 1984. "Minyuexi Jisi ji Xiqu Zhong Shenling Jiangling de Yanchu" [Religious Rituals and Chinese Opera of the Min and Yue Communities]. In *Guanyu Dongnanya Huaren Chuantong Xiju, Quyi Zonghe Diaocha Yanjiu* [Research on Southeast Asian Traditional Chinese Theatre]. Vol. 2, *Singapore and Malaysia,* ed. Onoe Kanehide, 1–16. Tokyo: Institute of Oriental Culture, University of Tokyo.

———. 1985. "The Social and Historical Context of Ming-Ch'ing Local Drama." In *Popular Culture in Late Imperial China*, ed. David Johnson, Andrew J. Nathan, and Evelyn S. Rawski, 188–218. Berkeley: University of California Press.

Tang, Wai Kuen. 1976. *The Chinese Wayang Playhouse in Singapore*. Elective study, School of Architecture, University of Singapore.

Taruskin, Richard. 1988. "The Pastness of the Present and the Presence of the Past." In *Authenticity and Early Music: A Symposium*, ed. Nicholas Kenyon, 137–207. Oxford: Oxford University Press.

Teo, Liang Chye. 1996. "Chaoju zai Xinjiapo" [Teochew Opera in Singapore]. *Singapore Chui Huay Lim Club 150th Anniversary Souvenir Journal*, 178–81.

Thio, Eunice. 1991. "The Syonan Years, 1942–1945." In *A History of Singapore*, ed. Ernest C. T. Chew and Edwin Lee, 95–114. Singapore: Oxford University Press.

Tomlinson, Gary. 1988. "The Historian, the Performer, and Authentic Meaning in Music." In *Authenticity and Early Music: A Symposium*, ed. Nicholas Kenyon, 115–36. Oxford: Oxford University Press.

Tong, Chee Kiong, Ho Kong Chong, and Lin Ting Kwong. 1992. "Traditional Chinese Customs in Modern Singapore." In *Asian Traditions and Modernization: Perspectives from Singapore*, ed. Yong Mun Cheong, 78–101. Singapore: Times Academic Press for the Centre for Advanced Studies, National University of Singapore.

Trocki, Carl A. 1990. *Opium and Empire: Chinese Society in Colonial Singapore, 1800–1910*. Ithaca: Cornell University Press.

Tsiang, Un-Kai. 1932. *K'ouen K'iu: Le Théatre Chinois Ancien*. Paris: Librairie Ernest Leroux.

Tu, Wei-Ming, ed. 1996. *Confucian Traditions in East Asian Modernity: Moral Education and Economic Culture in Japan and the Four Mini-Dragons*. Cambridge, MA: Harvard University Press.

Tu, Weiming, Milan Hejtmanek, and Alan Wachman, ed. 1992. *The Confucian World Observed: A Contemporary Discussion of Confucian Humanism in East Asia*. Honolulu, HI: Program for Cultural Studies, East-West Center.

Turino, Thomas. 2000. *Nationalists, Cosmopolitans, and Popular Music in Zimbabwe*. Chicago: University of Chicago Press.

Turnbull, C. Mary. 1989. *A History of Singapore, 1819–1988*. 2nd ed. Singapore: Oxford University Press.

Turner, Victor W. 1982a. "Dramatic Ritual/Ritual Drama: Performative and Reflexive Anthropology." In *A Crack in the Mirror: Reflexive Perspectives in Anthropology*, ed. Jay Ruby, 83–97. Philadelphia: University of Pennsylvania Press.

———. 1982b. *From Ritual to Theatre: The Human Seriousness of Play*. New York: PAJ Publications.

Vasil, Raj. 1995. *Asianising Singapore: The PAP's Management of Ethnicity*. Singapore: Heinemann Asia.

Vaughan, Jonas Daniel. 1971. *The Manners and Customs of the Chinese*. Singapore: Oxford University Press. Originally published as *The Manners and Customs of the Chinese of the Straits Settlements*. Singapore: Mission Press, 1879.

Vente, Ines, and Lim Geok Eng. 1984. *Wayang: Chinese Street Opera in Singapore*. Singapore: MPH.

Vincent, Joan. 1974. "The Structuring of Ethnicity." *Human Organization* 33, no. 4: 375–78.

Wan, Chiew Inn. 1996. "Qiongju (Hainanxi) zai Xinjiapo: Koushu Lishi Gean Diaocha" [Hainanese Opera in Singapore: Case Studies through Oral History]. Honors thesis, Department of Chinese Studies, National University of Singapore.

Wang, Fang. 2004. *Jingju zai Xinjiapo* [Beijing Opera in Singapore]. Singapore: Chinese Opera Institute.

Wang, Gungwu. 1989. "The Chinese as Immigrants and Settlers." In *Management of Success: The Moulding of Modern Singapore,* ed. Kernial Singh Sandhu and Paul Wheatley, 552–62. Singapore: Institute of Southeast Asian Studies.

Wang, Quigui, ed. 1992a. "Liyuanxi Zhuanji" [Special Issue on Liyuan Opera]. *Minsu Quyi* [Chinese Folklore: Reports and Studies] 75 and 76.

———. 1992b. "Mulianxi Zhuanji" [Special Issue on Mulian Opera]. *Minsu Quyi* [Chinese Folklore: Reports and Studies] 77 and 78.

Wang, Zhengchun. 1988. *Gen de Xilie* [The Roots Series]. Singapore: Seng Yew Book Store.

———. 1990. *Gen de Xilie Zhi Er* [The Roots Series 2]. Singapore: Sinmin Ribao and Seng Yew Book Store.

———. 1992. *Gen de Xilie Zhi San* [The Roots Series 3]. Singapore: Sinmin Ribao and Seng Yew Book Store.

———. 1997. *Shile Laojie* [Streets of Old Singapore]. The Roots Series 4. Singapore: Seng Yew Book Store.

———. 2000. *Liyuan Huadangnian* [Historical Narratives through Chinese Opera]. The Roots Series 5. Singapore: Lingzi Mass Media.

Ward, Barbara E. 1977. "Readers and Audiences: An Exploration of the Spread of Traditional Chinese Culture." In *Text and Context: The Social Anthropology of Tradition,* ed. Ravindra K. Jain, 181–203. Philadelphia: Institute for the Study of Human Issues.

———. 1979. "Not Merely Players: Drama, Art, and Ritual in Traditional China." *Man* 14, no. 1: 18–39.

———. 1985. "Regional Operas and Their Audiences: Evidence from Hong Kong." In *Popular Culture in Late Imperial China,* ed. David Johnson, Andrew J. Nathan, and Evelyn S. Rawski, 161–87. Berkeley: University of California Press.

Waterman, Christopher A. 1990. *Jújù: A Social History and Ethnography of an African Popular Music.* Chicago: University of Chicago Press.

Wee, C. J. W.-L. 2002a. "From Universal to Local Culture: The State, Ethnic Identity, and Capitalism in Singapore." In *Local Cultures and the "New Asia": The State, Culture, and Capitalism in Southeast Asia,* ed. C. J. W.-L Wee, 129–57. Singapore: Institute of Southeast Asian Studies.

———. 2002b. "National Identity, the Arts, and the Global City." In *Singapore in the New Millennium: Challenges Facing the City-State,* ed. Derek da Cunha, 221–42. Singapore: Institute of Southeast Asian Studies.

Wichmann, Elizabeth. 1991. *Listening to Theatre: The Aural Dimension of Beijing Opera.* Honolulu: University of Hawaii Press.

Wilkes, Charles. 1984. *The Singapore Chapter of the Narrative of the United States Exploring Expedition During the Years 1838, 1839, 1840, 1841, 1842.* Singapore: Antiques of the Orient Private Limited. Originally published in 1845, Philadelphia, PA: Lea and Blanchard.

Williams, Brackette F. 1989. "A Class Act: Anthropology and the Race to Nation across Ethnic Terrain." *Annual Review in Anthropology* 18: 401–44.

Williams, Raymond. 1961. *The Long Revolution.* London: Chatto and Windus.

———. 1976. *Keywords: A Vocabulary of Culture and Society.* New York: Oxford University Press.

Wise, Michael, with Mun Him Wise, eds. 1996. *Travellers' Tales of Old Singapore.* Brighton, UK: In Print Publishing. Originally published in 1985, Singapore by Times Books International.

Witzleben, J. Lawrence. 1995. *"Silk and Bamboo" Music in Shanghai: The Jiangnan Sizhu Instrumental Ensemble Tradition.* Kent, OH: Kent State University Press.

Wong, Chung Lin, Pi Shu Ming, Lai Yen Yuan, and Hsieh Yun Fei. 1972. *Sida Chuanqi ji Dongnanya Huaren Difangxi* [A Study of Four Chinese Classical Operatic Dramas and Their Popularity in Southeast Asian Countries]. Singapore: Institute of Asian Studies, Nanyang University.

Wong, Joanna Quee Heng. 1976. "Still Alive and Kicking." *New Directions* 3, no. 2: 32–33.

———. 1985. "Revival of Chinese Opera in Singapore." *Performing Arts* 2: 25–27.

———. 1995. "Chinese Opera in Singapore: An Overview." In *Traditional Theatre in Southeast Asia,* ed. Chua Soo Pong, 103–8. Singapore: UniPress.

Wong, Sui-Lun. 1988. "The Applicability of Asian Family Values to Other Sociocultural Settings." In *In Search of an East Asian Development Model,* ed. Peter L. Berger and Hsin-Huang Michael Hsiao, 134–52. New Brunswick, NJ: Transaction Books.

Wong, Wun Chyen. 1994. "Guoli Daxue Zhongwen Tushuguan Soucang Zhongguo Gudian Xiqu Shuji Mulu (1953–1993) jiqi Xuanlei Tiyao" [A Catalogue and Selected Annotations of Chinese Books on Traditional Chinese Drama (1953–1993) in the NUS Chinese Library]. Academic exercise, Department of Chinese Studies, National University of Singapore.

Wong, Yunn Chii, and Tan Kar Lin. 2004. "Emergence of a Cosmopolitan Space for Culture and Consumption: The New World Amusement Park-Singapore (1923–70) in the Inter-war Years." *Inter-Asia Cultural Studies* 5, no. 2: 279–304.

Wu, Fengwu, ed. 1993. *Dongnanya Huaqiao Tongshi* [History of Overseas Chinese in Southeast Asia]. Fuzhou, Fujian: Fujian Renmin Chubanshe.

Wu, Zhao, and Liu Dongsheng. 1993. *Zhongguo Yinyue Shilue* [History of Chinese Music]. Beijing: Renmin Yinyue Chubanshe.

Xinmin Ribao [Xinmin Daily News]. 2004. "Zhongxuesheng Yan Huangmeixi: Malai Nusheng Dang Gongzhu" [Secondary School Students Perform Huangmei Opera: Malay Girl in the Role of Princess]. April 19.

Yang, Yinliu. 1981. *Zhongguo Gudai Yinyue Shigao* [Draft History of Ancient Chinese Music]. Beijing: Renmin Yinyue Chubanshe.

Yen, Ching-Hwang. 1976. *The Overseas Chinese and the 1911 Revolution: With Special Reference to Singapore and Malaya.* Kuala Lumpur, Malaysia: Oxford University Press.

———. 1981. "Early Chinese Clan Organizations in Singapore and Malaya, 1819–1911." *Journal of Southeast Asian Studies* 12, no. 1: 62–92.

———. 1986. *A Social History of the Chinese in Singapore and Malaya 1800–1911.* Singapore: Oxford University Press.

Yeo, Kim Wah, and Albert Lau. 1991. "From Colonialism to Independence, 1945–1965." In *A History of Singapore,* ed. Ernest C. T. Chew and Edwin Lee, 117–53. Singapore: Oxford University Press.

Yong, Ching Fatt. 1987. *Tan Kah-Kee: The Making of an Overseas Chinese Legend.* Singapore: Oxford University Press.

Yung, Bell. 1989. *Cantonese Opera: Performance as Creative Process.* Cambridge Studies in Ethnomusicology, ed. John Blacking. Cambridge: Cambridge University Press.

Yung, Sai-Shing. 1997. *Xiqu Renleixue Chutan: Yishi, Juchang yu Shequn* [The Anthropology of Chinese Drama: Ritual, Theater and Community]. Taipei, Taiwan: Rye Field Publishing.

Zeng, Yongyi. 1976. "Zhongguo Difang Xiaoxi Xingcheng yu Fazhan de Jinglu" [Development and Changes in Chinese Regional Opera]. *Minsu Quyi* [Chinese Folklore: Reports and Studies] 46: 9–22.

Zhang, Bojie. 1980. "Chaoju Shengqiang de Xingcheng he Liubian" [The Origin and Development of Qiang in Chaozhou Opera]. *Xiju Yishu Zhiliao* [Information on Theatre Studies] 3: 48–58.

Zhang, Geng, and Guo Hancheng, eds. 1992. *Zhongguo Xiqu Tongshi* [A Complete History of Chinese Theatre]. Beijing: Zhongguo Xiju Chubanshe.

Zhou, Yibai. 1960. *Zhongguo Xiqu Lunji* [A Narrative on Chinese Theatre]. Beijing: Zhongguo Xiju Chubanshe.

———. 1979. *Zhongguo Xiqu Fazhanshi Gangyao* [An Outline of the Development of Chinese Opera]. Shanghai: Shanghai Guji Chubanshe.

INDEX

TONG SOON LEE is an associate professor of ethnomusicology at Emory University.

The University of Illinois Press
is a founding member of the
Association of American University Presses.

Composed in 9.5/12.5 Trump Mediaeval
by Jim Proefrock
at the University of Illinois Press
Manufactured by Thomson-Shore, Inc.

University of Illinois Press
1325 South Oak Street
Champaign, IL 61820-6903
www.press.uillinois.edu